Free to Travel

The Canadian Guide for
50 Plus Travellers

Free to Travel

The Canadian Guide for
50 Plus Travellers

· · · · ·

Pam Hobbs and Michael Algar

Doubleday Canada

Canadian Cataloguing in Publication Data

Hobbs, Pam

Free to travel: the Canadian guide for 50 plus travellers

ISBN 0-385-25479-2

1. Voyages and travels - Guidebooks. 2. Aged - Travel.
3. Middle-aged persons - Travel.

I. Algar, Michael. II. Title.

G151.II62 1994   910'.2'020846   C94-930986-9

Cover illustration by Eric Colquhoun
Cover and text design by Avril Orloff
Printed and bound in Canada
Printed on acid-free paper

Published in Canada by
Doubleday Canada Limited
105 Bond Street
Toronto, Ontario
M5B 1Y3

For Connie

who introduced me to travel so many years ago

P. H.

NOTE TO THE READER

We've gone to a lot of effort to ensure that the information in *Free to Travel* is up-to-date and accurate. At the time of going to press, dollar values were optimistically converted at the following exchange rates: Can. $1 to U.S. 74¢ and Can. $2 to £1 sterling. However, inflation being what it is worldwide, the dollar values given in this book cannot be guaranteed.

Countries change their names, their boundaries, their governments and their policies. On a smaller scale, hotels, restaurants, shops and other establishments come and go. These are just a few of the elements affecting tourism. If you have any suggestions, comments or corrections toward the next edition, please write to:

Pam Hobbs and Michael Algar
Free to Travel
c/o Doubleday Canada Limited
105 Bond Street
Toronto, Ontario
M5B 1Y3

*T*able of Contents

$\mathcal{P}$reface

$\mathcal{I}$n Roman times a person 28 years of age was considered old, and up until a few decades ago 40 was over the hill. Well, that was then. Now, as we near the twenty-first century, the growing population of older adults is a force to be reckoned with. And over the hill is fine, because most of us like what we see on the other side.

In Canada over a quarter of the population is 50 plus. More than three million Canadians are over the age of 65. Generally we are healthier, better educated and living longer than our parents and grandparents. And yet we are retiring or have chosen semi-retirement earlier. For many this time is a delightful landmark in our lives, with a home paid for, the children through school and off on their own and a retirement package that leaves us free to do our own thing.

The traditional interpretation of leisure has always been the opposite of work, but this doesn't seem to apply any more. Fifty, 65 and even 75-year-olds are no longer content to pass a few hours playing dominoes under a tree, or to "get through another day" with a visit to the local mall. Instead they are volunteering, taking up new sports and hobbies, earning university degrees, embarking on action and adventure tours, studying nature, learning a new language — and many are doing these things far from home.

There is no general profile for the 50 plus traveller. Some 55-year-olds enjoy the companionship of an escorted group, while others in their late 70s are virtually backpacking around the world. I see more single travellers these days, happy with their own company after years of family commitments. Also more grandparents are travelling and sharing their experiences with a child or teen. Many think nothing of laying out $7,000 for an exotic tour; others can travel the same route and enjoy the same experiences for less than half the price. No matter what the choice, it is clear that we are on the move, travelling more often than any other age group.

The purpose of this book is to inspire its readers to widen their horizons and, in consequence, enrich their lives through travel. I describe exciting travel adventures to be had beyond your family cottage. If you like to play bridge three afternoons a week, let's get you doing it on a cruise ship. If shopping is your pleasure we'll have you bargain hunting in bazaars and markets, and buying your favourite crafts at source. Sounds too tiring? Never fear. We know of some great little spas where you can take soothing time out during a busy tour.

With this book you will be informed and prepared, confident to set off on rewarding and worry-free travel in your retirement years, such as you used to dream about during your working life. I hope too that you'll find it a good read. Sprinkled with personal anecdotes from my 30 years of travel it gives lots of practical advice as well as useful names, addresses and telephone numbers. I show you how to get from here to there, how to get around when you arrive, what to do in an emergency, how to stretch your travel dollars and how to unravel the tangle of options for travel insurance.

Although *Free to Travel* is written in the first person there are actually two authors. Michael Algar has 45 years of travel experience. Many of his trips during the past two decades have been with me, and now his research and my writing have combined to produce a very comprehensive book. Our aim is to leave you so enthused, you will want to get up and go — NOW. If we have succeeded, *bon voyage!*

Pam Hobbs

ACKNOWLEDGMENTS

Special thanks to our agent Dean Cooke of Livingston Cooke, Inc., who saw our proposal for an article and encouraged us to turn it into a book.

Our friend Betty Fairbrass who read the manuscript before we submitted it to the professionals.

The staff of Doubleday Canada Limited, and in particular our editor Susan Folkins for her diligence and enthusiasm.

And the hundreds of people in the travel industry who gave their time so generously to answer our questions. Some were called on often, and we wish to thank them individually:

Val Austin, British Tourist Authority in London. Stephen Burnett, Horizon Holidays. Hal Burns, Goway Travel Ltd. Amanda Cashmore, John Ingle Travel Insurance. John Lang, The Cruise People Ltd. Sarah Lynch, British Airways. Elaine Maley, The Adventure Centre. Tov Mason, ElderTreks. Sue Moore, Canadian Pacific Hotels & Resorts. Valerie Schroder, British Tourist Authority in Toronto. Shirley Shelby, Travel Helpers. Catherine Smart, Ontario March of Dimes. Beverly Squires, Horizon Holidays (Special Care Escorted Holidays). Konstance Trainor, British Airways. Allan Trollope, P. Lawson Travel. Honor Verrier, British Airways. David Wood, I'm Proud To Be Me Travel.

The ever-helpful staff of Mississauga Library.

Part One
Before You Go

*W*hat Kind of a Traveller Are You?

*L*ike hunting and fishing and sewing your own clothes, travel used to be a means of survival. From times when pre-historic man had to follow his dinner across continents, to mass emigration to the New World and our own transient lifestyles, travel has often been a necessity — or at the very least a way to enhance everyday life. Now we have reached the age when we are free to go anywhere at any time, solely for our pleasure, usually bounded only by personal resources.

Inspiring though they are the countless travel options available can seem bewildering to the novice traveller, but they don't have to be. Simply ask yourself "What kind of traveller am I?" Then zero in on the opportunities from there.

If, from previous experience, you know you are nervous driving in unfamiliar cities or are permanently anxious in countries where English is seldom spoken, then group travel is probably the answer. On the other hand, if you are impatient with the needs of fellow travellers — the line-ups for hotel keys, meals and washrooms — you may prefer to travel alone.

Let's consider the numerous options.

THE TOUR PACKAGE

This is literally a **vacation package** with all or most of its travel components neatly tied together by a tour company. Some tours are more exciting than others, some more expensive. Usually you get what you pay for. For example, the two-week package to Mexico which costs $100 less than another to the same area may provide less attractive accommodation in a less desirable location. Or it could include five dinners, whereas the more expensive program gives you 10 — plus a series of free scuba lessons, a reception on arrival and an island tour. If this sounds good to you I suggest you take it, because paid for separately those extras amount to far more than $100. But if you want to try the local restaurants and rent a car to do your own tour, and really are not fussy about scuba diving — choose the lower-priced package and save some extra spending money.

It isn't a question of one tour company giving better value than another, so much as whether the package's contents are of value to you. There would be far fewer travellers, especially to exotic destinations if we didn't have tour companies whose business it is to put saleable travel programs together for public consumption. Here's how it works.

Imagine I am a tour company interested in selling Jamaican vacations. I go there, work with hoteliers and island tour people for the best rates in return for agreement to book 300 hotel rooms every day for the entire season. Similarly I book the island tours and reserve car rentals, all in bulk numbers. I charter an aircraft to get my passengers there and back, and because I want it every Friday, all winter, I can have this aircraft for a good price. As a wholesaler, I put it all together, promote it in a glossy brochure and pay travel agents a commission to sell my Jamaica package to the public.

As I build up a good reputation for my reliable, well-priced tours, I earn the loyalty of clients who can hardly wait to see where I want to take them next year. In Canada we have excellent tour companies, big and small.

Now, back to being a travel writer....

A real plus in buying a travel package is that almost everything is prepaid in advance, so you won't find your room rate hiked between booking and arrival. What's more you don't *have* to be herded all over the place with a group. Some tours provide air transportation, transfer to your hotel and accommodation. That's it. During your vacation you may recognize someone from your flight, and the same people you flew in with will assemble for the return journey. Otherwise you are on your own. Vacationing in Britain I always take advantage of a program which gives me a flight, car rental, theatre tickets and a couple of nights accommodation, even if I will be staying for two or three weeks.

Check the options and you will find travel savings that do nothing to impinge on your personal itinerary. Other packages offer you travel with a group on a pre-set itinerary, with professional escorts and guides. Or you may decide on one that is "all inclusive," in which case you stay put at a resort where all meals, accommodation and leisure facilities are included in the price.

An increasing number of tours are arranged specifically for 50 plus travellers. Many attract us because they are at a gentle pace, or because they are well organized and always use the best hotels.

Cruise programs are packaged to give us convenience and savings. Usually a tour company charters an aircraft or reserves blocks of its seats for transportation to the embarkation port, arranges transfers to the ship and passes on a good rate for on-board accommodation.

Once you start travelling you will have a favourite tour company. **Early bird discounts** may motivate you to book well in advance of your vacation. Having done that you can sit back and savour the joys of anticipation.

INDEPENDENT TRAVEL

For many, a large part of the pleasure is in planning a **customized itinerary.** With the help of a good travel agent, and knowledge of your destinations, this is relatively simple though time-consuming.

Remember that as an *independent* traveller you must be just that. When things go wrong you're the fixer. If you are working out your own itinerary on the assumption that it saves money (not necessarily true), but are inclined to fret over train cancellations, overbooked hotels and converting that funny money to Canadian dollars before parting with any, then the emotional expense will overshadow your vacation pleasure.

Do you prefer being with your own kind, or do you want to meet the locals? If you want to mix with the residents, you really need to deal with them directly and not through a Canadian tour representative who speaks for you. How about half and half? Perhaps you should consider a program that provides the essential ingredients, but lets you put them together as you choose. The most important assets for an independent traveller are a positive attitude, a sense of humour and the ability to be flexible. A little knowledge of the language goes a long way too.

For example, if, as part of a **European vacation**, you book a three-day excursion and arrive at the departure point to find it cancelled, it is no big deal. You simply find a local travel agency and inquire about alternatives. A few years ago we booked and prepaid a mini-tour of eastern Spain and reported to the given address in Malaga only to find a notice in Spanish on the door. A passer-by interpreted it as "Today is a holiday. Tour cancelled. Office closed for one week." Unable to find a travel agency or tourist office open, we returned to the hotel we had just left. The next morning we bought a tour to Morocco leaving that day. It cost roughly half of what we had paid for the original tour, and we had a wonderful time. Our original payment was refunded in Canada later.

VAGABONDING

The older I get the more vagabonding appeals to me. I love having the freedom to move on or to stay put according to mood, weather or chain of events. In the southern United States we have done this often when our condo stay has been extended from two days to five because the owner offered us a good deal. An advertisement in a South Carolina laundrette once alerted us to inexpensive lodgings which detained us there so long we never did reach Florida as planned. Visiting England's Blenheim Palace on assignment once I strayed into an art gallery in the neighbouring village of Woodstock. While I was there, the American owner put a sign in the window advertising an apartment over her store. I fell in love with the apartment and moved right in. It was a great location from which to take my tours of Oxford and I think I might be there still, had commitments not pulled me home a week later.

There are advantages to **travelling without a schedule**. You can be a stand-by passenger and turn up at the airport just prior to take-off. (I have to add that today fewer stand-by seats are available as more travellers buy their tickets at last-minute discount outlets.) Or you can be at a dock as a cruise ship prepares to leave with empty cabins. Or at one of the discount agencies where prices can be literally cut in half. If it is your nature to enjoy spur-of-the-moment action, you can take advantage of worthwhile savings this way, and visit exotic destinations ordinarily beyond your travel budget.

Vagabonders who have always dreamed of a **round-the-world trip** may now find it within their reach, as more airlines unite to combine routes and rates. The following examples will give you an idea of what is being offered.

Via British Airways/Quantas/United Airlines you can travel from Montreal, Toronto or Vancouver across the Atlantic to London. From there you can have a side trip to, say Paris, and fly back to London before taking off for Singapore, Perth, Melbourne, Sydney, Auckland, Papeete (Tahiti) or Nandi (Fiji). Then it's back to North America with a stopover in Los Angeles or San Francisco before returning to your Canadian gateway. The cost is $3,969 economy or $6,045 business class. If you want to bypass the Far East and go from London to Africa instead (before continuing to Australia) there is a small extra charge.

You must register your route and give your first departure date when booking, but you can leave the rest of your travel dates open until you are ready to move on. Should you decide to change the original route plan, it will cost you U.S. $25 (Can. $33) to have a new ticket issued. You must stop at a minimum of three destinations and have a year to complete all travel.

If that hasn't got you hunting for an atlas to figure out your own dream itinerary, here's another: Toronto-London-Paris-Bangkok-Hong Kong-Tokyo-Honolulu-Los Angeles and home. This fare is $3,139 economy and $4,572 business class. And with all the frequent flyer points earned, you can probably take off again soon after you've unpacked and stuck your photos in the family album.

TRAVELLING SOLO

There are people who wouldn't consider having a travel mate, especially on a long trip that's been months in the planning. On different occasions I have met Australian women roaming about Europe on trips lasting several months. Their stories are similar: having spent most of their adult lives looking out for others, they now relish this travel time on their own.

Older people do well travelling solo. They have learned to be resourceful. They are usually popular with other travellers of any age. They have a natural curiosity about the world around them. (In a group, watch to see who asks all the questions.) Locals tend to trust and like them.

Personally I prefer to travel with a friend or family member. Part of my pleasure is to share a perfect scene or a joke or a meal that can be enjoyed all the more for some good conversation. But I do travel on my own quite often, and these are trips during which I am invited to a local wedding or a family dinner or to visit someone's home that is ordinarily off-limits to foreigners. Remember Shirley Valentine, the subject of a stage play and movie about a middle-aged woman on her first holiday in the Greek Islands? Would she have had such an eventful week had her girlfriend not deserted her? Of course not.

If your status as a **single traveller** is not from choice, do look at escorted tours or a cruise package. Ask your travel agent about other singles on the tour. If there aren't any, you may choose to find another. Some companies will pair you with a traveller of the same sex or will put you in touch with someone before your trip. This way you can meet and, if you agree to share a room or cabin, avoid paying the wretchedly high single supplement fee.

TRAVELLING WITH A SPECIAL PURPOSE

Are you the kind of person who must have a definite reason for getting up in the morning? If so, you can certainly find it in your travels. **Learning vacations** (see Chapter 29) and **working vacations** (Chapter 30) give real purpose to a trip. So do those side excursions that take you to view wildlife, allow you to step back into history or help you to capture a perfect scene on film.

IT'S UP TO YOU

How, where, when and even why you want to travel are all questions to ask yourself. With the answers firmly in mind you can get on with the fun part.

$\mathcal{P}$lanning a Trip

$\mathcal{T}$ravelling is the geography lesson we used to dream about as youngsters at school. To study a far-off land and then conclude with a visit instead of an exam is surely the ultimate learning experience. Knowledge is an important tool in shaping any scheme, but where travel is concerned it is essential. This is where **time is on our side**. For one thing, we have lots of it in which to read about our proposed holiday destination and plan with care. For another, we are free to spend extra time in places of special appeal.

INFORMATION SOURCES

There are numerous information sources waiting to be tapped, but none is a worthy substitute for talking to someone who has been there. Once you start travelling you will meet people keen to give you advice based on their experiences. Soon you will be comparing notes with **fellow travellers**, exchanging ideas, recommending good value hotels and restaurants. Before that happens, ask your travel agent to put you in touch with clients who have enjoyed a trip such as the one you plan. They will probably answer your questions frankly and hopefully confirm most of what you have already read about your proposed destination.

In planning a trip your first journey should be to the **local library** to research guidebooks, magazine and newspaper articles. Many libraries also have videos. If produced for tourist offices the commentary may only tell you about the good stuff. Still, the scenery will be titillating, the history and geography correct and the facilities and attractions well documented. Slide shows and movies shown by independent travellers can be useful; the question and answer period afterwards is always enlightening.

Most countries have **tourist offices** in Canada or the United States. (See Appendix C for a list of contacts.) On request, they will send you travel literature free of charge. Some representatives have more resources than others. Canadian provincial tourism offices are terrific in this regard, sending out glossy books crammed with coloured pictures on every aspect of travel in their region. So is the British Tourist Authority, which has more than a thousand different pamphlets, all of them free for the asking. When sending for tourism material remember to ask about discounts for visitors over 50. The response could well determine your mode of travel.

Travel shows such as those organized by *Today's Seniors* are excellent information sources, since representatives of airlines, tourist offices, tour companies and cruise specialists are there for no other reason than to tell you about their products.

Finally, having garnered all the basic information, you now need to find yourself a nice, efficient **travel agent**. Drop by to collect brochures from their shelves and while there talk with one of the counsellors. If he or she appears disinterested in you and your proposed trip, go somewhere else. If you are well received make an appointment to return, with your travelling companion if there is to be one, and discuss details of your proposed adventure.

Your travel agent will not bill you for services rendered. He or she receives a commission from the suppliers: the airlines, hotels, cruise lines, car-rental agencies, travel-package wholesalers and the rest. On complicated itineraries you may be charged for long-distance telephone calls, but these you would pay if you did your own bookings anyway.

Older travellers are sometimes skeptical of agents, but truly when planning your travels, a good one can be your best friend. Make an appointment for mid-morning or mid-afternoon when she is least likely to be rushed. An agent has untold resources literally at her fingertips. A few taps on her trusty computer and she can provide you with the latest airfares, train routes, hotels offering discounts and much more.

Some travel agents belong to large chains with access to data banks of information. Some smaller agencies specialize, and when working with a difficult itinerary it is definitely wise to pay one of them a visit. For example, an agency specializing in South America can design a better tour of that continent than one whose staff once went to Rio on a four-day familiarization trip. The specialist agency can probably get you a better airfare since it deals constantly with airlines flying there. Staff members speak the language, accompany groups, spend time with relatives there and know which hotels and local tour companies will serve you best. Book with such an agency and you will be given the best possible prices, along with advice on where to shop and eat, how to use public transport and what areas to avoid at night. South America is on your counsellor's mind day after day. It isn't wedged between tours to Europe, Florida and Timbuktu.

WHEN TO GO

This is where *we* get really lucky. With all the time in the world (more or less) we can avoid the hurricane season, excessive cold and heat, school and other holiday periods when prices hit the roof.

Know about **special happenings** and **public holidays**. Do you want to be in Rio for its Carnival or in Munich for Oktoberfest? Or are these times when you'd prefer to be somewhere else? I try to avoid cities on Mondays when museums and similar attractions are often closed.

My last visit to Prague coincided with the arrival of the Pope. The joy his visit brought was wonderful to witness. It also resulted in roped-off roads, overflowing hotels and restaurants and a zillion tour buses, all of which did nothing for my nicely-planned walking tour of the city. In Moscow once when a foreign president was scheduled to come to town, I thought it would be fun to tour the city during his arrival. Instead I found Red Square and the Kremlin banned to all except this chap, his entourage and hundreds of Russian security guards (disguised as a Westerner's idea of a Russian security guard) during my only day there.

$ DISCOUNTS

They are everywhere but you won't know it unless you ask. So-called Seniors Discounts are not necessarily the greatest. Ten percent off a $120 room is not what you want when the mid-week rate is $65 and you plan to arrive on a Wednesday. In my experience hotel clerks offer little when it comes to rent reductions. Also, if you arrive in late afternoon, unannounced and with your luggage stacked up to your ears, they know you won't trudge off to another hotel because the rent is $10 higher than expected. So try to telephone ahead and ask for the very lowest rate given your **age** (if you are over 50) and your **membership** in CARP, AARP, CAA or any other organization that may afford discounts. Tell them your arrival date is flexible; city hotels often have specials on weekends when business people have returned to their homes, while resorts and country inns are busiest on weekends. At check-in time you could be asked for proof of age and membership, so be sure to have your documentation with you.

In the next chapter I discuss organizations whose members receive discounts. Also, Appendix D lists some hotel and motel chains which extend discounts of up to 40%, often favouring CARP and AARP members in particular.

Check out old newspapers and magazines received from these two organizations. A CARP newspaper I am looking at right now advertises member discounts of up to 30% at a certain hotel.

Hotel and motel chains have toll-free numbers which connect you with a central reservation system. However sometimes you must telephone the hotel directly to find out about a discounted rate. For example, when arranging a recent trip to Boston I dialed the hotel chain's toll-free number and was quoted U.S. $125 (Can. $167) per day. Unimpressed, I asked the operator for the telephone number of my selected hotel and next called them directly. This time I was quoted U.S. $87 (Can. $116). A confirmation slip showing the rate was received in the mail so there was no mistake when I checked in. Maybe the higher rate would have paid for a more desirable room. I don't know, and in any case what I had suited me just fine.

*U*seful Contacts

*T*hroughout this book I mention the names of organizations and companies useful to 50 plus travellers. Below are brief descriptions of those which I believe to be the most beneficial. I hope this information helps you to decide whether or not to contact them (see Appendix A for the addresses and telephone numbers).

- The 160,000 member **Canadian Association of Retired Persons** is open to anyone 50 and over. Membership currently costs $10 a year, less if you enroll for longer. Its general purpose is to improve the quality of life of its members and in doing so it covers a broad range of services. The rapidly growing organization now has 10 chapters across Canada with more being planned. It is becoming a powerful advocate for the rights of older citizens. Many of the specialized services to members are advertised in CARP's bi-monthly newspaper.

    For travellers CARP membership brings access to discounts on accommodation, package tours, cruises, car rentals and travel insurance. The CARP Toronto Dominion Visa card includes travel insurance benefits.

- The **American Association of Retired Persons** with over 32 million members in 4,000 chapters is open to anyone 50 and over. Annual membership is U.S. $10 (Can. $13.35). An impressive number of member services include insurance, the association's own Visa card, and membership in the Amoco Motor Club. AARP members receive the organization's bulletin, published 11 times a year, and the bi-monthly magazine *Modern Maturity*. Information is available upon request on subjects such as health, fitness and financial investments.

    Member discounts are available from 25 hotel/motel chains, major car rental companies and other travel-related companies. The AARP **Travel Experience from American Express Travel** includes a range of cruises and tours, some of which are offered at discounted prices.

- Readers with British connections may be interested in **ARP Over 50**, a British organization with more than 120,000 members. Travel benefits are similar to those with AARP and CARP. Annual membership costs $30, or $40 for two.

- **The Canadian Snowbird Association** represents Canadians wintering outside Canada. Annual membership is $5. Medipac International supplies health insurance to members, while Medipac International Publishing circulates the CSA *News*.

- Services provided by your local automobile club affiliate of the **Canadian Automobile Association** are touched on in Chapter 14. We have belonged to our local club for 35 years and believe the value of travel assistance received has more than reimbursed our dues. At present our basic single driver membership costs about $55. Member services include emergency road assistance, legal coverage (including a bail bond service in the United States) and various forms of insurance, discounts on accommodation, automobile inspections and repairs.

  In co-operation with the American Automobile Association, it inspects and grades accommodation, restaurants and automobile services. Member clubs operate full-service travel agencies. Some are also tour operators, making the association one of the country's larger travel organizations.

  The association's guidebooks (available free to members) are revised annually. They contain reliable descriptions of geographical features, communities and tourist attractions in the United States, Canada, Mexico and Europe. Recommended hotels and motels are listed with rates showing discounts for older guests. So are recommended restaurants. Separate campground guides are available. Clubs issue International Driving Permits and provide information on driving, car rentals and vehicle purchases abroad.

- **Elderhostel Canada** and its counterpart in the United States are dealt with in Chapter 29. They are, of course, deeply into travel.

- **The Globetrotters Club**, a British-based organization with chapters in New York, California and Toronto, specializes in what it terms "travel on an anaemic wallet." This club is a support group and clearing-house for inexpensive travel. It exchanges travel tips and addresses for fellow members and also matches like-minded adventurers of all ages. Subscriptions cost $24 annually, proportionately less for two or three years.

- On the **international scene**, some major companies specifically servicing the over 50s travel market are:

- **Saga Holidays,** with offices in Britain, the United States and Australia, has a minimum age of 60 for members but can be flexible. This organization provides inclusive tours to almost anywhere in the world. It also packages programs for individual travellers and customizes combinations of group and independent travel. Members have their own magazine, which includes advertisements for single travellers wanting companions. Saga deals with its members directly rather than through travel agents. Some programs are a little more expensive than comparable tours for clients of all ages, so you have good reason to expect quality. Unless you plan on booking from Britain, you should contact Saga's Boston office.

- **Trafalgar Tours,** a British firm with an office in New York has tours available through Canadian travel agents. It offers first-class escorted coach tours of Britain and Europe, for clients 55 and over. Their tours move at a relaxed pace and use first-class hotels.

- **Golden Age Travelers** is an American travel club on the west coast for those over the age of 50. It deals directly with its members, and its tours are a little more expensive than those of competitors catering to all ages. Members receive a newsletter and a special matching service for room-mates helps singles to avoid supplemental charges for accommodation.

- **Grand Circle Travel** of Boston provides tours for travellers 50 and over, and it too deals directly with the public instead of using the services of travel agents.

- **The Over The Hill Gang** is an American organization, with a Toronto chapter. It offers skiing expeditions and other sports activities as well as adventure tours for 50 plus travellers.

*Y*our Very Good Health

*A*re you feeling tired or generally out of sorts or do you have a mild toothache that may be getting worse? None of these things is particularly troublesome at home, but when you expect to enjoy one busy day after another even minor twinges can spoil your tour as you wait "a few more hours" to see if what ails you goes away without medical help.

Above all else then, when planning to do some travelling get all your bits and pieces checked out and in good repair. If you are out of breath before you reach the store three blocks from home you will never manage the walking tour of Old Jerusalem in the midday sun or those cobbled streets beckoning you through historic York. How can you tackle all those steps to the station platform, then hoist your bag aboard the train when you have a trick back? And what a shame to be there at the Great Wall of China, too weary to walk more than a few metres of it.

BEFORE YOUR TRIP

Begin an **exercise program** now, so that your body is ready along with the rest of you for that big trip. Nothing too strenuous. A 30-minute brisk walk most days keeps me in sufficiently good shape to get where I am going without too much huffing and puffing. As well, have **dental work** completed at least a month before your flight, because atmospheric pressure plays havoc with new fillings. The same applies to abdominal surgery. Try not to fly within a month of your operation. The gas build-up could cause your incision to burst open and then things may get a mite messy.

Prevention being better than a cure in most things, and definitely when we're talking about tropical diseases, **inoculations** are necessary for certain trips — even if it's only a flu shot to battle the latest strain. Your family doctor will direct you to your local tropical diseases clinic where your vaccinations and immunizations are recorded in an International Certificate of Vaccinations distributed by Health and Welfare Canada. Look in it every few months so you know when to renew the more general vaccinations — those for typhoid, tetanus, yellow fever, meningitis and en-cephalitis — as they become invalid.

Medical personnel at the tropical diseases clinics have up-to-date in-formation on new strains of old diseases currently showing up in areas you plan to visit. Start your program several weeks ahead of your trip, espe-cially when travelling in Asia, Africa, South and Central America and some Caribbean countries. They, or your own physician, may also suggest gamma globulin as short-term protection against hepatitis and perhaps a flu shot.

As I write this I wonder what became of the American woman on our tour of Kenya's game parks. There we were enjoying a moonlit meal out-doors serenaded by wildlife, when she leaned her ghostly white, perspiring face towards me and asked if I could spare her a malaria pill. Had I given her one it wouldn't have helped because for full effect they must be taken before, during and after the trip. Next day she was flown to a Nairobi hos-pital. I just hope health insurance had been one of her pre-vacation pri-orities even though a visit to the tropical diseases clinic was not.

The Canadian headquarters of **International Association for Medical Assistance to Travellers** (IAMAT) in Guelph, Ontario will send you world immunization and malaria charts describing the latest status of countries where you could be at risk. (This information is free, but a donation is ap-preciated.) IAMAT also publishes a very useful directory of overseas medical facilities; it lists doctors who will provide assistance in English, at your hotel if required. See Appendix A for IAMAT's address.

Commonplace over-the-counter medication is usually available in larger hotels even in isolated areas, but it can be expensive and gift shops selling it seem to keep odd hours. It's a good idea to bring Pepto-Bismol tablets, aspirin or Tylenol, Band-Aids and the like with you from home. Some travellers carry personal pouches of blood in areas where AIDS is ram-pant. I don't go to this extreme, but do carry a packet of single-use syringes when I'm travelling in countries where these are known to be in short supply.

One last thing before leaving home: if you are on a very precise med-ication schedule and will be flying through multiple time zones, consult your physician about adjusting the dosage. Also if you are taking tranquil-lizers, sleeping pills or sedatives, ask your family physician if they can have adverse effects when combined with long-distance flying.

A cold or allergies could develop into painful ear and sinus problems after experiencing cabin air pressure changes. Use of a nose spray or drops during landing helps.

JET LAG

All of your saving and planning and the overnight trans-Atlantic flight are behind you. Now it is around 9 a.m. in London, Paris or Amsterdam when you reach your hotel and (providing they let you in this early) all you want to do is obey your body's clock telling you to climb into bed.

Doctors call it circadian desychronization, laymen call it jet lag, the effect on your body of flying across time zones at something like 800 km (500 mi.) per hour. The condition is worse when travelling from west to east, since you lose five or more hours in the process. The added effects of sitting in a fairly cramped space in a cabin where the air is short on oxygen and drier than the Mojave Desert compound the resultant fatigue, light headedness, loss of appetite and constipation.

Jet lag can't be avoided. It can be minimized with a few simple precautions:

❑ If possible have a **nap** during the day of your flight and go easy on refreshments at those *bon voyage* parties.

❑ On a truly long flight try to break up your journey with a **stopover** of at least 48 hours. For example, when heading for Australia, arrange with your airline for a couple of days in Hawaii or Fiji. On trips to India or the Middle East, I often attend a London show and meet friends for dinner before continuing my journey. It is like having two trips for the price of one. Given enough time I repeat the exercise on my way home.

❑ Combat dehydration during your flight by drinking plenty of liquids, but avoid excessive quantities of the complementary bubbly and pretty little bottles of liqueurs. Even caffeine should be limited. Instead try to consume plenty of water, in addition to the usual juices and soft drinks served during a six-hour flight.

❑ Follow that last bit of advice and I won't need to tell you to walk along the aisle every hour or so. (About the only thing I envy youth these days is their strong bladders.) In any event, get yourself a convenient aisle seat so it's easy to stretch your legs. Even while sitting you can wiggle your toes, flex your arm, leg or neck muscles to good effect.

❑ Upon arrival, try to adapt to the new time zone. No telling yourself "It's four in the morning at home so I am tired." An afternoon nap on your first day will probably be all you need before your body clicks into local time.

❑ When you have come through several time zones be prepared to abstain from tiring physical activities for approximately 48 hours. In tropical countries the heat is likely to be too oppressive for tiring activity until you become acclimatized. Whatever the temperature, be conservative about the distance you walk, remembering you have to get back again. And recognize that you may be constipated for the first few days, a condition better alleviated through consumption of fluids than by a harsh laxative.

DIETARY NEEDS

Older travellers often have special dietary needs. Airlines are pretty good about catering to these, as long as they know of them in advance of departure. **Self-catering accommodation** is better than all others when you are on a really strict diet. **Multi-vitamins** will help supplement diets of vegetarians in regions where a balanced meal may not always be available.

I sometimes carry my own supply of pre-wrapped snacks so as to avoid horribly expensive mini-bars and vending machines. These hold me over until we hit a town and I can buy more in a local supermarket. If you suffer from blood sugar problems, it can be crucial to have your own snacks on hand. Even if you don't, packaged crackers, granola or fruit bars can prove useful. On my first visit to Moscow about ten years ago I relied on my snacks for lunch, after several abortive attempts to find a place which would serve me. Tramping from one hotel restaurant to the next, I was told "no groupa, no food." Finally I concluded this to be the only city in the world where hotel dining rooms close at lunchtime unless they have a tour group booked. On subsequent visits I took my snacks to city parks and sat with weathered old residents watching pre-school groups at play. Now there are privately-owned and independently-operated restaurants where you can buy a good meal. If you really must, there's always McDonalds.

DIARRHEA AND SUNBURN

These are the two most common health problems of travellers overseas, and once again **precaution** is the magic word.

Diarrhea

Call it what you will — traveller's diarrhea, Montezuma's revenge, tourista,

Delhi belly — it always strikes at the most inconvenient times. Low-risk areas are the United States and Canada, northern Europe, Australia and New Zealand and some Caribbean islands. At high risk are vacationers in some 200 developing countries, especially those of Latin America, Africa, the Middle East and Asia.

When contracted, Pepto-Bismol or Imodium and lots of good clean water should clear it up. More severe cases which last three or four days should be treated with an antibiotic such as Norfloxacin, Septra or Bactrim. When you plan to tour a medium- or high-risk area, have a prescription filled before leaving home.

Diarrhea is most prevalent in countries where sanitation isn't what we are used to at home. Not that every newcomer is affected. I tend to be cautious when it comes to street foods, yet all over India I see tourists munching on terrific looking snacks cooked by roadside vendors. In exotic destinations you will frequently see invitingly colourful salads — and eating them may not affect you adversely at all. For my part, just knowing the saladstuff could have been grown in soil cultivated with human excrement, and that handlers don't have the facilities to be squeaky clean, puts me off. Every guidebook advises its readers to eat only fruit they themselves have peeled. Now, having peeled that straight-from-the-tree mango or persimmon, remember to wash your hands before tucking in.

Unless you know your stomach to be made from cast iron, try to avoid certain foods in risk areas. Make sure your meat, especially pork, is well cooked. Baked or broiled foods are better than those fried in old fat. Pass up the uncooked fish, unpasteurized milk and dairy products generally.

In regions where tap and well water is contaminated, you will probably find **bottled water** in your room, or on sale in the hotel. Make sure the bottle you buy is sealed, to ensure it isn't tap water. Refrain from using ice in your drinks. On a trip to Upper Egypt one idea I was glad to borrow from Japanese travellers was bottled water in a thermos carried on a shoulder strap.

SUNBURN

Avoiding sunburn should be commonsense, but most of us find the sun difficult to resist. It takes superhuman will-power not to spend too much time in the sun when arriving in a warm climate, especially when you've just left snow and ice behind. Try to remember, though, that in the tropics and at high altitudes, two hours of sunbathing can lead to five days with second-degree burns. And, unfair though it is, you can still be burned when the sky is overcast. So take it easy. Stay out of the fierce sunshine between noon and 3 p.m. when possible. Cover up with a long-sleeved shirt, wear a hat with a three-inch mimimum brim and use a sunblock appropriate to local conditions.

The array of **sunscreen** products on the market now is quite dizzying. Sun Protector Factor (SPF) indicates the number of times the product exceeds your skin's own natural protective powers. (For example, SPF 15 is 15 times as powerful as your own natural defences.) Higher numbers provide greater protection, but can cause skin irritation.

Your local pharmacist can advise you. In view of my fair skin, I was directed to a product with an SPF of 29 or 30 and was told it should be applied 30 to 60 minutes before exposure to allow the chemicals time to penetrate. A fresh application is necessary every two to four hours, more frequently when you swim. Water-resistant products should protect up to 40 minutes, waterproof products last twice as long.

Remember too that altitude increases the intensity of light — by 40% at 3,000 m (10,000 ft.) — so you need to take extra precautions when hiking in mountainous regions. To soothe a burn use cool compresses soaked in water or milk, followed by an antiseptic lotion to lessen the pain and prevent infection. Once the burn has cooled, over-the-counter cream or foam will help the healing process.

If all of these health precautions make you think it's easier to stay at home, you are right. But imagine how boring that would be. Believe me, a lot of this becomes second nature as you travel more frequently. And it's great to wake up each day in top form, eager to absorb new sights and experiences.

$\mathcal{P}$hysically Challenged Travellers

$\mathcal{T}$hose of us who heard the thunk, thunk, thunk of Terry Fox's prosthetic leg on the pavement as he attempted his run across Canada for charity couldn't fail to be stirred by his courage. And who could be anything but inspired by pictures of Rick Hansen, grinning from his wheelchair at the Great Wall of China during his world tour?

Around the globe I see travellers overcoming physical impairments of varying degrees, and their triumphs hold me in awe. It no longer makes the evening news when groups in wheelchairs conquer mountains and go exploring in Nepal. Or when individuals, who in other times would be confined to hospitals, now take on marathon tours. I recently read of a sightless woman on a one-year tour of India. It wasn't her blindness that almost did her in, she said, but because she was a woman travelling on her own. My mother-in-law who just turned ninety still crosses the Atlantic to attend family weddings and christenings. She travels unescorted and doesn't even acknowledge that she's hearing impaired.

Generally speaking, airlines, cruise ship companies and hoteliers are finally recognizing the needs of physically challenged travellers, and those for whom advancing years have brought limiting, though not severe, impediments. If you have very special needs, you probably belong to an association which has addresses of helpful organizations and medical facilities overseas. Their newsletters report on organized tours, and fellow members can give travel tips from personal experience. Below are some leads to follow, as you pursue your travel plans.

AIR TRAVEL

All travellers should check around to find the best airline for their needs. For disabled travellers requiring special assistance this is essential. Each airline has its own rules regarding things like wheelchairs, use of oxygen on board and discounts for an accompanying attendant.

An airline may require a **medical certificate** attesting to your ability to travel. If you plan to travel often it could be worth applying for a Frequent

Traveller's Medical Card (FREMEC) from your airline. This serves as a permanent medical record accepted by all International Air Transport Association (IATA) member airlines, and you simply produce it when booking future flights.

If there isn't a direct flight to your destination, make sure you know what is involved in making a connection. When booking your flight tell your travel agent, or someone in the airline's Special Services department, about your requirements. Usually they will do everything they can to make your journey comfortable. If your hearing is impaired tell the person who checks you in at the airport. Then you will be alerted to important announcements you may otherwise miss.

RAIL TRAVEL

Long-distance trains can be very convenient for physically challenged travellers, especially when you reserve a private bedroom. Most large stations have elevators, so you can avoid a lot of stairs. Train steps can be awfully high and difficult for even slightly arthritic passengers. Usually you can get a leg up with a stool and assistance from a porter.

Under certain circumstances **Via Rail** gives free transportation to an accompanying attendant. A telephone call to one of their offices will tell you whether you qualify for this, and you can ask for their publication *Services for Special Needs*, which is available in braille and large print. It can be obtained from local offices or by writing to their customer service department in Montreal. Similar information is available from **Amtrak**'s customer relations department in Washington D.C. and **British Rail**'s Toronto office (addresses and telephone numbers are listed in Appendix B).

CRUISE-SHIP TRAVEL

With so much competition these days, almost all cruise ships are adapted to accommodate disabled passengers. One very popular Caribbean cruise last winter was organized by Horizon Holidays of Toronto; the company arranged for a group of oxygen-dependent travellers to be accompanied by medical experts. Personal oxygen bottles were attached to seats on the flight from Toronto to Florida for embarkation. Medical staff from an Ontario hospital's respiratory division stayed with them at all times: during the flights, on the ship and on shore excursions. This tour was such a success a repeat is scheduled and others are being planned.

BUS TRAVEL

Like aircraft and trains, modern buses can be fairly user-friendly, depending on the severity of your disability and where you are travelling. If possible reserve your seat in advance and inform the booking agent of your needs. Some bus lines permit a companion to travel free if he or she is essential to the disabled traveller's well-being. Covering North American routes, **Greyhound Bus Lines** has a Helping Hand Service for their physically challenged passengers.

CAR TRAVEL

Most car rental companies in Europe and North America have specially equipped cars and vans for physically challenged drivers. Britain's Automobile Association publishes a *Guide for the Disabled,* for its members and anyone else belonging to affiliated clubs worldwide.

HOTELS AND MOTELS

Almost all of North America's new hotels and motels, and the old ones which have been renovated, have rooms designed for guests with disabilities. For example, **Canadian Pacific**'s resorts and grand old railway hotels have recently emerged from complete overhauls and upgrading of facilities. Now they have curbside and garage access for wheelchairs. All hotel public areas, including restaurants, lounges, banquet facilities and public washrooms are redesigned to permit wheelchair access. Special guest rooms have space for wheelchairs to move freely throughout. Closet rods and shelves can be lowered. Light switches, thermostats and security peepholes in the door are accessible from a wheelchair. Ensuite bathrooms have grab bars, lowered sinks, hand held showers and higher toilets. Portable bath benches and chairs and stout poles to help guests get into bed are available upon request. In addition, some guest rooms are equipped with visual alarms for the hard-of-hearing and have braille instructions and verbal alerts for blind visitors. Guests can make their special needs known when reserving rooms on Canadian Pacific's toll-free line 1-800-441-1414.

This is one example of user-friendly facilities which are provided by enlightened hoteliers. Other hotel chains to look for are: Best Western, Journey's End, Hilton, Holiday Inn, Howard Johnson, Hyatt International, Marriott, Sheraton, Travelodge and Westin.

SIGHTLESS TRAVELLERS

Air and cruise lines, railway and bus companies all have their own rules regarding **guide dogs**. When it comes to taking your dog out of the country you will likely run into quarantine regulations, so it is well to inquire before launching plans for an overseas trip. (Bermuda is one place I know where cruise passengers can take a guide dog ashore.) When you are accompanied by your dog, she should have all necessary shots. A veterinarian's certificate to this effect should be among your important documents.

Before departure for foreign destinations, try to become familiar with the feel of foreign currencies. Some have raised dots in their bills for identification by the blind.

MEDICAL ASSISTANCE

The International Association for Medical Assistance to Travellers (IAMAT) distributes a directory of English-speaking doctors in 120 countries. It suggests you carry a detailed record of your physical disabilities and medications prescribed for them and recommends you wear a Medic-Alert bracelet. The IAMAT directory states common medical problems and also gives a 24-hour hot-line telephone number your attending physician abroad can dial for further medical data.

Tips

Although I am not permanently disabled, more than once I have pulled a back or leg muscle while attempting to plug small appliances in hotel electrical outlets coyly hiding behind dressers and beds. Now I have no need for such acrobatics because I travel with drip-dry clothes and a wash'n wear haircut that doesn't scream for a hot curling iron to tame it. If this sounds too drastic for you, consider purchasing a butane curling iron. Battery-powered shavers are useful too, although most hotel bathrooms come with "shaver only" outlets above the counter.

I once shared a hotel room with a woman below average height who has learned to cope admirably. Out of her voluminous handbag came a rope with suction cups, which enabled her to hang up her clothes. She propped a portable mirror on the night table, then sat on the bed to apply her make-up. A folding lightweight stool (also carried in her purse) allowed her to reach sinks in the ensuite bathroom and public facilities.

A fascinating selection of **travel aids** are available through mail-order catalogues and travel shops: rubber caps to ease removal of stubborn bottle tops and tiny but effective reading lights and magnifying glasses for small print, just to mention a few.

☎ USEFUL CONTACTS

The Ontario March of Dimes organizes annual vacations close to home as well as great trips to various parts of the world for travellers with disabilities. People from other provinces are welcome. See Appendix A for the address and phone number.

Shirley Shelby of **Travel Helpers** in Don Mills, Ontario (see Appendix B) is very experienced in arranging trips for physically challenged travellers. In fact when Michael last spoke to her she had just returned from Toronto International Airport, where she had taken a stretcher patient for his second trip to Bermuda this year.

Another contact is **Travellin' Talk** of Clarksville, Tennesee, which coordinates a network of people around the world who offer information and help to disabled travellers visiting their area. It circulates a newsletter and offers a directory of services available to disabled travellers in the United States, Canada and several other countries. The address and telephone number are listed in Appendix A.

FURTHER READING

■ Cinnie Noble's *Handi-Travel: A Resource Book for Disabled and Elderly Travellers* (Toronto: Canadian Rehabilitation Council For The Disabled, 1987) is a well-organized manual which provides information sources and the names of organizations available to persons with specific disabilities.

■ *Access to the World: A Travel Guide for the Handicapped* (New York: Henry Holt & Co. Inc., 1986) by Louise Weiss is also very helpful.

*P*apers, **Please**

*S*ince most of us have plenty of time, it shouldn't be difficult to keep **travel documents** up-to-date. Human nature being what it is, few of us are so organized. Too bad, because in these times of sell-offs and last minute discounts, tremendous travel bargains are to be had when you are ready to get up and go with little notice. Here's what we need:

PASSPORTS

Every Canadian citizen is entitled to a passport and requires one for overseas travel. **Application forms** may be obtained from post offices and regional passport offices. To locate the passport office nearest you, or for automated information, you can telephone 1-800-567-6868 toll free, 24 hours a day from anywhere in Canada. For a more personal touch call Monday to Friday between 9 a.m. and 5 p.m.

Completion of your application calls for two passport photographs (you can have these taken at most camera stores), your birth certificate and, if you are a naturalized citizen, your citizenship certificate. Applications and photographs must be countersigned by a professional person who has known you for at least two years. Passports, valid for five years from date of issue, currently cost $35.

If you mail your completed application and accompanying documents to the Passport Office, Department of External Affairs, Ottawa, ON K1A 0G3, you should receive your passport in approximately two weeks — although it can take twice as long. If you take it personally to a passport office, your application will be processed within five working days. Should you be unable to get your own passport, your travel agent can do the legwork for you.

Having obtained a passport, do keep it in a safe place. Often it is as valuable to thieves as cash or cameras, and if it is lost or stolen you can be stranded until a replacement is obtained. (Your Canadian citizenship card or birth certificate will get you back into Canada but not necessarily across other borders.)

You should carry your passport in a **moneybelt** or **neck pouch** worn under your clothing, or stow it in a **hotel safe**. Many hotels have room safes, for which you choose the combination. Other hotels have safes behind the check-in counter. If they are in a place anywhere more public than this, I tend to pass them up and carry all my valuables (passport, rail-pass, credit cards, traveller's cheques and airline tickets) in a pouch under my shirt or sweater — not outside where it can be grabbed.

Try not to give your passport to anyone, especially in a place where they can take it into a back room and pass it on to someone else then swear they never saw it. Instead have a copy of those pages with your photo and pertinent data (pages 2 and 3) readily available for ID when using credit cards and so on. (Leave an extra copy at home, to be faxed to you if needed.) In some countries, the law requires hoteliers to keep your passport for the first 24 hours of your stay or until you leave, so you have no choice but to give it to them.

Make sure your passport is always current, and replace it well before the expiry date. (Some countries insist you travel with a passport that's valid for up to six months after you have left them.) Then if someone invites you on a whirlwind tour of India, leaving on Friday week, you can tell them "yes please."

VISAS

Canadians need only a current passport to enter many European and British Commonwealth countries. Simple identification (birth certificate or citizenship card) is required for Canadians to enter the United States, although a passport is recommended. Other countries may require a **tourist visa**, which is essentially written permission to enter a country; it also states the purpose of your visit. Within these countries your visas are as important as passports. If you have dual citizenship, tell your travel agent because in some countries Canadians require visas whereas holders of EEC passports do not.

When travelling as part of an organized tour your group may be covered by one visa obtained by the organizer.

Travel agents will obtain visas for you, in return for a service fee. Or you can contact the consulates of countries on your itinerary. Some countries will issue a visa when you arrive there. Others insist you have one in advance of your trip.

Your visa application must be accompanied by your passport, and since embassies and consulates keep your documents for seven to ten days you won't be able to travel overseas during this period. They insist on having the actual passport, not a photocopy. This means that if you need three or four visas you must wait for return of your passport from one embassy before sending it to another, and the whole exercise can take four or five weeks.

As a journalist I was once given an assignment which was to take me into three Eastern European countries, and I had to be back in Canada with my stories written within a month. There was a lot of nail-biting on my part, and much persuasion on the part of my tour company, but still I was able to get only two visas before my departure. And this was only after couriers had dashed between Ottawa and Toronto at my newspaper's expense. Things may have eased up in some countries now, but the problem still exists for others — it's best to inquire while your trip is in the early planning stage.

GETTING IT ALL TOGETHER

Whether you are planning a trip soon or not, it's a good idea to have an **Important Documents Envelope** containing nothing but your up-to-date travel documents. It should include the following items:

❑ Passport and photocopies of pages 2 and 3.

❑ Extra photos of yourself for use on train passes and so on.

❑ Canadian citizenship certificate or Canadian birth certificate (useful if your passport is lost or stolen on a trip).

❑ International Certificate of Vaccination which, like your passport, should be kept current.

❑ Medical prescriptions, including one for eye glasses if you wear them.

❑ If you are taking underage grandchildren along, a letter of agreement from their parents (see p. 50).

❑ Green customs card recording valuables in your possession, such as cameras, lenses, camcorder, jewellery, expensive wrist watches. (It is obtainable from the customs office at your Canadian departure airport.)

❑ Important numbers, that is home telephone numbers for emergency contacts, passport numbers, credit card numbers, driver's licence numbers, as well as telephone contact numbers in case of loss.

❏ Make a note to add your travel insurance policy and claim forms as soon as you get them. Also an extra copy of your itinerary with telephone numbers of places where you'll be staying.

Have all of the above handy. Then when your best friend calls and says her husband wants to attend the thingamajig show downtown next week instead of going on their Oriental tour, you can tell her you'll be ready in no time flat.

*M*oney Matters

*N*o matter how carefully you plan your holiday budget, you are likely to spend more money than anticipated. What I save on general expenses I tend to blow on a souvenir I really don't need, a tourist-priced feast and folklore evening advertised in my hotel or an impromptu casino visit even though I don't gamble at home. I tell myself this is all part of the happy travel experience.

Still, there are ways to be prudent with your travel money. You will establish your own methods; until then here are some general guidelines.

TRAVELLER'S CHEQUES

This is the safest way to carry your money. And depending on where you buy and exchange your cheques, you can save a few additional dollars.

When purchasing traveller's cheques commission or service charges can be at least 1%, plus as much again when you cash them in. Such charges can be avoided. Your bank's service plan may allow you to purchase cheques without a fee. Some travel agencies, including your automobile club, may waive their commission when you buy from them. If you purchase from **Thomas Cook** or **American Express** in Canada, and then cash the cheques at one of their overseas agencies you pay no charge at either end. Stores and restaurants rarely charge a commission for cashing your cheques when you do business with them. On the other hand some offer a discount of up to 10% for payment in cash.

When buying traveller's cheques you will be given two lists recording their numbers. Leave one list at home. Keep the other in a safe place, separate from the cheques because you will need it if they are lost or stolen.

CREDIT CARDS

Of all the useful aids that make travelling easier, can there be anything more convenient than a credit card? Think about it for a minute. Until we get home and start receiving the bills, it is akin to magic. We can dine and shop, change routes or wardrobes, replace a stolen camera and see the best theatre, just about anywhere, with a flash of our plastic cards.

A word of warning. Prices sometimes mean little when our signature substitutes for cash, especially when the currency on that tag is foreign. In Harrods once I picked up a pair of canary-yellow pumps from a barrel marked five pounds. I didn't even bother trying on the left shoe since I intended using them as slippers and they didn't have to be a perfect fit. When the bill arrived it was for fifty pounds. Even worse, the left shoe was too small.

I have learned to carry several credit cards following a shopping experience in Staffordshire. There one day a dinner service was bought and packed at 9.15 a.m. and almost paid for with my MasterCard. Then came the rub. For credit approval a call to Canada meant a delay of five hours because of the time difference. Instead of hanging around, I whipped my Visa card out from its separate hiding place, found it required no such call and was on my way in ten minutes.

If you will be away from home for some months, the interest on unpaid bills can be a shock to come home to. This can be avoided if you leave postdated cheques with a friend and have him pay your bills when they are due. Or, you can arrange for your bank to take a series of payments from your account. Or, you can send the credit card company postdated cheques in amounts you estimate spending.

ELECTRONIC BANKING

Bank and credit cards can be used creatively to save you money. For example, while away, transfer money from your checking account through an automatic teller machine just as you would at home. The advantage in doing so is in the exchange rate. This way, in return for a charge of $3 or so to use the system, you pay the interbank wholesale rate rather than retail rates, and so receive up to 5% more than if you had converted Canadian dollars or travellers cheques. But don't rely entirely on plastic. If your cards are stolen it will be at least 24 hours before they are replaced, depending where your lose you cards and the company which issued them. (More on this in Chapter 25.)

Automated teller machines which are connected to the Plus or Cirrus networks, can be found worldwide in almost every location that attracts tourists. When relying on these, first try to use them during banking hours.

Recently my card was refused by a machine. As a real live teller completed the transaction he explained that airport metal detectors sometimes damage the card's magnetic encoding. You may also find you cannot use your card while your bank's computer system is down.

$\mathcal{T}ips$ . . . .

❏ Not all credit cards are created equal. MasterCard and Visa are most widely accepted in stores and restaurants. Sometimes I find merchants reluctant to accept American Express.

❏ Check expiry dates and apply for a new card if necessary to see you through your trip.

❏ Keep card numbers recorded in your Important Documents Envelope or file. Also note telephone numbers to call in case of loss or theft.

❏ Credit card fraud is rampant. Try not to let your card out of your sight when using it. On my return from Argentina once I received an American Express bill for several hundred dollars, supposedly spent during my tour. I figured the only time this fraud could have occurred was in my very exclusive hotel, when a clerk disappeared with my card as I paid my bill. Luckily I was in another country by nightfall and couldn't have signed for tours in Argentina charged on the date shown. (If you are leaving postdated cheques with a friend, give him some idea of what the bill he pays should be.)

❏ Often small establishments refuse some or all credit cards. Even large stores, Marks and Spencer in Britain to name one, can require payment by cash, traveller's cheques or their own company card.

CASH

With the exception of those countries where the American dollar is welcomed as if it were their own, I find it best to convert some cash into the local currencies before leaving home. If you are travelling independently try to arrive with $100 or so in small denominations to get you through the airport and to your hotel. If the currency you need is not available in Canada, carry American five and one dollar bills for taxi fares and tips. In these countries, when you convert your currency buy small amounts, since it cannot be changed back once you have left.

Exchange your dollars or traveller's cheques into local money at official agencies. There you are likely to receive an established rate, less a commission or service charge. I find banks usually give the best overall value. Those storefront exchange bureaus you see in tourist areas may be more accessible and have more convenient hours, but local money there usually costs you more. Changing money at your hotel can be even more expensive.

Although street dealers work quite openly in some places, what they are doing is usually illegal. In countries where Western currencies are in huge demand you will be offered very exciting rates on the street. Don't fall for the dealer's line, however sweet. Chances are the bills are counterfeit and so closely resembling the real thing you won't notice.

A guide once told me that con men consider older travellers to be easy marks. According to him we are too trusting, easily flattered and readily distracted during a transaction. At the time I scoffed at his commentary. Then I saw it happen. Outside the Budapest Hilton, I refused an unrealistically high rate for my dollars but through a shop window watched as a tout worked on a middle-aged American couple. During the swap, the dealer's friend chatted up the woman, and with polite good-byes all round the locals sauntered into oblivion provided by a German tour group.

The tourists couldn't believe that fate had dealt them such a blow. It wasn't even counterfeit money, but newspaper sheets cut to size and sandwiched between a few genuine looking bills. You say you wouldn't be so gullible? Don't count on it. Not in a busy foreign street, with the dealer's mate telling you how his brother lives in your beautiful city. In this instance the friend pocketed the American dollars, while his pal counted out the funny money furtively under his jacket. Had the law stepped in, I suppose the chap with the dollars could have hurried off, claiming no knowledge of the deal or the swindler.

In the neighbouring Czech Republic street dealers are palming off worthless old federal Czechoslovak koruna bills. In Israel you could be given old shekel notes of 500 and 1,000 denominations. Although they are no longer in circulation they look similar to current notes of lower denominations.

So **play it safe** and give your business to the official money changers.

In countries with currency restrictions you will often find Tourist Shops, where prices are in U.S. dollars and clerks convert your tab to any Western currency with enviable speed. Try to pay the exact amount in dollars. In a Russian Berioska store I handed over a $20 bill and received $6 change in French and German coins that were useless to me.

CONVERSION

By the time you reach your fourth country in ten days you will find yourself trying your key in the door of your Amsterdam hotel's room number though you are now in Antwerp and calculating your Belgian francs at the rate paid you in France. (Since you receive 4 francs for the dollar in France and 24 in Belgium at this time, you could pass up that Bruges lace hanky in the mistaken belief it would cost you a week's wage.) A pocket electronic converter has helped solve my ineptitude in calculating costs. I set it at the new rate when crossing the border, and so long as I have it handy, I no longer buy $50 earrings which I thought were costing me $5.

EMERGENCY FUNDS

With a good friend and money back home, you can easily have additional funds sent to you. Your friend simply visits a Western Union or American Express office and for a fee, arranges for the required cash to be transferred to an outlet near you. He can pay with cash or a credit card, and if both you and your pal are close to an office (and you need less than $10,000) you can have the money within an hour. If not, a transfer can take several days to complete.

TIPPING AND TAXES

Tipping should be included in your reckoning. Porters and bellmen expect $1 per bag carried, chambermaids $1 per day. Although some cruise lines advertise that tipping is entirely optional, $10 to $13 per passenger per day is suggested on most ships (see more in Chapter 16, p. 96).

Tour guides typically receive $2 per day. Local guides and coach drivers half that sum.

At least in Europe you will not be reminded of taxes, because they are included in the prices. In Canada it is embarrassing to hear visitors from overseas gasp at their bill, presented with GST and PST plus special hotel levies tacked onto the amount they were expecting to pay. Also in restaurants where a further 15% service charge has been added before the various taxes. (Remember too that parking at city hotels can add another $10 to $15 a day to your bill come check-out time.)

Tips

❏ If you choose to splurge on a $350 a night hotel room, remember that your expenses don't stop there. In any five-star hotel you will tip someone to park your car, someone else to show you to your room and a third person to carry your bag. You will be charged for parking, and probably for breakfast. Morning coffee or a mid-afternoon snack can cost as much as a meal in that nice little restaurant around the corner. In fact everything from a visit to the in-house beauty salon to a drink in the lounge costs more than you need to pay.

❏ Increase your buying power by joining organizations such as CARP and AARP and your local automobile club, because membership brings travel discounts among the many perks. (The trick here is to ask for them when making your reservations.)

❏ Take advantage of the buying power of airlines, tour companies and some of the larger travel agency chains. They "buy" hotel rooms, theatre tickets, rental cars, etc., in bulk and then pass the savings on to their clients.

❏ Use **travel passes** instead of individual tickets for air, rail and road transportation. Flexipasses which limit travel to a specified number of days within a fixed period are probably your greatest travel bargain — if you can plan your travels to use them wisely.

❏ Most large cities have reduced-fare passes on public transport for travel outside rush hours. One-day excursion rates can often be combined with discounts awarded travellers over 55, or to visitors from abroad.

❏ Shop where the locals do. If you are budget conscious enough at home to choose a supermarket over the local convenience store, you can do so as easily while away.

❏ There are seldom any bargains to be had at tourist stores, and with very few exceptions airports are notoriously expensive even in so-called duty-free shops.

❏ Take advantage of national promotions. An example is the **Holland Wallet.** This leather wallet contains things important to an arriving tourist: train pass to take you from the airport into Amsterdam; Dutch coins and pre-stamped postcards; fonecard (for prepaid phone calls because few telephones there take coins); and admission passes, maps and vouchers for shopping discounts. Total value is about $150 and the wallets cost $83.95 for one person, $94.65 for two. Copenhagen and Helsinki are two cities where inexpensive passes provide public transportation and admissions. Tourist bureaus will tell you of other promotions in effect during your visit.

❑ Some museums and cultural attractions have free access one day a week. Cards for multiple admissions such as those for National Trust properties in Britain provide big savings so long as you make good use of them.

❑ That long-distance feeling can work out to be outrageously expensive when you use your in-room telephone. Avoid it by using **public telephones** in the lobby or beyond. (Post offices or telegraph offices are a good bet). A telephone company credit card, used in conjunction with the company's local number, allows you to call overseas without paying a trans-ocean surcharge.

❑ Don't even open that mini-bar in your room unless it is to store films or snacks and soft drinks from the grocery store. In modern hotels the contents may be accounted for by computer, which is clever enough to charge for anything removed but doesn't necessarily credit your account when you put it back. Since the maid restocks the mini-bar daily you can't prove you didn't consume the entire contents at the beginning of your stay.

❑ Finally don't clean out your wallet completely during that last night in town. You may have to pay an airport departure tax, which can be as high as $35 per person. On arrival I usually check this out and tuck the required amount away with my return air ticket so I am sure of it on the way back out of the country.

Cutting corners to conserve on expenses isn't always a joy, but it can be done painlessly when you know where the savings are and determine their value to you. If you have always wanted Afternoon Tea at the Dorchester Hotel, or long to see *Miss Saigon*, or dream of being pampered for a day at some fabulous spa, I hope you will do these things. If this means delaying your trip for a month or two, or skimping on something else, or even bringing home fewer presents, take a leaf from the book of those youngsters on television who advertise hair colouring. Tell yourself "I'm Worth It."

$\mathcal{I}$nsurance

$\mathcal{T}$he television commercials are dead wrong. It is not the traveller's cheques you mustn't leave home without, it is medical insurance. We all have horror stories to tell about friends, if not ourselves, when it comes to $2,000 to $3,000 a day hospital costs and having to sell the house or kids to pay a surgeon's fee. For your vacation to be cut short by hospitalization is tough enough, without the fear of rising costs every time your blood pressure is recorded or a new bandage applied.

While the following will give you some ideas on what to look for, only you and a travel insurance expert can determine your exact needs.

WHAT TO BUY

There are three broad categories of insurance usually required by travellers and they are often contained in one policy:

- **Trip cancellation** insurance, to protect you against the costs of cancellation, interruption or delay
- **Personal effects**, for protection against loss of your belongings
- **Health** and **accident** or **medical** insurance

In addition, for those travelling on a tour package, default insurance is necessary in case of a company declaring bankruptcy (this is unlikely, but it does happen.) In Ontario, British Columbia and Quebec, compensation funds offer partial, not necessarily total, protection.

Premium type credit cards often entitle holders to a specified amount of travel health insurance, which can be reason enough to make their annual membership fee worthwhile. Such policies usually contain age exclusions or can otherwise be inadequate to a traveller's needs. If you have such a card, establish what insurance benefits come with it and purchase extra coverage where necessary.

Trip Cancellation and Personal Effects Insurance

The trip cancellation portion of your insurance covers the cost of alternative routing or transportation when your flight is cancelled, or the cost of returning home for an emergency before the scheduled date. The personal effects portion covers loss or theft of your belongings *en route*. In practice, both travel and trip cancellation insurance are often included in the policy for health and accident insurance.

This type of insurance is quite inexpensive. Ask for the policy to be explained. Perhaps it entitles you to only $200 for your camcorder which cost five or six times that amount. If you have a prosthetic limb or wheelchair, its coverage could be grossly inadequate. In such instances you can buy additional coverage from your travel insurance vendor, or add these items to your homeowner's policy as we do with our cameras.

Health Insurance

This is the Big One, absence of which can put you in hock for ever and beyond. Your credit cards, employee health insurance plan and automobile club memberships may provide some health and accident insurance, but they are unlikely to cover a hospital stay in a foreign country. Canadian residents are covered by provincial health insurance plans so long as we remain in the country. Once we leave it, the situation changes dramatically.

Be aware that regular hospital care in the United States and Europe will cost you upwards of $2,000 a day. Using myself, an Ontario resident, as an example of government insurance coverage: OHIP currently pays $400 a day maximum for acute care services. This is for hospital room, surgery, drugs and all other treatment. Two hundred dollars a day is allowed for less intensive service provided outside Canada. (OHIP's current plan to reduce payments for out of country hospital care to $100 per day is being vigorously contested.) Regardless of fees charged by overseas physicians, OHIP will reimburse them in the amount Ontario doctors receive for similar treatment. OHIP also covers out-patient services overseas, at the rate paid for the same medical procedures in Canada.

To qualify for even this coverage I must be physically present in Ontario for at least six months of the year. (Excepted are people working or studying outside the province temporarily.) Obviously then I am well advised to have additional insurance to span the very large gap between OHIP payments and medical charges outside the country.

Other provinces and territories have similar financial restrictions, with residency requirements between four and eight months. Moreover some provincial governments want notification to the health department when you plan to be away for a month or longer.

In summing up, check your situation with your provincial Ministry of Health before selecting additional health and accident insurance. It is a costly but essential travel expense, and you simply can't afford to leave home without it.

WHERE TO BUY YOUR INSURANCE

Take time to check out your options when buying travel insurance. Recently we had an emergency trip to Britain and in the turmoil forgot to buy insurance coverage before arriving at the airport. There we were charged $50 for a week's coverage for two when it would have cost $30 from our regular insurer.

The sources are as numerous as gophers on a prairie field: travel agents, automobile clubs, 50 plus organizations, some banks and trust companies. Or you can purchase your insurance from one of the specialist companies such as **Blue Cross** and **John Ingle Travel Insurance**. Coverage can be for a day, a week or months. Frequent travellers may find it advantageous to buy an annual policy instead of a different policy for each trip.

Something else to consider is the "managed care program" policy of the kind offered through travel agencies by the **Voyageur Insurance Company.** Under Voyageur's program, insurance costs are reduced by approximately 40% because policy holders agree to accept medical care from health specialists and hospitals within Voyageur's worldwide group. The list of participating facilities is extensive, especially in North America. For example, in our favourite part of Florida, the hospital where my sister checked in with a fractured ankle is not included, but another listed with Voyageur is only five or six minutes away. If the distance between participating hospitals is a concern, I suggest you inquire about their locations before buying.

? QUESTIONS TO ASK

? Since we are talking fairly big money here, you might look for answers to the following questions:

❑ When insurance is provided through a credit card, are you covered even if you haven't used the card to pay for your vacation?

❑ If your credit card covers you for a maximum of three weeks and you are travelling for six, does that three weeks begin when you leave home or when you first require medical treatment? In stacking two credit cards to cover the total period, are you in fact insured twice for the first three weeks and not at all for the remainder of your trip?

❑ Will you be eligible for credit card insurance coverage at the time of your trip? Since some companies place an age limit of 65 or 70 years, this may be the time to apply for a different credit card.

❑ What is the insurer's ruling regarding any chronic or pre-existing health conditions? Or if you travel against medical advice? Are specific illnesses, such as AIDS, covered?

❑ Are certain activities excluded? I wouldn't lose sleep if I had to refrain from mountain climbing or participating in the Boston marathon, but for some this may be the highlight, if not the sole purpose of their trip. Are countries on your planned itineraries excluded because to venture into them is considered a high risk?

❑ Does the insurance company pay for your expenses directly to the hospital and doctors, or are you required to settle your bills and wait to be reimbursed later?

❑ If necessary, will your return to Canada with a medical escort be covered? If you are driving, is the cost of returning your car or RV covered? If you die while travelling, does the policy pay for the return of your body? Is your travelling companion's journey home covered in any of these situations?

❑ Is there a 24-hour toll-free telephone line to your insurance company, to be used in time of emergency?

❑ How does the cost compare with rates quoted by other companies? If it is much lower, perhaps you have to pay the first $250 or $500, or a proportion of the claim. Is there a ceiling on payments by the insurance company? Is the price lower because potentially important and expensive eventualities are excluded?

❑ Can you extend your coverage if you change your travel plans and decide to stay out of the country longer? If so, determine the extra cost when buying the original policy.

❑ If you are planning a number of short trips out of the country, does one single policy keep you covered for the entire period abroad, saving renewal costs?

❑ How well established is the insurance company? That lovely cheap rate won't be worth much if the company's not there when you need it.

It is your responsibility to understand your policy. Given any doubts, you can talk to someone in your provincial health department or call the **Canadian Life and Health Association** on their toll-free line: 1-800-268-8099.

Recognize that you must be up front with your insurance company when asked about previous illness, chronic conditions and anything else that could effect your coverage. Insurance policies invariably have "pre-existing condition" clauses and if the information you give is not 100% you could find yourself without support just when you need it.

COSTS

Health insurance costs are based on so many factors there is no such thing as an average price. To give you some indication of this, here is a list of some current rates quoted to me in 1994:

■ A 30-day comprehensive deluxe policy with no deduction for Ontario residents through Ontario Blue Cross costs:
$76 for someone 54 years and under;
$112 for someone between 55 and 69 years;
$176 for someone 70 years and older.
(Blue Cross rates in other provinces should be obtained locally.)

■ For 33 days' coverage, John Ingle – Nomad quotes for residents of Ontario and most western provinces:
$129 for someone between 55 years and 64;
$222 for someone between 65 and 75;
$348 for someone 76 and older.

■ For Voyageur Insurance Company's managed care plan up to 30 days I was quoted for Ontario residents:
$50.50 for someone 59 years and under;
$93 for someone 60 to 69;
$124 for someone 70 to 79;
$181 for someone 80 years and older.

Voyageur's rates vary somewhat for residents of other provinces and territories. For example Quebeckers pay $44, $81, $108.50 and $162.50 respectively. Residents of the Atlantic provinces pay $27, $45.50, $76.50 and $91.50 respectively, while those who live in British Columbia and the

Yukon pay $44, $81, $108.50 and $162.50. There are similar variations for residents of the Northwest Territories and the Prairie provinces.

The best rates are for Canadians travelling in Australia and New Zealand, where health and accident insurance costs can be very low when compared with all others. Even here it is important to find the right insurance company.

Always carry proof of your provincial and private insurance plans (the insurer usually gives you an ID card) and a few insurance claim forms.

MAKING A CLAIM

Read your policy carefully in the comfort of your home. Then at the time of crisis you aren't scrambling around wondering what your first move should be.

In the event of loss or theft, call the police and register details with them. Ask for a copy of the police report for your insurance company. Hang on to receipts for any replacements purchased. (If you buy a new camera, camcorder or piece of luggage before your trip, keep these receipts too. They will be useful when claiming for their loss.)

If your health insurance coverage requires you to take care of your hospital expenses and collect later, be prepared with an acceptable method of payment. When you leave the hospital request a legible, itemized statement, preferably one in English, to satisfy your insurance company.

FURTHER READING

■ Canadians travelling to the United States and snowbirds bound for Florida and Arizona in particular, will find the *Traveller's Medical Services Directory* (Fort Lauderdale: International Medical Services Director Publishing Co., 1993) an invaluable source of information.

Taking It With You

A friend of mine packs all her belongings for a two-week vacation in a carry-on flight bag, yet returns with photos showing how fresh and perky she looked during her entire tour. A cheeky little cap here, a scarf artfully tied there, a coloured belt to match her shoes — it's nice when you know how. The first time I tried this I set off with no more than a huge shoulder bag and came home lopsided. (I also had two huge carrier bags filled with clothes I bought when the weather turned unseasonably cold, and gifts I simply couldn't resist.) Since then I have learned the joy of travelling unencumbered, of being able to carry everything without help. Well, without manual help at least. The invention of luggage with strong wheels changed my life.

THE RIGHT STUFF

If your luggage dates back to World War II, I suggest you put a new suitcase on your list for Santa. While at it give him the make and model number of your choice, so he gets it right. Gone are the days when we carried three-piece matching sets, plus a little square cosmetic case that banged the thigh mercilessly unless carried at arm's length. Now nobody needs more than one good suitcase plus a flight bag or hold-all.

Hard-shell cases are durable but quite heavy even when empty. I find a deeper case more manageable than a larger shallow one that flops about on the hotel room stand and plays dead like our dear departed dachshund when attached to a leash. Cases made of coarse fabric show stains more readily than those with smooth nylon surfaces which are easily wiped off. Check out the zippers to ensure they are heavy duty. A cheap suitcase will not serve you well, but do look for a sale because luggage is frequently available at 40% to 50% off the regular price.

I always carry a nylon shopping bag which can fold into a small package. When we stay in a self-catering unit, it is useful for groceries in places where shopkeepers don't provide plastic or paper bags. It's also handy when buying small items like grandchildren's clothes. I skip from one store to the next, stuffing it with the soft little parcels and have my hands free to examine more.

There are all manner of expandable bags on the market. Some are no more than the size of a purse or large envelope when folded but grow into fair-sized totes on wheels, and even to fully-grown suitcases. If you have to buy an extra bag during your trip, try to get to a street market. Whatever country you are in, among those strange looking root vegetables and brass pots and sticky cakes someone will be selling luggage.

I don't travel with a portable luggage carrier on wheels because I find them awkward to carry, but in this regard I think I am in the minority. I prefer a suitcase with sturdy wheels, large enough to take the bumps on uneven sidewalks. The latest in carry-on luggage is a rectangular case with retractable wheels and walking handle. It can be carried or walked, fits under the seat of an aircraft and upon deplaning the chap who's first in line for a taxi usually has one.

Lock your luggage, then pocket the key where it will be safe yet easy to reach if a customs official asks you to open up. Tie a ribbon around the handle for easy recognition. Have your home address inside as well as out. Over the years, I have had three Canadian flag tags stolen from my case while in transit. Now I use unobtrusive brown leather tags, with a flap over my home address.

CLOTHES TO GO

That old traveller's rule about taking **twice the money and half the clothes** you think you'll need still holds true. You actually require roughly the same amount of clothing for a two week's vacation as you do for a long weekend away. Travelling light means to dress around one colour and to mix and match outfits. If your jacket can be worn only with those grey slacks or skirt, put it back in the cupboard. Everything has to be versatile, including you.

I remember the days when we used to buy a new outfit to wear on the plane. I can only think that was when we were met by relatives who hadn't seen us in donkeys years. Now, with the exception of something like hiking boots for your first trekking adventure, or a newer style of swimsuit when you are off to the Caribbean, I suggest you rely on clothes you consider to be old friends. Broken-in shoes, everyday slacks comfortably contoured to your shape, a favourite broad-brimmed hat to fit into a purse or pocket, T-shirts and sweaters are all must go's. Have you noticed how manufacturers are how returning to the polyester blends which were once considered old fuddy-duddies, remnants of the sixties? Could this be because they travel well, while raw silks and cottons don't? Let wash'n wear be your motto for travel clothes.

Comfortable shoes are vital. You can loosen belts, undo jackets, get by with unmatched colours, but if your feet hurt there's not much you can do.

As the years speed relentlessly by, my feet tend to swell more on long-distance flights. To avoid walking barefoot off the plane I carry flat shoes a size bigger than usual in my flight bag for that marathon walk through the airport on arrival. For touring, do take a good pair of walking shoes with thick soles to blunt the impact of cobbled streets and uneven paths on your feet. Also bring a pair of dress shoes (not sandals, they quickly become uncomfortable when walking far) and thongs for the beach or poolside.

You will need a raincoat, one that is lightweight, dark-coloured and wrinkle-free. It can double as a dressing gown if your hotel room and the nearest bathroom are not connected. I usually have a simple cotton cover-all dress for sitting around my hotel room, the beach or pool. Socks can double as slippers. Lounging pyjamas are useful for sleeping and for day wear in a suite or apartment. Those big sloppy T-shirts can do double duty as bed and loungewear. Actually, almost every item of clothing should be up to double duty or stay home.

Learn to dress in layers. On a cold morning a T-shirt under your cotton shirt, topped by a sweater and lightweight jacket will keep you warm without the bulk of a down-filled parka. As the day wears on, and hopefully the sun comes out to warm you, the layers can be peeled and stuffed into your shoulder bag.

Any clothing made for a specific purpose, whether a sports outfit, school uniform or travel wear is bound to be more costly than everyday duds. But, it can be fun. At the dude ranch who wants to be the only city slicker not wearing a check shirt, cowboy boots and ten-gallon hat? On safari, tourists get all decked out in khaki multi-pocketed jackets, flapping shorts, high woolen socks and the mandatory hat — even though their weapon is a camcorder and they shoot from a mini-van with the top raised.

Shirts and jackets with lots of closed pockets, a lightweight hold-all shoulder bag with zippered interior pocket and a wide-brimmed hat for hot weather destinations are what constitute good travel gear for me. Women's jackets seldom come with a secure inside pocket so I often create one. If shirt pockets are open I sew a velcro strip in to close them, making them secure enough to hold my credit cards and a few bills. If you can afford it, you will find **Tilley Endurables' travelwear** virtually indestructable: jackets, slacks and even dress blazers, have hidden thief-proof pockets. Dresswear is smart enough to wear on almost any occasion.

I seldom carry a purse when touring for the day. Cash, ID, credit cards and the like are all stashed in my secure pockets. (A good alternative is the durable money belt, or small pouch worn around the neck under your shirt.) This way I have my hands free and don't worry about absentmindedly leaving something on a cafeteria counter or bus seat.

ACCESSORIES

I positively drool in travel shops stocked with handsome little gadgets designed to make the traveller's lot easier. Then I tell myself "it's one more thing to carry" and pass most of them by.

It's as well to ask yourself how often you will use that handy accessory before buying it. The portable door lock may give you peace of mind in a city hotel room (so will a chair pushed under the door handle) but it's quite unnecessary for the farm vacations you take most years. And those bright plastic cylinders to wear round your neck? They are great for holding keys and ice cream money at the pool or beach, but you won't have much use for them at Aunt Helen's in Chicago.

Travel shops have catalogues packed with gifts for $10 and under, such as a retractable hair brush and self-storing tooth brush; a little cap to protect your regular toothbrush when you leave it on the hotel bathroom counter (I found a beetle nibbling my toothbrush once, and couldn't wait to buy a new one); foam earplugs; plastic clothes hangers; a stain eraser guaranteed to take out coffee, red wine, sauce, lipstick and ink stains; an inflatabale neck pillow, good for bumpy train rides; a portable cutlery set, water purification filter straw, various types of personal alarms; waterproof moneybelts, travel wallets and document pouches to fit around your leg, waist or neck; and the Linguaphone European Translator which can display some 2,400 commonly used basic phrases in 12 languages in its screen.

The items mentioned above are taken from a catalogue distributed by Toronto's **The Way To Go** travel shop, which stocks more than 2,000 travel aids. Two other catalogues, focused more on the outdoor vacation are **Europe Bound Travel Outfitters**, which provides super camping and sports gear, outdoor clothing, cookware, backpacks and the like at its four

Ontario stores. And **Mountain Equipment Co-op** with stores in Vancouver, Calgary, Toronto and Ottawa. These stores are also good sources of travel guides, as are specialist travel bookstores such as **Ulysses Travel Bookshop** of Montreal and Toronto and **Gulliver's Travel Book Shop** of Toronto.

In our basement I keep a cardboard box which is my personal travel store from which I shop for every trip. Items used most include:

❏ An all-purpose drain stopper, face cloth and regular-sized cake of **soap** in a plastic container. (A surprising number of first-class hotels provide soap the size of a postage stamp, and even five star properties where thick fluffy towels and bathrobes hang in the bathroom are shy of face-cloths.)

❏ A **Swiss army knife**, with corkscrew, bottle opener, nail scissors and a tiny pair of pliers, in addition to the usual blades.

❏ **Binoculars**. Mine serve me well to focus on many things from a distant volcanic eruption to the Pope, from bald eagles to concert performers, just in case my seat isn't as good as the ticket price promises.

❏ **A first-aid kit**. Very important. Travel shops stock complete kits. If you make your own in a plastic food container or toffee tin, it should contain nail scissors, tweezers, all-purpose ointment for cuts and blisters, sunburn salve, plasters and syringes. (Syringes are for when you have an infection requiring an injected antibiotic, in countries where they have to be reused because of short supply.)

❏ A small **flashlight**. This is useful in those darkened theatres, at museums and at night in dimly lit streets where I am unsure of curbs and steps. Mostly I use mine for lighting my way to the bathroom, so I don't flood-light the bedroom by pressing the wrong light switch and wake my buddy.

❏ An old-fashioned style **alarm clock**, with large luminous digits. (The inexpensive sort that folds into a hard covered case. I have been let down too often to rely on wake-up calls, and in-room clocks which call for an engineer to set them.)

❏ **Adapters**, which allow me to use small electrical appliances bought from home. About the only thing I use these for is a battered little coffee percolator left over from our camping days, and which boils water for tea faster than the immersion heaters. Inside it I stuff a small mug, tea bags and a set of cutlery so I can avoid plastic when having a deli lunch or supper.

❑ **Laundry supplies**. A portable clothes-line and miniature pegs can be bought in a neat package, but I use a piece of sturdy twine, regular pegs and a couple of folding dress hangers. Once opened, small containers of laundry powder are not easy to reseal. Instead I pour a small supply into a Ziploc bag.

❑ In a **nylon pouch**, roughly 12 cm x 18 cm (5 in. x 7 in.) I carry adhesive tape, a tiny screwdriver set to fix my camera and reading glasses, safety pins, needle and thread, nail scissors, elastic bands, string, extra pens and a pocket-sized notebook. If you send postcards home, you could keep addressed labels here, and postage stamps. (Buy a supply at a post office and use them throughout the country. It saves hunting down stamp machines for two or three at a time. Hotels sell stamps, but who wants to line up at the desk for a couple of stamps?)

❑ **Plastic bags** or grocery shopping bags to wrap muddy shoes, swimsuits and dampish laundry that hasn't dried quite as quickly as expected. Small amounts of currency for countries to be visited, costume jewellery, a spare wristwatch, and even make-up are easily recognized when carried in Ziploc bags.

❑ A **rain poncho** that folds into a pouch.

Experienced travellers agree that clothes can emerge from your suitcase virtually crease-free when you pack them rolled into cylinders. Put heavy items at the bottom, and clothes you won't be wearing right away in the next layer. Some people I know stuff socks, hose and underwear in shoes and spare corners. I prefer to keep them together in a plastic see-through bag so I can find them easily.

When checking in for an overnight at a country hotel, B & B or some other accommodation where I know my car is secure, I pack so that I can take a hold-all or flight bag with me, and leave my main luggage in the trunk. Sometimes I leave my larger case in storage at a railway station or airport and go off on a three- or four-day excursion with only a large shoulder bag. Better still if I can return to the same city hotel I put my luggage in the storage room. Once in a while, in hotels where I am known, my case will be in my room when I return, and that really makes me feel I have come home.

CARRY ON

Air passengers are permitted one carry-on bag approximately 50 cm x 37 cm x 25 cm (20 in. x 16 in. x 9 in.) though you wouldn't know it as passengers lug several bags along the aircraft's aisle, each one large enough to hide a stowaway. As the rules require, mine does fit under the seat in front, and I prefer it there where I can use it as a footrest. (Overhead bins are good for coats, but I hate wrestling with anything heavier up there.)

Your carry-on bag should contain travel documents, traveller's cheques, sunglasses and a change of clothes in case your main luggage goes A.W.O.L. for a day or two. You should also include all medication and prescriptions, ear plugs and eye shades (if you want to sleep before lights out) and your reading material, toiletries and camera (preferably unloaded).

The nature of your trip and the destination's climate are crucial to your choice of clothes and accessories. Bear in mind that if you have neglected to bring everything you need, you can probably buy it there. In Britain we always stock up on underwear, socks, T-shirts, sweaters and even slacks at Marks and Spencer which has branches in about every town.

CHAPTER 10

*O*n the Home Front

*I*f you have traded the family home for a condo and concierge, off you go. If not, you have a few things to take care of first. There are the obvious precautions: arranging for your grass to be cut or driveway plowed, cancelling newspaper delivery and having the post office hold your mail. But, the fewer people who know of your absence the better, and this is where good neighbours come in. Automatic lighting and security alarm systems help, but it takes a watchful neighbour to give your home an authentic lived-in look. Not only does our neighbour pick up the mail and countless flyers slung onto the porch, she also puts her garbage on our driveway for collection and asks her visitors to park here. Sometimes she opens and closes curtains as the sun moves around the house just as I would if I were home, and occasionally she hangs her washing on my backyard line. Whether a prospective robber knows I am away isn't important, so long as he understands someone is around keeping an eye on the place.

Maybe this is the time to make it easier to leave home. We stopped buying house plants long ago, and as yet have not replaced our family pet. Our garden requires minimum care. (That same neighbour puts the hose on if it looks dry.)

SAFETY DEVICES

The yellow pages of your telephone directory list installers of professional security systems. In addition to such a system, or instead of it, you can do other things to safeguard your property while away.

Make sure you have strong, well-fitting doors with deadbolt locks on them. If your windows slide upwards, insert a long screw where the two sections meet. Tighten it when you're going away so the lower part can't be raised. A bar inserted in the groove of sliding doors and windows make them less easy to access. Your pet's door should be no larger than necessary, and preferably kept locked during your absence.

There was a time when we left a spare front door key under the mat. Sadly, not any more. Don't even stash it in a little magnetic box attached to something in your garage, because burglars know all the secret places.

Cut back shrubs so would-be thieves have nowhere to hide. Secure your garage, especially if it contains ladders or tools. A timed electrical system, which turns on porchlights, interior lights and a radio or television, will make your home appear occupied when it isn't. Unplug all appliances in case an electrical storm occurs during your absence. Close connecting doors so that anyone peeping through windows can't see whether a room is occupied or not. Turn down your telephone bell — a ringing telephone is a sure sign nobody is home.

VALUABLES AND PAPERWORK

Rent a safety deposit box for private papers and valuables. Also ensure that your home insurance provides adequate coverage against loss. Have an up-to-date inventory of your possessions and record any serial number on them. Hang on to receipts that establish the value of things you bought yourself, and try to determine the commercial worth of gifts. Where bills are missing, photograph those items so that in the event of a break-in you can better describe what is stolen. Keep all of these in your safety deposit box, away from your home.

This is a good time to review your will and if necessary revise it. If you are thinking of taking underaged grandchildren on your travels, have your lawyer draw up a simple letter of agreement signed by their parents; this agreement should permit you to take them out of the country and allow you to obtain medical treatment for them in an emergency. (It may seem unnecessary, but airlines and other carriers, immigration officers and even physicians could require it at the most inconvenient times.)

Make a up a list of addresses and telephone numbers for use in your absence. This list should include your family members, your lawyer and physician and a repairman you call when things go wrong with your house. Give the list to whoever is looking after your home.

HOUSE SITTERS

If you haven't a neighbour to keep an eye on things, is there a friend who would like to move in? As a country dweller, I jump at the chance of a couple of weeks in my daughter's city apartment when she is away.

Services of a professional house sitter can be hired through an agency. This person will be bonded, and can move right in or visit daily to water the plants, feed the cat, take in mail and so on. Your travel agent probably knows of a local service, or you can find one in the yellow pages.

PETS

Concern for rabies and other contagious diseases has prompted almost all countries to prohibit the entry of animals from overseas. Where it is permitted, they must be kept in quarantine for six months or longer. In reality then, you cannot take your pet overseas on vacation with you.

On North American flights some airlines allow small pets in the passenger cabin if their container (maximum size 23 cm x 40 cm x 50 cm or 9 in. x 16 in. x 20 in.) fits under your seat. More often, cats and dogs and other pets of similar size are carried in the baggage hold. Airline personnel have told me that animals are usually not over-stressed by their flight in the belly of the aircraft, especially if they have a favourite blanket or toy with them. This is something you will doubtless discuss with your veterinarian. Motorhomes are terrific for transporting pets. Ours carried a guinea pig called Penny to the east coast one time, and we were into New Brunswick before I knew about it.

A booklet called *Travelling With Your Pet* (Don Mills: Patrick Communications Ltd., 1993) is sold in pet stores and through mail order; it lists more than 2,000 hotels and motels in Canada where pets are permitted. The information is arranged by province, then community, so it is a handy guide to carry with you on tour.

Room and board at local kennels can become expensive when you plan a long trip. It costs approximately $6.50 to board a medium-sized dog per day, $4.50 for a cat per day, or approximately $350 per month if you have one of each. Hopefully, you have a friend Fido is comfortable with, or who will come to your home to keep him comfortable.

KEEPING IN TOUCH

Give a detailed copy of your itinerary to a friend or relative and to the neighbour caring for your home. If you haven't pre-booked your hotels, they can write to you c/o the main post office (Poste Restante) at points along your route as shown in your itinerary. All mail should have your last name in prominent block letters and underlined on the envelope. The address should read: Post Restante, name of city, then country. It should be marked Hold. American Express or Thomas Cook clients can arrange to have mail sent to their offices on their route, ready for pick-up when they are in the neighbourhood.

$\mathcal{A}$ Place to Stay

$\mathcal{C}$hoice of vacation accommodation can make or mar a trip, and this is where 50 plus travellers are lucky. Possibly for the first time ever we aren't bound by school holidays, facilities for kids or even cost. If in your working life you were automatically put into prestigious hotels with corporate rates, capacious lobbies and front desk robots, you are in for a treat now. The variety, in every price range, is quite wonderful. The research is fun too.

GETTING THE BEST RENT

Development of resorts and hotels the size of small towns were part of the eighties boom. Now with less business travel and a preference for no-frills accommodation, many hoteliers are desperate for our business. Remember this when shopping for a hotel room and you could be a winner.

In Canada and the United States **discounts** of up to 30% are often available to guests 62 or over, (CARP and AARP members need only be 50 or over; participating chains are listed in Appendix D). Savings may be even greater for mid-week stays, or for weekends when business people have gone home. Shoulder and off-season rates are substantially lower than summertime rates in resort areas. The important thing is to ask for the lowest rate, given your age and arrival date. Telephone in advance if possible (you are not as likely to get a deal when you arrive looking weary, suitcases in hand) and when booking ask for a confirmation number so there is no argument when you get there.

In southern resort areas we occasionally arrive without hotel reservations and find condominium owners hanging about in the hope that new arrivals will drop by. They welcome our patronage for a price lower than the advertised rate. On the other hand, highway motels on the drive south are often full even at midweek. Time and again we used to pull into a decent looking place with restaurant attached and no more than one or two cars outside, only to find it totally booked by a tour group or prudent independents who had telephoned in advance. Now we too make reservations, to ensure our driving doesn't continue into the night.

OVERSEAS HOTELS

Look into **airline packages** before arranging your flight. To lure you from their competitors airlines provide far more than a reasonably comfortable journey. National airlines usually have the best programs in their home country when it comes to good deals for hotels, car rentals tours and even theatre tickets. Researching a travel article on the cost of staying in London, I once visited five hotels and asked for the lowest price of a double room for a three-night stay. These were compared with rates at the same hotels offered by British Airways to their passengers from Canada. Savings on luxury hotels were greatest, but overall the airline's rates averaged 35% lower than off-the-street prices.

? QUESTIONS TO ASK

Travel brochure writers sometimes speak a different language from the rest of us. It can be prudent then to ask a few questions before selecting that modern hotel "overlooking the ocean."

How near is "near," as in "near the beach" or "near the golf course"? Does "across from the beach" mean there's a six-lane highway separating your hotel from it? If so, you may have to use a pedestrian overpass to reach the sea so artfully photographed in the publicity pictures. How new is "new"? We have all heard miserable tales of vacationers arriving at resorts so new they aren't quite finished. It's nice to know your room will be "gently kissed by the ocean breeze," but is there also air-conditioning for when the temperature tops 32°C (90° F)?

How much will all the extras amount to? A chocolate mint on your pillow at night, an orchid floating in your toilet and a note from the maid saying her name is Elsie are designed to make you feel welcome. And I guess they do. But I would feel more warmth in the welcome if that $8 a day parking fee was waived. Or when free coffee and Danish are provided first thing in the morning for those with a flight to catch before the dining-room opens. If breakfast is included, is it continental or cooked? Are taxes and service charges included in the price quoted? Is use of sports and recreational equipment complimentary? It all sounds pernickety I know, but extras tend to add up.

In my experience, the higher the rent the higher the cost of extras. At one $300 a day resort the manager told me he charges for a glass of tap water because it would offend guests to give it to them free. How he came to that conclusion I don't know.

INDIGENOUS LODGINGS

For something different consider indigenous lodging. This could be a castle on the Rhine, a pousada in Portugal, a Spanish parador, a Japanese ryokan, an English mansion, an Israeli kibbutz or a monastery in Asia. All are far more exciting than a standard hotel room and some even cost less. If they do pop your budget, I suggest skimping on something else to spend a night or two at such special places.

Few things will immerse you in local culture more than to "go native," even if accommodation is modified to provide a few traditional comforts of home. Obviously some indigenous lodging is so primitive all but the most adventurous will want to give it a miss. Here are a few types of lodgings that require no heroism to stay in overnight. In fact, I guarantee you'll love them.

Pousadas

These provide guest accommodation in monasteries, convents and castles throughout Portugal. Usually the number of guest rooms is limited, so you may have to book weeks or even months in advance. Accommodation is in character with the building and its locale, which means that a convent's rooms retain original stone walls and tiny arched doors. Usually two cells have been made into one room with ensuite bath. Bedroom furniture here is heavily carved and dressed in plain white linens, whereas palace guest rooms are richly endowed with velvet and brass. Government operated and immaculately maintained, the pousadas' public areas display antiques and period artifacts. Some have lovely courtyards and cloisters, manicured gardens and swimming pools. Their dining-rooms are open to all; if you can't stay overnight, do at least come for a meal. Double rooms run from $100 – $200, depending on the season, location and facilities. A cooked lunch for two costs around $40.

Portugal's first pousada, the **Pousada do Castelo**, opened in the fairytale town of Obidos some 80 km (50 mi.) north of Lisbon during the 1950s, and remains a favourite today. Others to look for: the **Pousada da Rainha Santa Isabel** at Estremoz is considered the country's finest pousada. Located in a thirteenth-century castle, it has bedrooms furnished with four-poster beds bearing the insignia of the royal household to which they once belonged. South of Estremoz, Evora was Portugal's cultural centre between the twelfth and fifteenth centuries and now its **Pousada dos Loios** is in a splendid convent from this era. At Sagres, the southernmost tip of

Portugal, the **Pousada do Infante** is on the windswept promonotory where Prince Henry conducted his school for navigators in the early 1400s.

Paradores

You will find them throughout Spain. Similar to Portugal's pousadas, they reflect the history, culture and cooking of their region, and usually are found in historic palaces and castles. In Puerto Rico the island's Spanish heritage is reflected in paradores established on working coffee plantations, on historic sites and even in the rain forest. Spanish paradores cost $100 to $150 per double room. In Puerto Rico you pay $45 to $90, depending on the location and season.

The site for Spain's first parador was chosen by King Alfonso XIII at his favourite hunting grounds in the **Sierra de Gredos**, west of Madrid. Constructed as a hunting lodge in 1928 it still provides a retreat for outdoors sportsmen. The most popular parador in all of Spain is the **San Francisco**, part of the Alhambra complex high on a hilltop above the city of Granada. And one of our favourites is Carmona's **Parador Nacional Alcazar Del Rey Don Pedro** in a hilltop fortress some 33 km (21 mi.) from Seville.

Ryokans

At $700 to $1,000 a night some of Japan's ryokan's are prohibitively expensive, but a little digging will unearth others that cost no more than the average hotel. In Kyoto I stayed in a real charmer that cost around $120 for a double. I wasn't pampered beyond belief as are guests of the more expensive ryokans, but was comfortably housed in traditional Japanese style. The only concession to Western ways here was an ensuite bath and a television in my room. I slept on a futon and ate Japanese style sitting cross-legged at a table no more than 70 cm (2 ft.) high. (If this is uncomfortable, you will be offered a chair and regular-height table.) Fresh kimonos and sandals were provided each day. This ryokan, the **Three Sisters Inn**, is the centuries old family home of three very gracious sisters whose American schooling and Japanese good manners combine to make them perfect hosts. The hard part of any ryokan stay comes at check-out time, when you have to face the noisy, crowded, polluted world outside.

Kibbutzim

When I first booked into an Israeli kibbutz I knew I would have a single room with bath because that's what I had paid for, but I fully expected to eat at a trestle table alongside sweating workers in from pulling up veggies in the fields. Not so. Kibbutzim represent big business in this tiny country. Although still devoted largely to farming, some operate manufacturing plants. Some process fruit grown in their orchards, and turkeys raised on their farms. Some have three- or four-star hotels and restaurants.

While guest accommodation can be quite plain, the historical and often stunningly beautiful locations are unmatched. You will find kibbutz hotels in ancient cities, at seaside resorts, in orange groves and close to world-famous landmarks. One of the most popular is **En Gedi**, with air-conditioned tourist cottages above the Dead Sea and a shuttle to a spa on its shores.

Rents vary, depending on locations and facilities, and whether or not you are travelling with a group. Independent travellers pay $60 to $150 for a double (most are $80 to $90), which includes a traditional Israeli break-fast. The above-mentioned En Gedi is $66 for a double.

The original co-operative concept of the kibbutz established 90 years ago remains intact, but now rules for residents are more relaxed. The most important break with tradition is the housing of families in apartments, whereas children used to sleep and eat with their peers. During the past three years more kibbutzim have utilized these former childrens' quarters with cottage and dormitory style accommodation for visitors. Rent here is around $25 per person, breakfast (eaten in the kibbutz residents' dining hall) is included, and if you want to sample life as a kibbutznik you can lend a hand with the chores.

Ireland's Castles, England's Mansions

Some castles and mansions have been converted to luxurious hotels, while others are virtually top-of-the-line bed and breakfast establishments with resident aristocrats earning a few extra bob by hosting paying guests. Local pursuits such as fox hunting, duck shooting and salmon fishing are easily arranged. If that's not your bag, on the premises there are usually lovely country walks, golf courses, tennis courts and swimming pools. Meals are graciously served, sherry decanters are kept filled in the lounge and fires crackle in giant stone hearths. And for all the opulence your hosts will strive to make you feel as though you belong. The price tag can be high, maybe $400 a day for a double with breakfast, and even more if you have dinner.

To name two favourites in Ireland: **Adare Manor** 32 km (20 mi.) from Shannon Airport is on a 340 ha (840 acre) estate in the village of Adare, a picturesque community which is sprinkled with picture-postcard thatched cottages; and **Waterford Castle** 2 km (about a mile) from Waterford City on the south coast is unique for its lavish use of local crystal in guest and public rooms. Located on an island, it is reached by the hotel launch and a car ferry.

Canada's Grand Railway Hotels

Overseas visitors have told me that when they think of Canada it is of Rocky Mountains, trees, mounties on horseback — and our castle-type hotels with their distinctive green roofs. We do have more than that, folks. But for starters I'll settle on those grand old hotels displaying native art, paintings of historic battles and regional artifacts in their capacious lobbies.

In the late 1800s William Van Horne, then general manager of Canadian Pacific, started the CP hotel chain, which soon had links across the country. Having finished the railway coast to coast, he realized the enormous tourist potential, and supposedly announced that if he couldn't bring the scenery to the people he would bring the people to it. He then set about doing just that by building these great hotels and resorts across the country.

All have recently undergone lengthy restoration programs which have included the upgrading of facilities to meet modern demands. Last year, the oldest, **Le Château Frontenac**, celebrated its centennial with the addition of a new wing, indoor pool and health club. Access for disabled guests is taken seriously in these hotels. Mid-week and low-season packages are very affordable, as are programs combining rail transportation and hotel accommodation.

Favourites with vacationers, for the glorious settings and historic sites, include **The Empress** in Victoria, British Columbia, **Banff Springs Hotel**, **Jasper Park Lodge** and **Chateau Lake Louise** in Alberta, **Le Château Montebello** and **Le Château Frontenac** in Quebec, and **The Algonquin** in New Brunswick's St. Andrews by the Sea.

HISTORIC INNS

These can be adorable when restored to combine original character with discreetly hidden modern conveniences. When a third of your room has been used up for installation of an airless bathroom, and walls are so wafer thin you can hear your neighbour getting undressed, they aren't so much fun. A drawback to the oldies are wickedly steep and winding stairs, the warren of narrow hallways, sharp corners and heavy fire doors, all combining to produce an obstacle course encountered whenever you leave your room.

In central Amsterdam I stayed in a jewel of a canal house. My fourth floor room was everything I had hoped, but there was no elevator to reach it. A mistaken assumption on the manager's part was that all his guests would be as agile as mountain goats. Some of those tall skinny hotels do have elevators, so if you have trouble with stairs it can pay to check.

I hate to be negative, but those precious coaching inns, all vine-covered outside, smouldering fires reflected in mirror bright brass within, have their drawbacks too. If there's a pub under your room you won't get to sleep early, and if a wedding is being catered to maybe not at all, as guests dash from one friend's room to another for drinks after the bar has closed.

BED AND BREAKFAST

If you prefer the personal touch, B & Bs can be for you. Prices are often as high as a room in a hotel, but then they will provide exceptional comfort and service. Tourist boards give details of organizations handling bookings, or lists of addresses for you to contact them directly. In tourist areas B & B signs are everywhere, telling of ensuite baths, tea and coffee making machines and TV in spacious rooms with full breakfasts included in the rent.

Interestingly these hard economic times are causing more home owners to open up to paying guests, something they wouldn't have considered a decade ago: children's rooms have become vacant, investments are less lucrative, or a single person may have inherited a spacious, centrally-located house.

B & B guests tend to be courteous yet friendly, ready to give touring tips to each other. Outside school holidays, most are well over 50. I like the hosts too. They're quick to help with telephone numbers, emergencies and tourist information.

Canada has a far-reaching network of B & Bs, listed in provincial tourist material and commercial guides. Ontario farms, ranches in the Alberta foothills, homes of fisher-families in the Maritimes — all will give you a peep into the daily lives of Canadians.

We have paid as little as $40 and as much as $100 double at B & Bs, have never had a bad experience and seldom had to share a bathroom. Prices are similar in the United States, where you will find B & Bs in most of the grand old cities from San Francisco to Savannah, from Key West to Fairbanks and Honolulu. They are extremely well represented too, in the country's numerous beauty spots from Massachusetts' Berkshires to California's Napa Valley. Always regional tourist offices are a good source for local B & Bs.

Overseas, a knowledge of the language is helpful but not essential. You will be shown the accommodation, the rent will be written down, and you can indicate agreement or not.

In Britain B & Bs have come a long way in the past 20 years. The old seafront houses are here still, but now they are joined by country estates and smart city homes. The British Tourist Authority has information. **Wolsey Lodges** is a non-profit organization with 220 properties throughout Britain and a few in Europe. These are upscale and unusual historic homes in which owners rent no more than one or two rooms. Their idea is to give guests a look at English life. Rent is around $100 a day double, with cooked breakfast. These outstanding properties are identified by coloured photographs in the Wolsey Lodges free booklet obtained from the organization's head office (address in Appendix B). In London recently I discovered **Uptown Reservations**, a booking service for upscale B & Bs in London's most prestigious areas (Chelsea, Knightsbridge, Kensington, Hampstead). Hosts are usually artists, writers and other professionals. Rents are $120 for a double, $60 for a single per night for a minimum of two nights. Rooms are elegant, baths ensuite, and locations are very convenient (for Uptown's address see Appendix B).

Similarly, **The Bulldog Club** has fabulous B & Bs in London and other areas across Britain. Membership costs £25 (approx. $52) per annum, and overnight rates are £53 (approx. $108) single with private bath, £73 ($150) double with private bath. Most have private sitting rooms too, and the rent includes a full English breakfast. In London my favourite is on Gloucester Road, steps to the subway's Piccadilly line with direct access to West End theatres and Heathrow airport in an area peppered with intimate restaurants and shops. This club has a North American representative in southern Ontario, whose address is listed in Appendix B.

SELF-CATERING ACCOMMODATION

I love it. Even if it's only for a few days, I settle right in and become part of the neighbourhood. I enjoy shopping for new taste experiences as well as familiar foods, talking to neighbours and generally acting as if I were there to stay. Obviously some properties are more attractive than others. In Europe especially, purpose-built vacation homes can be marshalled in rows like army barracks, and have about as much charm. And then there are real jewels.

The classified section of Canadian newspapers advertise privately-owned properties. Ask to see photographs, preferably a video, if you are considering these. Word of mouth is one of the best routes to a good rental. There are the usual travel sources too: tourist offices and guidebooks. Particularly helpful are guides dedicated to self-catering properties in the part of the world you plan to visit.

Britain has a very workable scheme called **"Book-a-Bed-Ahead."** The idea is that you can drop by any British Tourist Authority office and request accommodation in that town, or for wherever you will be in the next few days. The staff will locate a caravan, a flat, a farmhouse, a room in a guest house or hotel or whatever else you want. Cost of the service is the long-distance telephone call, if one is required.

A few years ago we tested the system en route to Wales. First we telephoned Swansea's tourist office from a motorway service centre and requested an historic house for four days in North Wales. Two hours later we called back and were given the number of a rental agency in Bangor. They in turn agreed to have a representative meet us in a castle car park the next afternoon, with keys to a property. (This was a case of getting there being half the fun.) As promised we found our contact waiting in a small white sports car, and were instructed to follow her to our temporary home. It proved to be a tourist's dream. Built in 1580 and set in 5.6 ha (14 acres), Pen-y-Bryn was large enough to house 12 although we were only three. Antiques lined an upper gallery, the music room was sun-filled in the mornings, the modern kitchen and dining-room could have catered a feast. It even had a room in the tower, for heaven's sake, and a "local" at the end of the lane. Our collective gloom at having to leave after four days was lifted with promise to return for longer next time. This is a promise we still hope to keep.

The British Tourist Authority will send you a book detailing self-catering rentals ranging from around $400 per week for a one bedroom mews townhouse to picture postcard thatched cottages and seaside family homes furnished to sleep six adults and several children for approximately $1,500. Something to note when renting a large property in Europe is that you may have six bedrooms but only one full bath and one or two toilets.

Other successful self-catering rentals for us have been **condos** in Waikiki and Maui, an adorable **stone cottage** in Virginia, a two-storied **apartment** on Georgia's Jekyll Island, a **villa** in Jamaica and assorted properties in Florida. In London we sometimes try for a small flat. Conveniently-packaged foods in Sainsburys, Marks and Spencer and wine shops on just about every corner, make entertaining a breeze.

HOSTELS

Hostels too have changed over the years. Now you will find them in country mansions nestled in grand estates and in national parks. Some have double and single rooms as well as traditional dormitories. Most have kitchens where you can get to know other guests while preparing yourself a light meal. In the country districts scenic walking paths often go right past the front door and wardens conduct nature programs.

London has seven hostels, including the modern Rotherhythe Hostel with ensuite facilities. I am told Hong Kong's downtown hostel occupies one of city's finest waterfront sites. Jerusalem has hostels in its historic area. There is no age limit at any of these and if you travel when most under 60s are back at school or work, you will find lots of other guests in our age group.

The **Canadian Hostelling Association** operates hostels in every province. If you are planning to stay in one of these, you should obtain a Youth Hostel Association membership card from the association's head office before leaving home. (Cost is $26.75 per person annually and it isn't essential but does bring discounts.) The **American Youth Hostel Association** is expanding its program all the time. At present they include cycling and hiking tours with van transportation through the United States and Canada. North American members are invited to join Europeans for tours of continental Europe, Britain and Israel. Programs are available to four different age groups, one of which is for hostellers **over 50.** The association's head office is in Washington (see Appendix A).

World travellers contemplating hostel stays will find the two-volume International Youth Hostel Federation's *The Guide to Budget Accommodation* (Welwyn Garden City: I.Y.H.F., 1991) invaluable. In four languages, it provides details of 1,400 hostels in 25 countries. It's published in Britain, but Canadians can buy it through the Canadian Hostelling Association (address in Appendix A) and at some local hostels.

BACK TO SCHOOL

City accommodation can be terribly expensive, especially during school holidays when families are on the move. But there is a way, because this is the very time when campus accommodation becomes available to non-students. It is usually comfortable and centrally located, and guests are free to make use of the cafeteria and sports and leisure facilities. There can be learning programs, including those of Elderhostel, but if you simply want a few days away — say in Toronto, Ottawa or New York or any other city during school break periods — campus living can be an inexpensive and enjoyable answer to otherwise high accommodation costs.

RETREAT HOUSES

Guest accommodation in monasteries, convents and similar religious centres is an age-old Christian tradition which continues to this day. Ostensibly it welcomes travellers who want to escape from the harried pace of everyday life to an oasis of simple comfort, reflection and spiritual renewal.

Retreat houses differ widely, ranging from mountain cabins to big city estates. Guests may be housed with monastic residents or have their own quarters. As a guest you are free to do as you please: spend time alone in contemplation, look for spiritual guidance or perform light chores. Often such guest houses are in favoured vacation locations, with hiking trails and sports facilities nearby. Currently the rent is around $40 per person daily, meals included.

Tourist boards will know of more retreat houses, and I am familiar with two other sources: *The U.S. and World Guide to Retreat Houses* (Newport Beach: Campus Travel Service, 1992), which lists 225 retreat houses in North America, and a few elsewhere, and *A Guide to Monastic Guest Houses* (Harrisburg: Morehouse Publishing, 1991), which lists retreat houses in the United States and Canada.

Part Two

Getting There

$\mathcal{F}$lying High

*W*e older travellers are very important to airlines; they court us royally to retain our loyalty and affection. Lovely as it feels to be so wanted, it's wise to do a little investigating before take-off. Most major airlines have clubs or programs entitling members over a certain age to special privileges and discounts.

Promotional fares for mid-week and off-season travel can be even more worthwhile to those of us free to travel. And because we aren't in a hurry, we can fill seats on aircraft travelling the long way round, paying less than passengers on more direct flights. Rock bottom of all are the sell-offs, for snapping up a week or so before departure. It is a savvy flyer who shops carefully (preferably with the help of a travel agent) weighing the discounts against convenience, an airline's reliability versus the additional perks being offered.

Something to remember when paying a discounted fare is that certain conditions apply, and usually there is one saying your fare is not refundable. This is where trip cancellation insurance can come in handy.

$ DISCOUNTS FOR OLDER PASSENGERS

Marketing experts are well aware that people over 50 are free to travel a lot, and in fact many do. We tend towards more than one vacation a year, in addition to visits to friends or relatives across the country and overseas. In consequence, airlines are out to woo us away from their competitors by dangling a few carrots. The following are just some of the privileges given specifically to our age group.

- **Air Canada's Freedom Flyer Program**, available to travellers 60 and over, plus a companion of any age, offers a 10% discount on almost all fares in North America and to Great Britain. This airline also has a four-destination pass to anywhere in North American for $599, eight stops for $799, to be used within 12 months. Another plan offers flight coupons for $649 for any four one-way flights in North America during the course of a year, e.g. Los Angeles and return count as two flights. Eight coupons cost $1,049. These flights can be used for flying with Air Canada, Continental Airlines and United Airlines.

■ **Canadian Airlines International's Golden Discount Program** is for passengers 60 and over with a companion of any age. It gives a 10% discount on return flights within Canada, and the United States (except Hawaii) and on select fares to Britain. Additional promotions are made available from time to time to travellers over 60 or 65. An example is a program effective at the time of writing this. Called 60/60 it gives a 60% discount on economy fares within Canada to 60 plus travellers and a companion of any age.

■ **British Airways has a Privileged Traveller Club** for passengers 55 years and over. Members receive a 10% discount on most trans-Atlantic flights, and the same for a travel mate regardless of his or her age. The discount also applies to almost any land arrangements in Britain; that is, any car rentals, coach tours, hotels, promoted in current brochures. This means two people on a $3,000 per person tour of Britain can save $600 in return for an annual $30 Privileged Traveller membership fee. British Airways keeps a record of each member's health conditions, need for boarding assistance or special diet, seating preference and other important information. Moreover members are not penalized for changing flight dates, or even cancelling, and that is a very comfortable cushion for older passengers to fall back on.

■ **American Airlines, Continental Airlines, Delta Air Lines, North-west Airlines** and **US Air** usually offer some form of reduced fares to passengers over 62, (or in some instances 65) years. As do international flag carriers such as **Alitalia, Cathay Pacific Airways, KLM Royal Dutch Airlines** and **Lufthansa German Airlines**.

So it really pays to examine your options. Stack the airline discounts against your personal requirements, and you are bound to find something better than the regular airfare.

A TOUCH OF CLASS

Flights from Toronto to London can take less than seven hours, which is a little over half the time of a trans-Atlantic crossing in those early years of scheduled passenger flights when we stopped at

Shannon or Gander for refuelling. What with meal service, drinks and snacks, and a movie or brief nap, these few hours pass quickly. Still, travel is tiring. There is the stress of getting to the airport on time, and the airport wait. Even I, a seasoned traveller, am happier once I have my boarding card in hand and luggage out of the way.

With an aisle seat, one small carry-on bag under my feet, and a paperback I am anxious to read, I am comfortable enough for seven or eight hours in the tourist-class section of any aircraft. Even so, if I could afford it I would fly business class on such overnight journeys. It is quieter up front, the seats are armchair size with retractable footrests, meals are more digestable and service attentive. In consequence business-class passengers arrive at their destination rested.

For longer journeys I would urge any older travellers to treat themselves to business or even first-class travel if the budget can stand the cost.

There is little if any profit for the airlines when they carry passengers across the Atlantic for around $500, which is the promotional fare at the time of writing this. (As a 55 plus traveller receiving 10% discount off that, I can cross the Atlantic now for less than I paid ten years ago.) Accordingly airlines are out to win business- and first-class passengers with VIP lounges, individual TV screens with a selection of movies to choose from during the flight, healthy meals and unhurried service. British Airways now go a step further, providing its first-class passengers with pyjamas and duvets for the overnight flights from Canada. First- and business-class passengers are also invited to sleep through breakfast on the aircraft. If they do, then upon arrival they can head for a new VIP lounge at London's Heathrow airport where a complimentary breakfast buffet is ready; facilities to shower, to change their clothes and a full valet service are also available. This is terrific not only for people with an early business meeting, but also for tourists whose hotel rooms may not be ready until noon. With this kind of a start, they are rested and keen to get on with their tour.

I remember my very first flight at the front of the plane. It was with **Air France** from Montreal to Paris, en route to Cairo. To say I was impressed is an understatement. Especially with the dining experience, because, believe me Air France's inflight cuisine in first class is as good as it gets. Dinner seemed to go on for hours. (Just when I thought we were through, the main course was served.) Finally, the cheese trolley arrived. As a lifelong old-cheddar fan, I didn't know the names of many other cheeses offered and the waiter was too snooty to explain. So, I simply pointed to "some of that" and "a little of this please." "And?" he asked imperiously, his knife poised in the air. "That's it, thanks," I demurred. His lip curled with a sneer. "But Madame has chosen only butter," he said a little too loudly. "I like butter," I replied, I hope with some aplomb, and lifted a couple of crackers to help it down.

These days personnel directors are too smart to choose snooty cabin crews. Competition is so fierce they can't possibly risk offending passengers. Every single one is important, even ignoramuses who can't tell cheese from butter.

CHARTERED FLIGHTS

Why does that flight to Vancouver or Nassau aboard Canada 3000 Airlines cost less than Air Canada's? Because passengers aren't paying for the convenience of a scheduled service which will allow them to catch another flight if the original flight is delayed or cancelled.

More often than not, a chartered flight will get you to your vacation destination and back, on time. If it doesn't there can be lots of hanging around. In winter charter flights to sun destinations in particular fly back-to-back, meaning they take a load of passengers to say, Kingston, Jamaica, and bring back last week's vacationers that same day. If a heavy snowfall delays departure of the aircraft from Toronto or Montreal, you are kept waiting at the Kingston airport until it eventually arrives to take you home. If there is a mechanical hitch in Kingston and no spare part to fix it, you may be delayed in Canada until the part is flown in and the aircraft can return home.

Most charter companies have all of their aircraft busy all of the time, with no spares to call in for rescue of stranded passengers. If they can't repair an aircraft in a hurry they will scramble around and rent another or put their passengers on scheduled flights. Either way you will be delayed, but not stranded. I must emphasize that this is not a frequent occurrence. If it were, then charter aircraft wouldn't be packed to capacity as they are. But it does happen, and if you find yourself waiting around for what seems like a lifetime, remember that nice low fare you paid.

Charters often travel to vacation destinations not on scheduled routes. As the lifeline to tour operators, they negotiate very affordable hotel/air packages. If these companies relied on scheduled flights, the package prices would be out of reach for many a vacationer.

LOW, LOW FARES

Some airlines have very low stand-by fares. These are terrific if you can live with the uncertainty of not knowing whether you will board, until minutes before the flight is closed for take-off.

If you are truly flexible, you might consider flying as a freelance courier. You pay very little, if anything, for your flight. In return you give up all or most of your checked baggage allowance to the courier company. (You pack your travel necessities in your carry-on bag.) The courier company uses your baggage space to transport time-sensitive items which cost far more to ship by air freight. Their baggage is delivered to the check-in counter for you, and taken off the carousel at the other end. Usually you do nothing more than receive the paperwork and hand it over on arrival.

Courier travel is a somewhat secretive business, and only certain companies prefer freelancers to their own employees. If you are interested, I suggest you look for **Air Courier Services** (or a similar name) in the yellow pages of your telephone directory. Kelly Monaghan's *The Insider's Guide to Air Courier Bargains* (New York: Inwood Training Publications, 1991) is a must for prospective freelance couriers.

ONWARD FLIGHTS

In most countries, on a mileage basis domestic air travel is far more expensive than the long-distance routes. With this in mind, you can save by including local flights in the ticket taking you overseas. For example, if you are flying Lufthansa, Toronto – Frankfurt, and anticipate continuing to Hamburg or Berlin a few days later, it's better to add the ongoing flight to your trans-Atlantic ticket than to purchase it in Germany. If you plan an excursion to Iguazu Falls on the Brazil/Argentina border during your visit to Rio, have the extension put on your Varig Brazilian Airlines ticket from Canada.

AIR PASSES

Domestic air passes, sometimes available only to overseas travellers, give big savings over regular airfares. Price is not everything though. Check the alternatives to see if you really want to skim over a particularly scenic chunk of territory at 800 km (500 mi.) per hour, when a leisurely train or coach journey would be very enjoyable.

To give full value, air passes must be used wisely. For my first trip to India, I bought an **Indian Airlines** pass allowing 21 days of unlimited domestic travel (the current cost is $480). Some of the flights I wanted were fully booked. Against my travel agent's advice I arrived "wait listed" for the most important journeys, and wasted a lot of time in airline offices where promises of reservations never did materialize. I met other travellers who had seen most of the country courtesy their air passes. Sensibly they had checked availability several weeks before departure and planned their itinerary around those flights.

In Argentina, a four flight 30-day air pass from **Aerolineas Argentinas** which currently costs U.S. $450 (Can. $600) took me from one end of the country to the other, flying from Buenos Aires to Iguazu Falls, then Mendoza and Bariloche, before returning to Buenos Aires. I could never have done this in my brief visit had I travelled by car or rail. The pass does not allow passengers to back-track, so my travel agent devised an itinerary to keep me travelling always in the same direction.

In Australia, by all means use the **Australian Airpass** for four flights (it currently costs $532 or $632 if you take in Perth). But, don't use it up with trips from Sydney to Canberra and Melbourne when you can go much further and take in Darwin 3,000 km (1,864 mi.) away.

AIRLINE TICKETS

Airline tickets are complex contracts established over the years as the result of agreements between governments and airlines. Rights and responsibilities of the passenger as well as those of the airline are spelled out on the back of the ticket. Included are such eventualities as overbooking and loss of luggage.

Currently the airline's financial responsibility on most flights is limited to $13,000 for deaths, and $27,000 for injury, and to $100,000 for death or personal injury on flights involving a stop in the United States. Usually passengers are entitled to fair market value replacement for lost or damaged luggage up to $27 per kilo (2.2 lb.) if it was checked, and a total of $532 for carry-on items.

For newcomers to air travel, the following pointers will show you how easy it can be.

❑ Keep your ticket safe. In the event of loss, advise your travel agent, tour company or the airline immediately. Normally you will be issued a replacement, but this is a time-consuming and worrisome business, especially in the middle of a tour, so its best to hang on to the original.

❏ **Confirm** your return flight by telephone if you have been asked to do so.

❏ Before leaving for the airport, telephone the airline to make sure your flight is on schedule. I might add that this can be easier said then done, because hundreds of other passengers are trying to get through at the same time.

❏ Plan to arrive at the airport on time. Airlines request that you arrive two hours prior to departure for an international flight, one hour for domestic travel.

❏ Avoid driving yourself to the airport. Long-term parking can be a distance from the terminal and sometimes very expensive. A better idea is to have a friend deliver you there, or take a bus or cab.

❏ If there's a porter nearby, his service is preferable to finding your own luggage cart. Not only will he take you the shortest route to your check-in counter, but may lift your luggage onto the scales as well. (Tip $1 per bag, a little more if he has had a long walk or is particularly helpful.)

❏ Take advantage of curbside check-ins offered in many U.S. airports, also at some airport car-rental offices.

❏ When flying to Switzerland or Germany via their national airlines you can check luggage through to the railway station closest to your destination, and do the same in reverse on your homeward journey.

❏ At the airline's counter your heavy luggage will be taken for stowage on the aircraft, and you will receive a boarding card. This shows your departure gate number, the time by which you must have passed through airport security, and your seat number.

❏ If you feel the need, take advantage of pre-boarding announcements which allow anyone requiring a little extra time to get settled on the aircraft ahead of the other passengers.

SEAT SELECTION

When you buy your ticket, ask if the airline permits seat selection at that time. If not, you have to make your choice when checking in. Some couples choose aisle seats across from each other so they both have that additional leg room. Others, on aircraft with three seats abreast, will take an aisle and window seat and hope the middle one is left empty. If you make frequent stops to a washroom, you may want to sit fairly close to one, but this can be noisy when passengers standing in line are beside you. Seats by emergency exits have a little extra leg room.

ARRIVAL

On arrival in a foreign country you will pass through immigration, collect your luggage and then continue through customs. Usually you simply follow the signs, answer a few easy questions and in a matter of minutes you are out on the sidewalk ready for your adventure to begin.

Because you are in unfamiliar territory, you should make sure you hire a reliable cab into town. If there is a dispatcher curbside, let him hail you one. Or, ask if there is a shuttle to your hotel or a point nearby. Such services are reliable and their fares far lower than a cab. Establish ahead of time if there is a bus service, and whether it is worth your while to use it.

DELAYED FLIGHTS

Relax, because there is very little you can do, except perhaps look around for other airlines going to the same destination. A competing airline may well take you if you have a regular unrestricted ticket. They will settle with your original airline later.

GETTING BUMPED

Let's assume you are looking forward to your vacation, and although flexible want to get going on time. For this reason you arrive at the airport at the appointed hour. Unfathomable as it may seem to you, some passengers who bought a refundable ticket won't turn up at all. For this reason all airlines hedge their bets and sell more seats than they actually have. And once in a while, come departure time, they find themselves with passengers left over. If you already have your boarding card, you are guaranteed a seat unless you volunteer to give it up in return for compensation. If you arrive for the flight and find no seats left you will be offered "denied boarding compensation" for the inconvenience and put on the next available flight.

Because airlines like to be free to negotiate, they are reticent to discuss the amount of compensation involved, but you can expect to receive more if you were involuntarily bumped, than if you volunteer to give up your seat. Your airline will pay all extra hotel and meal expenses, and if you are an economy-class passenger, perhaps an extra $200 on a North American flight or $400 on an overseas flight for volunteering to give up your seat. Business and first-class passengers receive more compensation than tourist passengers.

Riding the Rails

Ask me to write 25 words or less on what I like about rail travel, and I would be hard pressed to do so. Give me ten pages though, and I will fill them with raves for those silver ribbons of track that opened up countries and continents, and now lead us through some of the world's most glorious scenery.

For one thing, as train passengers we know where we are going. I was reminded of this in a supermarket line-up last fall after my Toronto-Vancouver trip by rail. A customer ahead of me commented on the cashier's tan, which she learned came from a vacation in the Canary Islands. "Where exactly are they?" asked the shopper. "I don't know. We flew there," was the reply. That's the difference you see. On a train we have an awareness of distance and changing terrain, and when we get there nobody could fool us as to the destination.

As well, it is nostalgia time for us. Most people over 50 have memories of train journeys in times when this was practically the only way to travel. Certainly I remember childhood trips to London from the suburbs, when getting there was more than half the fun. Also vivid in my memory is a traumatic trip as a World War II evacuee with a label pinned to my coat. On the boat train from London to Liverpool, the clickety-click of the wheels — like Dick Whittington's bells — seemed to be saying it wasn't too late to turn back. The train ride from Quebec City to Toronto, with "landed immigrant" stamped on my passport is one I shall never forget.

Now, in 80 words or less? I like arriving to board just ten minutes before departure. I like settling in, perhaps for days, with my own thoughts and memories called up by the rhythm of the wheels. I like having time to read and the walkabouts at stops along the way, and that the train has its own parking spot when we arrive in a big city. Try it, I know you'll like it too.

CANADA

Via Rail, Canada's national passenger rail system, operates from Toronto, Montreal, the Gaspé and Halifax on the east coast, to Churchill on the

Arctic Ocean and Vancouver and Prince Rupert on the west coast. It has direct connections with Amtrak to New York, Chicago and Seattle.

By the eighties Via's reputation had become slightly tarnished. Service was spotty as employees' low morale became evident, and car interiors looked decidedly shabby. Now, all long-distance trains have been handsomely refurbished (there are even on-board showers). Service is attentive and friendly, and while meals aren't exactly gourmet or haute cuisine they are tasty enough and nicely presented. The trains are clean and bright, comfortably warm in winter and cool in summer, and that viewing coach with its clear domed ceiling gives an all-around look at some of the world's loveliest vistas.

Discounts of 40% for off-peak travel apply to some Via Rail routes, 33% for advance booking on others. An additional discount of 10% is given to passengers aged 60 and up. Sleeping accommodation is extra.

Via Rail's **Canrailpass** gives you 12 days of coach-class travel within 30 days. Between June 7th and September 30th the cost is $489 or $439 for passengers 60 and over. Low-season rates are $329 and $299 respectively. For more information, contact your travel agent, or telephone Via Rail direct (see Appendix B).

Canada also has private and provincially-operated lines popular with vacationers. Here are some I know you will enjoy even though few, if any, offer discounts for older travellers.

■ British Columbia's steam-powered **Royal Hudson** excursion train between North Vancouver and Squamish.

■ The **Polar Bear Express** on Ontario Northland Railway's line from Cochrane to Moosonee, 300km (186 miles) beyond all highways, at James Bay on the Arctic Ocean. (There is a Toronto-Cochrane connection.)

■ **Rocky Mountain Railroad** has sightseeing trains travelling the mountain ranges between Vancouver and Banff in the Rocky Mountains.

■ **The White Pass and Yukon Route**'s narrow gauge line connects Whitehorse in the Yukon to Skagway on Alaska's Pacific coast.

UNITED STATES

Amtrak operates national passenger rail services in the United States. They reach out to link all major cities with a network 40,000 km (25,000 mi.) long. This makes rail travel very easy for Canadians who can connect through Via Rail from Vancouver, Toronto and Montreal.

Amtrak's programs are designed to lower the cost of rail travel for vacationers, and for such purposes the country is divided into three zones: all of the country east of Mississippi, and east and west of a dividing line roughly north and south of Denver. **All Aboard America** tickets permit three stops with prior reservations. Currently a one-zone ticket costs U.S. $138 (Can. $184). A ticket for travel in all three zones is U.S. $218 (Can. $291). Passengers 62 and over receive a 15% discount on the lowest fare on most routes. It does not extend to sleeping accommodation. Disabled travellers should inquire about special discounts.

In addition to coach seats, on-board sleeping accommodation comes in several varieties, from bedrooms to curtained bunk-bed sections. Snacks and full meals are available, depending on the route.

Of importance to snowbirds from Canada, Amtrak will carry your car from Lorton, Virginia, (near Washington) to Daytona Beach in Florida while you ride the train.

With basic fares and accommodation as complicated as the train schedules themselves, I suggest you have a travel agent work out details of your proposed trip. As well as a regular service, Amtrak has a range of vacation packages. These include fly-ride and rail-sail programs, rail-hotel and escorted tours. For information you can call Amtrak directly at their toll-free number: 1-800-USA-RAIL.

EUROPE

Rail passes for use in Europe almost always have to be purchased before leaving Canada and are validated on the first day of use. Some are for travel within a country or two, while the Eurailpass covers most of the continent.

Europe is so well served by its fast, efficient passenger rail network, the train is often a preferred method of transportation. The **Eurailpass,** which currently costs $672 for 15 days and $876 for 21 days or $1,888 for three months, gives unlimited first-class travel in 17 countries, including Austria, Belgium, Denmark, Finland, France, Germany, Greece, Holland, Hungary, Ireland, Italy, Luxembourg, Norway, Portugal, Spain, Sweden, Switzerland, but not Great Britain. There are special youth rates (under 26-year-olds can buy a second-class pass), but no discounts for older passengers.

A less expensive variant is the **Eurail Flexipass**, which can be used in a 60-day period. A pass for any 5 days' first-class travel within that period costs $470, 10 days $756 and 15 days $1,000. Also two people travelling together between April and September, or a group of three or more people during the rest of the year, can travel on a single **Eurail Saverpass** which permits 15 consecutive days unlimited travel for $582, 21 days $744 and 30 days $916.

A tremendous advantage of multi-country passes is that you pay only once, in Canadian currency. In consequence you're not constantly sorting out different currencies for different tickets, and can avoid those long line-ups at ticket windows. Eurailpasses also open up access to hotels and tour programs, similar to those offered by airlines.

Rail travel devotees reckon that Eurailpass is worthwhile if you use it in more than two countries, and cover at least 2,400 km (1,500 mi.) in 15 days or 3,500 km (2,200 mi.) in 20. So if your travels are confined to a limited part of the continent, it's well to look at alternatives.

Young travellers usually like to buy a Eurailpass and visit all the countries possible. I see more sense in getting to know one, two or at most three countries well, and returning next year to explore more. Some countries issue rail passes for use within their borders, or their own and neighbouring countries. Discounts for passengers from 60, 65 or 67 years of age may apply.

A Eurailpass will give you free or reduced-rate travel on selected ferries and buses. It is also possible to buy combined rail and car rental, or rail/air programs.

When travelling by rail in Europe, ask your airline about luggage transfer. Some European airlines will check your luggage for flights within the continent, or from Canada, through to the railway station at your destination (see Chapter 11). Another service — offered in Switzerland and Germany, and perhaps other countries as well — has your luggage forwarded by van from one hotel to the next so you are less encumbered on the train. You pay for the service, and your suitcase probably won't arrive ahead of you, but if your stay is for several days the system works well.

The **Russian Flexipass** is useful because it provides unlimited travel for four days in any two-week period. This means you can travel on your Eurailpass, or on a one or two country pass to the Russian border from Finland, Hungary, Czech Republic, Slovakia and other Eastern European countries, then the flexipass takes over. The basic cost is U.S. $298 (Can. $397) first, U.S. $198 (Can. $264) second class.

Information on European (except British) train travel, including Eurailpass can be obtained from Rail Europe's Canadian office, telephone

1-800-361-RAIL. When contemplating serious rail travel in Europe you will enjoy the informative *Berlitz Handbook to Train Travel in Europe* (Lausanne: Berlitz Publishing, 1994).

BRITAIN

Despite cut-backs in rail services, Britain still has more intensive rail services than any other country, with approximately 16,000 trains calling at 2,400 stations every day. The **Britrail Pass**, which must be purchased in Canada, provides unlimited travel in Great Britain. Passes for first and standard classes are available for a number of different periods. For example, an 8-day pass costs $339 first class, and $259 standard, a 22-day pass costs $709 and $489 respectively. **Britrail Flexipasses** cover a 30-day period. Any four days of travel within that period costs $279 first class and $219 standard, 8 days of travel costs $435 and $315 and 15 days of travel costs $650 and $450 respectively. Travellers 60 years and older receive a discount of approximately 10%. Various permutations on Britrail passes include travel to France and rail/drive programs.

British Rail's Senior Railcard (currently $35) entitles passengers 60 years and over to a discount of one third of the fare on many routes. There are also rail passes for one to 14 days of travel within a special region. Purchased at stations in the area to be travelled, these usually include bus and ferry travel. Discounts may be given to 60 plus travellers. Britrail's Canadian office has details, if you are interested in exploring this further.

OTHER PARTS OF THE WORLD

Australia's rail network provides a large part of that country with a comfortable and reliable service. **Austrailpass**, purchased outside the country is available from Goway Travel or Quantas Airways. It comes in a number of variations. For example, a first-class pass for 14 days costs $667, 21 days $823. Budget class is $400, and $520 respectively. The **Austrail Flexipass** provides travel on any eight days within a 60-day period. It costs $488 first class, $294 budget.

India's railways carry 10 million passengers daily on their trains, a figure readily believed by anyone who has travelled on them. They are crowded, hot, grubby and quite unreliable, but this matters little when the countryside they take you through is so extraordinarily vivid, so alive with unfamiliar scenes. The secret of success here is to be flexible, and patient.

The **Indrailpass** must be paid for in U.S. funds. First-class travel for 7 days costs U.S. $270 (Can. $359), 15 days U.S. $330 (Can. $440), 30 days U.S. $500 (Can. $667). Second-class fares are one half the cost of first-class fares. While it is possible to buy this pass in India (in U.S. funds only), purchase is more easily arranged in Canada. Agents are Hari-World Travel of Toronto. You or your travel agent must provide a photocopy of your passport details with your application. I also recommend that you book at least your first journey or two before leaving Canada, because seats on trains to the more popular areas fill up fast.

Japan's famous bullet trains will speed you across this country at up to 210 km (130 mi.) per hour. Passes, also good for some buses and ferries, must be purchased in Canada, from a travel agent or **JAL** (Japan Air Lines). A 7-day first-class pass costs $480, 14 days $780 and 21 days $1015. Economy class is $360 for 7 days, $575 for 14 days and $735 for 21 days.

New Zealand's Travelpass provides unlimited coach/train/ferry one-class travel. With this pass, 8 days of travel costs $273, 15 days $340 and 22 days $444. A further $143 brings you a **Complete Pass**, which gives you all of the above plus one air pass. Its value is that after arrival in Auckland (in the North Island) from Canada, you can then travel by train, ferry and bus as far as Invercargill in the South Island, and use your air ticket to get back to Auckland for your flight home. More information on these travelpasses is available from the Canadian agents, Goway Travel.

The rail information I've provided is for the most-travelled countries. Tourist offices and guidebooks are good sources of information for others. So, hopefully, is your travel agent's computer.

A TOUCH OF CLASS

What's in a little class? Plenty, when it comes to rail travel. If you are taking a long-distance train and want to sleep, I urge you to consider comfort over cost, which translates into first class. In some places even first class can be uncomfortable by Western standards. You may have to share an on-board bedroom with strangers, and on luxury trains such as India's Palace on Wheels an ensuite toilet is for use by six or eight passengers.

Travelling from Tallinn, Estonia to St. Petersburg, Russia my first-class ticket gave me space on a wooden seat, and I had a none-too-friendly looking Alsatian dog at my feet while its owner snored in an overhead rack.

On the other hand, travelling in Japan in August, the busiest time for rail travellers, I found economy-class coaches super-clean and comfortable. Fellow passengers were friendly and quick to give useful travel advice. Box lunches available on board were tasty. Only problem was that I didn't always get a seat and was embarrassed by my suitcase blocking the aisle. Another time I travelled first class, which meant reserved reclining seats, hot towels, magazines in several languages and very courteous attention from staff. Fellow passengers then were mostly business people or fellow tourists who added nothing to my journey.

IN FOREIGN PLACES

Can you travel by train in countries where you don't speak the language? You bet. Let's take Japan, because its language is totally foreign to Western ears. This is where I make good use of my pocket-sized notebook. Every morning I write questions in English, and ask a hotel clerk to put a Japanese translation underneath. Say I am off to Hiroshima. My first note asks the cabbie to take me to the railway station. Another saying "Which platform to Hiroshima, please?" is shown to a railway employee. In major stations porters will take you and your luggage to the exact spot on the platform where you need to be. In the absence of a porter, other passengers will point you in the right direction or escort you. A phrasebook also will serve you well. Memorize a few pleasantries, including "please" and "thank you" in the language of your host country and you will be just fine.

Tips •

■ Most cities tend to have more than one train station, so make sure you know the name of yours.

■ Railway stations may have as many as 15 platforms, all reached by steep steps. Try to allow plenty of time to change trains and if the one you are on arrives only three or four minutes before your connection leaves, let it go. It isn't worth inflicting personal injury by way of a fall.

■ In some countries timetables mean little. In others, such as Switzerland, trains arrive and depart on the minute.

■ Train food can be surprisingly tasty, even in Britain where travellers long ago resigned themselves to cardboard buns with leather fillings. When travelling with a friend, you don't have to settle on train or station food unless you fancy it. One of you can sit on the luggage while the other goes to the nearest deli.

THE SPECIALS

What about those **extra-special train trips**, the ones you read about in glossy magazines and thought would never materialize? Some aren't all *that* expensive. Few of us could afford them for family holidays, but maybe now it's time to treat yourself.

Most train specials are for travellers rather than tourists — people looking for the Great Train Experience, not just for a way of getting from here to there. Tour companies snap up space on the world's most famous trains, often months in advance of departure, so before that dream gets too exciting you'd better check with your travel agent about availability. If you like train rides, keep the following in mind when you're in the neighbourhood.

India's Palace on Wheels consists of 14 one-of-a-kind sleeping cars formerly owned by maharajas, hauled by a richly-decorated steam engine. Service is so attentive you will forgive the dust and lack of air-conditioning. Departing from New Delhi, this journey follows an 8-day itinerary through Rajasthan, with day trips to local palaces and world-famous landmarks such as Agra's Taj Mahal. Most meals are served on the train, others in the palace hotels. As the week continues, you sense what it is like to be visiting royalty, as local bands, decorated elephants and street entertainers herald your every stop.

South Africa's luxurious Blue Train is legendary. In fact, there are two, running in opposite directions between Cape Town and Pretoria via Kimberley and Johannesburg, a distance of over 1,600 km (1,000 mi.). In spite of political turmoil and resultant drop in tourism, these trains have been booked up to a year in advance.

Australia's famous Indian-Pacific covers the 3,960 km (2,460 mi.) between these two oceans in four days. Soon after leaving Sydney, it passes through the Blue Mountains, then makes several stops — including Broken Hill and Adelaide — before travelling the longest straight rail line in the world, 478 km (298 mi.) across the Nullabor Plain to Kalgoorlie and on to Perth.

If you enjoy this train ride, you should consider riding **The Ghan**, a desert train operating between Adelaide and Alice Springs in the continent's core. Or you might want to try **The Queenslander** which runs between Brisbane and Cairns through tropical oceanside country — magnificent scenery all the way.

New Zealand's **Silver Fern** is a daytime commuter special. It travels through achingly beautiful scenery which links Auckland and Wellington, covering 680km (422 mi.) in 10 hours. Another favourite with tourists is the **TranzAlpine Express**. Its five-hour journey takes it daily from Christchurch over the Arthur's Pass in the Southern Alps to Greymouth. Impressive engineering includes 20 tunnels, one of which is 8 km (5 mi.) long.

Russia's Trans-Siberian train from Moscow (which can be reached by rail from Helsinki, Warsaw or Bucharest) to Vladivostok or into China through Mongolia is far from luxurious and recommended only for the most adventurous travellers.

As well as this scheduled service, a "deluxe" tourist version known as the **Trans-Siberian Special** is chartered by tour operators for all or part of this route. Russia also has an elaborately restored steam train, the **Bolshoi Express**. It once provided transport for President Brezhnev (who didn't like air travel) and now plies between Moscow and St. Petersburg. Passengers stop off at good hotels for overnights, visit landmarks on the way, and take five days for a journey which on scheduled trains is done in about 10 hours.

The Orient Express, which once provided deluxe Wagon-Lits service between London and Istanbul, never really recovered from World War II. Several versions now evoke memories of these grand long-distance trains. Two well worth considering are: the **China Orient Express**, which follows part of the ancient Silk Road, and the **Eastern Oriental Express**, which will take you in style from Bangkok to Singapore.

Mexico has numerous passenger services, connecting with Amtrak trains through El Paso, Texas or Calexico in California. Best known is the **Copper Canyon Express** between Chihuahua and Los Mochis on the Pacific coast, a 645km (400 mi.) route which crosses the Continental Divide three times and rises over 2,400km (7,875 ft.) above dramatic canyons. People who know their trains say this is the best ride in the Americas.

Peru's rail trip between Cuzco and Machu Pichu is far from comfortable but when it gets you to the Lost City of the Incas, who cares? Locals board the train to hawk their crafts. Seamstresses will take your order for a new dress or shirt on the way there, and deliver it to you on the journey back. It won't be the greatest fit, but will be light and cool and gives you a cover-up for the beach, while contributing to the needlewoman's family income.

For my money, Canada has one of the world's best train rides, north of Superior and through the Rockies to the west coast. This can be part of Via Rail's four-day trip from Toronto, or you can disembark at stops along the way. My recent trip to Vancouver took ten days, with stopovers in Winnipeg and Jasper. Using rented cars to explore the prairies, and to drive the fabulous Icefields Parkway from Jasper to Lake Louise, I saw a great deal of this country in a week and a half. I stayed at spectacular railway hotels and resorts, and rubbed shoulders with tourists from Britain, Japan, America and Australia. There were very few Canadians though, which is too bad, because you can do this one without crossing oceans and continents.

$\mathcal{T}$he Open Road

$\mathcal{G}$one are the days of being asked "how much farther?" — as if it's our fault Fort Lauderdale is another 1,000 km (620 mi.) along the road. No more urgent calls for pit stops. No more fights "she started." No more packing an endless supply of games. No more counting green cars or sing-alongs.... Actually I miss those family trips, which is not to say I don't enjoy keeping the car radio tuned to my favourite adult station, or having an uninterrupted conversation. And just for old times, we do slip *Winnie the Pooh* into the tape deck once in a while, along with Vivaldi and Anne Murray.

GETTING READY

If you plan on doing some long-distance driving in North America and your Canadian Automobile Association membership has lapsed, now is the time to renew it and to study the many services this organization provides. Visit your local CAA office to tell a counsellor about your upcoming trip, and he or she will arrange to get you a **triptik**. This is a road map laid out as a strip which, along with the association's road maps and guidebooks, is the handiest travel companion a motorist could ask for. The association's travel guides are as explicit as any you can buy, with restaurant, hotel and tourist attraction listings for your proposed route. All this is in addition to member discounts, emergency services and so on (more about that in Chapter 3).

Consider getting a **cellular telephone**. It will be useful for emergency calls, making reservations or confirming arrival times and keeping in touch with home. Basic units which either plug into your car's cigarette lighter socket or depend on rechargeable batteries, and can be used outside the car, cost as little as $200–$250. A basic emergency phone service to cover a large area of your home region can be $10 per month. To use the telephone anywhere else in North America you simply dial in the local telephone company's code on a pay per call basis. If you prefer a service allowing longer air time, the basic cost increases to between $30 and $150 per month, plus fees for calls outside your area.

Have your car checked over and serviced by a neighbourhood mechanic before leaving home. Remember to include a check of the air pressure in your automobile's spare tire.

Pack an **emergency kit**. Its contents depend largely on where you are going, and possible weather conditions. Your regular medications, bottled water and dry food snacks, plus a blanket and first-aid kit are mandatory. You should also bring a flashlight, a Call Police sign and two reflective triangles. Keep this kit inside the car, not the trunk, so you can use some of it without facing outside elements which may be causing your emergency.

If you are going south and don't relish the long drive to reach your destination, you might consider using a drive-away service. These are listed in your yellow pages, under Automobile and Truck Drive-away services. For example, one Toronto company will deliver a car from Toronto to Florida for $467, to California for $500. If you are going to Florida, you can also use Amtrak's Autotrain service from northern Virginia.

ON THE ROAD

Know your limits. Even the fittest among us tire more quickly as we get older. When touring by car, try to take every third day off. Even with two drivers, fatigue can set in, since the passenger seldom relaxes totally. If you have always driven to your vacation destination in three days, and it is now more comfortable to do it in four, so what? Find a country inn off the highway and consider the extra night as part of your vacation.

Our routine is to set off soon after daylight, usually within 15 minutes of waking. I used to make tea first, but with all-night diners along highways now we tend to stop for take-out coffee, then again for breakfast around 9:30 a.m. Our next stop is early afternoon, as restaurants empty of local workers. Overnight accommodation is reached no later than 4 p.m., so there's time to relax by a pool or go for a walk. An early night after a light meal, and we are ready for the same routine next day. We carry a supply of talking books from our local library and favourite tapes from home, and the miles are lapped up easily.

SECURITY

For the best security, try to look as if you live there, and by this I mean pack your vacation gear in the trunk. Maps, guidebooks, triptik, hotel reservation vouchers and similar travel documents should be kept in an envelope, so that they can be easily carried to the restaurant or hotel in your purse or a briefcase. With doors locked and everything out of sight, thieves will find your car less tempting than another with cameras and luggage on the rear seat.

Highway restaurants are often easy targets for thieves. Park between cars where your vehicle isn't obscured from view by a van or wall and at night try to park under a light. On well-travelled routes reserve your overnight accommodation so you aren't crawling around back streets looking for lodging after dark. Check out security before leaving your heavy luggage in your car trunk overnight. It's easier to get by with nightclothes and a few toiletries, but not always smart.

IN CASE OF BREAKDOWN

If your car malfunctions, try to keep driving until you reach a service station, convenience store or some other well-lighted area when you can.

If you have a cellular telephone, now is the time to use it. If not, try to get to a call box and ask the operator to send help. In the United States, request the operator to send a police officer. He will contact an automobile club or towing company and stay with you until assistance arrives.

When you can't find a telephone box, drive onto the shoulder, display your reflective triangles and Call Police sign. Then lock yourself in your car to wait for the police or a highway patrolman to come by.

Should strangers approach, speak only through a slightly-lowered window. If they appear trustworthy, ask them to drive on and send help. If not, tell them help is on the way.

RENTING A CAR

I know you can identify a rented car by its licence plates, but I have come to recognize other signs. Like the windshield wipers going full tilt on a sunny afternoon. The car that dashes through a yellow light permitting its driver to stay in gear is a rental. The windows stuck open in heavy rain is another giveaway. So is a sudden blast of loud music as the driver frantically fiddles with different knobs. The first rule is to try it all out before leaving the rental lot.

Give your age at the outset, because some companies will not rent to drivers 70 years and over. When overseas, remember to ask for automatic transmission if this is what you are used to. Driving those squiggly roads on the "wrong" side is fun enough without having an unfamiliar gear shift to play with.

In most countries your Canadian driver's licence is sufficient. In others you may require an **International Driving Permit,** so do check with your travel agent when planning to drive overseas. Permits are available from automobile clubs, to non-members as well as members.

For the lowest rates, book your car before leaving home. Airlines have good rates, as an incentive for you to fly with them. CARP, AARP and CAA are three of many organizations offering discounts.

Look at the total cost of renting a car. The automobile insurance policies you have at home are unlikely to cover you, and while certain credit cards provide some insurance, you must make sure you are protected against liability to others and theft and damage to the car. Add all the bits and pieces — GST or VAT and other taxes plus insurance — and your advertised $25 a day car rental bargain is up to $40.

When driving abroad read up on local rules of the road before you leave Canada. In some countries you will drive on the left, which doesn't take much getting used to since everyone else is on your side. If there is no traffic around, those right turns can be a little dodgy for the first day or so, after which it all becomes automatic. Carry some local currency. Once in a while you will be expected to pay fines for infractions on the spot. Not to do so only causes delays.

Where to collect the car? We try to pick up a car and return it at an airport. Then, in congested places such as London, we begin and conclude a trip by taking public transport into the city where there is no need for private wheels.

Usually rental companies will hold your car for only two hours beyond the arranged time. Try to telephone ahead if you are going to be delayed.

Do you really want one? A nervous driver, or someone who's easily lost, may find self-driving too much of a headache. In some countries where drivers have little regard for the law, and police are not too zealous about traffic control, you may be better off using public transportation or joining a tour for part of your trip. This is after all a vacation, and if you don't like to drive, there are happy alternatives.

*B*us Travel

I've always found bus travel a friendly way to go. Especially overseas where passengers inevitably move over to make room for anyone over 50 to sit down. And if you ask the driver to point out your stop, at least four people will beat him to it. On bus journeys I have sat next to hens going to market, and sacks of flour from the mill. Once I was asked to hold a baby in return for her father's seat. In Mexico members of a mariachi band on their way to work at a tourist hotel played for us, and in Brazil a missionary from South Carolina prayed for us.

In most of the world bus services have grown up to expand on passenger rail services and, increasingly, to take their place. Scheduled services frequent most roads shown on maps, and their standard of reliability generally reflects a country's quality of life.

In the Third World, buses present an enormous variety. Often resembling Canadian school buses, they are painted in riotous colours, sometimes with elaborate pictures on the sides. Cab areas are treated as the driver's private domain, decorated with assorted miniature shrines, rosaries, family pictures and good-luck charms. On mountain tracks where roadside shrines in memory of accident victims stand at every curve in the road, I have said a prayer or two myself.

Some island buses are trucks fitted with padded bench seats in the back. They look like a lark, and do provide local colour, but if you've ever had a spinal problem I can guarantee it will reappear after 20 minutes of bouncing in one of these vehicles.

In Mexico, where the driver's cab is often outlined in velvet bobbles as well as religious objects, and where driving can be hazardous to one's health, I hired a driver with car to take me from Cancun to the Mayan ruins at Chichen Itza. Later I learned that first-class air-conditioned buses serve the same route for a small fraction of my car fare. Once again, check out your options if you want to save on expenses.

EUROPE

European buses are very reliable. They have to be, because they are frequently the lifeline between towns and isolated farmhouses. Inter-city buses are often interconnected with rail services, and during off-peak periods may operate in place of trains. Rail passes issued for use within one or two countries are usually valid on inter-city buses, but the Eurail-pass is not.

To travel any distance by bus can be relatively inexpensive. For example, the **Europabus** service, which leaves London's Victoria Coach Station three times daily, crosses the channel from Dover to Zeebrugge, continues through Belgium and Holland to Cologne in Germany, takes 15 hours. The fare is $80 one way, $140 return. This same bus continues to Mannheim, Stuttgart and Munich. The entire 23-hour journey from London to Munich costs $110 one way or $185 return. The lowest British Airways Apex return fare London to Munich is $345. The equivalent journey by second-class rail costs $310 one way, $620 return, although that amount can be cut virtually in half when using a four-day Rhineland Flexipass package for two people costing $609 with a day's car rental at no additional cost.

Similar bus services exist to most of continental Europe from London, the most popular with Brits are those to Spain's Costa del Sol and Portugal's Algarve.

National Express-Eurolines also operates a full service between London and the continent. For information contact their London office at telephone: 071 730 0202. Europabus information is available from the same number.

I suggest then that you look at all the options. Bus travel is leisurely, cheap and shows you a lot of countryside into the bargain. Long-distance buses are comfortable with roomy reclining seats and air-conditioning; some have on-board hostesses, snacks, videos and toilets. But if you are impatient to reach your destination and likely to ache from the inactivity of sitting for hours on end, long-distance bus travel may not be for you.

BRITAIN

In Britain it is reckoned that a journey by bus takes twice as long as by rail, and costs half as much. Distances are short here and town or city bus depots centrally located, which makes for convenient and reasonably-priced day-tripping.

The country-wide **National Express** network of scheduled coach services links over 1,000 destinations. Nearly all operate daily; and often there are hourly departures. Frequent services from Heathrow, Gatwick and Stansted airports to London's Victoria Coach Station will connect you with all parts of Britain and continental Europe.

Britain has some particularly good deals for its bus travellers from overseas. One is the **Britexpress Card**. It costs $24, and gives a reduction of approximately 30% on every journey made in any 30-day period. Another is the **Seniors Coach Card** for travellers 60 and over. Costing $12, it is valid for 12 months, and offers the same discounts as the Britexpress Card.

The **Tourist Trail Pass** provides unlimited travel on all bus services. Passengers under 60 years of age pay between $130 for five days and $380 for 30 days. If you are 60 or over, you pay $90 for five days and $266 for 30 days.

When planning day-trips out of London, you will find the Green Line *Days Out* brochure valuable. It describes inexpensive day-return outings by coach to places like Stratford-Upon-Avon, Hampton Court Palace, Oxford, Cambridge and other tourist favourites. No reservations are necessary. Simply turn up at Victoria Station with your umbrella.

AUSTRALIA AND NEW ZEALAND

Bus travel is extremely popular for touring these countries. In Australia distances are so formidable few visitors choose to drive them and the bus services are superior by any standards. When planning your itinerary you will want to consider the many opportunities described in travel planner books distributed by the Australian Tourist Commission, or from travel agents specializing in that country.

To give you an idea of the costs: the **Greyhound Aussie Pass** provides unlimited travel from $316 for 7 days to $1,932 for 90 days. Regional passes are less. And there is a handy **Kangaroo Road'n Rail Pass**: 14 days' first-class travel $832, economy $524 or 28 days' first-class travel for $1,224, economy $920.

New Zealand's Travelpass (see also p. 79) provides unlimited bus/train/ferry travel for 8 days at $273 to 22 days for $444. The Complete Pass, which includes one air pass, is from $417 for 8 days to $587 for 22 days. The system has only one class. The Travelpass must be purchased in Canada — Goway Travel of Toronto and Vancouver are the agents. Once you are in New Zealand, specific travel reservations are required. Since this pass covers train, ferry and most inter-city and suburban bus services, it takes you just about anywhere you want to go in New Zealand.

NORTH AMERICA

On this continent, students and retirees are the mainstay of bus lines, and for good reason. Bus routes are far more extensive than those of passenger trains, fares are lower and these two age groups both have more time to sit back and relax on the open road.

Recognizing their market, bus companies offer substantial discounts. The **Greyhound** system which covers the United States and Canada west of Toronto gives a 10% discount to all passengers 65 and over. **Voyageur Colonial** lines which operate in Ontario and Quebec have discounts of 10% to 30% for travellers over 60. Some other regional services offer similar incentives.

Available to travellers of any age are a variety of other incentives and travel passes. For example, Greyhound Canada has a series of passes for unlimited travel which must be purchased seven days in advance. A pass for 7 days costs $179, 14 days $239, 30 days $329 and 60 days $429. Voyageur Colonial and some other regional lines have similar passes, although they may be available only at certain times of the year.

In the United States, Greyhound Bus Lines' **Ameripass** gives 7 days of unlimited travel on its own and many subsidiary companies' lines for $333, 15 days for $467 and 30 days for $600.

If you are thinking of using North America's bus lines extensively, you should read *Russell's Official National Motor Coach Guide* (Cedar Rapids: Russell's Guides Inc., 1994) and its various supplements, for its complete listings of bus lines, routes, stations and schedules. If you plan on travelling with visitors from overseas, have them inquire about low-cost Greyhound Bus passes available from travel agents outside North America.

Bus Charters

These are different from coach tours in that the bus is chartered to go to a special event or destination. You pay your fare, get taken there and report back to the bus in time for your return home.

Bus charters can be great fun, especially when you take the same trip each year, as do so many passengers to Las Vegas, Atlantic City, Nashville (for an annual fix of country music at the Grand Ole Opry) or Memphis (for the anniversary of the "King's" death).

Because chartered bus excursions are advertised in recreational halls and meeting places attended by retirees, they attract a high percentage of people in our age group. In consequence, the music and board games played en route are geared to older travellers, and fellow passengers will be compatible.

Shipping Out

According to the surveys, 50 plus passengers are well represented on most ships and outnumber all other travellers on both round-the-world luxury cruises and small ships sailing to exotic destinations. It is easy to see why. A cruise offers excellent vacation value. It is the most relaxing way to tour. You unpack only once, even on a month-long voyage, and you can rest any time without interfering with the itinerary. Also, there are no unpleasant surprises with your bill when you leave, because a large portion (70% for most cruise passengers) of your vacation costs are prepaid.

Since older passengers are in the majority, few cruise lines offer us discounts. Loyalty is rewarded though, and as a former passenger you will receive notice of upcoming bargains. You might keep an eye open for last minute sell-offs, but more likely these days are discounts for booking early — at which time cabin selection is at its best.

CHECK IT OUT

Unless your best friend assures you there is no cruise line like hers, and continues to tell you why she travels with it regularly, find yourself a travel agent who is a cruise specialist. He or she is kept up to date with all the latest cruise news such as new itineraries and specials like the D-Day anniversary cruises to Europe.

Make an appointment to visit the agent so there's time to talk. Establish your budget, explain your interests and hobbies and, if you have any infirmities, let them know. (If you can manage a short walk to the elevator, but not three flights of stairs to reach your cabin, your needs can be accommodated if you book early enough.)

For older passengers the ship's size may be important, in that some of the larger vessels can't get into every port. Going ashore in a tender can be tedious and tiring, especially when you have to wait in line beneath a hot Caribbean sun. Passengers on monster ships number in the thousands, and disembarkation queues are long enough to make you think twice about going ashore.

Once again the novice traveller must ask some questions of him or herself. Do you want a floating resort with endless on-board entertainment? A different port every day, or night sailings followed by two or three days in each place? Is food important? I hope so because it can play a dominant role in the success of a memorable cruise.

Check the ship's registry and crew's nationality. It may be cruising in the Caribbean but if it's registered in Italy, its crew will be Italian and the dining-room fare will be continental with strong Italian overtones. I happen to love Italian and French cuisine — especially beneath the Caribbean moon sometime around February and March. If you crave a steak and fries consider a U.S. flag American Hawaiian Cruise Line ship. For continental cuisine, with all those French sauces, how about a Club Med sailing ship?

These days, the Russian ships are said to give the best value in cruises of the Mediterranean. Leaving or returning to Tilbury, England their 15-day tours of the Greek Islands are approximately $2,200 including the one-way airfare between their Mediterranean port and London. A former Soviet ship, *Gruziya* (now flying the Ukrainian flag), offers particularly good value on its one-week cruise out of Tampa, Florida to Belize, Honduras and Mexico's Yucatan Peninsula. The price is approximately $2,000 including airfare from such U.S. gateways as Buffalo and Seattle.

Where To Go
Anywhere. Cruise business is big business. Last year more than 4.5 million North Americans took cruises with the Caribbean, the Pacific coast and Hawaii as favoured destinations of 50 plus passengers. Alaska is extremely popular since many of us have given up chasing the sun and more wrinkles, and the scenery is incredibly beautiful. Exotic destinations are ideally reached by cruise ship because they provide their passengers with clean and comfortable accommodation, and well-prepared meals in areas where sanitation may not be up to Western standards. If you are free to travel at any time, do study weather patterns. Prices are lower in shoulder season, but this can be hurricane time. Danger may be minimal, but foul weather can result in a very rough ride and a change of itinerary.

How Formal Should You Be?
Few cruise ships are very formal these days, and there is no need for men to take more than a suit for evening wear and women a cocktail outfit or two. On the other hand, if you love to dress up, your travel agent can steer you to a ship where this is encouraged.

A Short Cruise as Part of a Longer Tour

I like to use a cruise as part of a longer trip. As with the spa, a ship can give you a few days R & R during a hectic tour and it can also take you to places not easily reached on your own. A Mediterranean, Rhine or Danube cruise during your big tour of Europe — an Alaskan cruise followed by a bus tour through the Yukon and British Columbia — a three-day Hawaiian Island cruise preceded by a few days in Honolulu and followed by two more in Maui (or en route to Australia) — a Nile cruise to get you to Luxor and the Valley of the Kings after your Cairo visit — are all delightful alternatives to land and air travel.

ON-BOARD ACCOMMODATION

As a rather shy and certainly unworldly young woman I crossed the Atlantic from Britain in the early 1950s, when a ship's passage cost far less than the airfare.

It was hell. My cabin way down below all other decks, was shared with four strangers, of whom at least two were seasick all the time. Air-conditioning, if there was any, didn't reach this far. We kept the door open for quick access to toilets along the corridor. After nine days of this, I was reluctant to travel by ship again.

When I finally woke up to the pleasure of cruising, it was to queen-sized beds, full-sized windows in the cabins, large bathroom ensuite and more closet and drawer space than I was used to at home. Mealtime was relaxed and friendly, the food good to excellent and with a warm aquamarine ocean out there instead of the slate grey Atlantic, I decided hell had been transformed to heaven.

Although cabins and staterooms on upper decks cost more than those down below, they may not be much larger. On any level, a cabin beside the main stairway can be noisy in late evening. Staterooms facing the promenade decks have nice big windows, (and pedestrians outside who wouldn't think of peering in your windows at home but now look in to compare your cabin with theirs). I prefer an outside cabin to one without a window or porthole, but have no objection to lower decks.

My agent always recommends a middle-priced cabin or stateroom. If that's too expensive or unavailable, but the itinerary is what you want, settle on the best accommodation you can get. After all, entertainment, meals, on-board lectures and shore excursions are the same for all passengers.

Everyone has use of all public areas. Lounges and decks are well furnished with comfortable seating. Evening shows, or a casino, will keep you out of your cabin after dinner. Really then, the size and luxury level of your cabin isn't all that important — you will spend few waking hours there.

ON-BOARD DINING

I can't think of any place other than a cruise ship where you are tempted with so much food day after day. It starts with breakfast buffets piled high with tropical fruits, fresh juices, traditional cooked dishes and ends with a grand midnight buffet. In between there are mid-morning and afternoon snacks, a lunch chosen from the dining room menu and possibly hamburgers cooked on deck in early afternoon for passengers returning from shore excursions. Give the barbecue a miss, and you may just have room for afternoon tea a couple of hours before dinner.

Most dining-rooms have tables for eight to ten passengers. If you are with your family, or a small group, special arrangements can be made for you to sit together. Otherwise you will be allotted your table on boarding, often being matched to compatible guests by the purser's office. If, during the cruise, you want to move to another table, it can probably be arranged.

Passengers are free to arrive for breakfast and lunch at any time it is being served. For dinner there are two sittings, usually at 7:00 p.m. and 8:30 p.m. and you can make your choice when booking. Whichever sitting you decide on, you will find plenty of after-dinner entertainment timed for when you are through with your meal.

CRUISE COSTS

Most staterooms are furnished to sleep two, and some have an overhead bunk or fold-up couch for third and fourth passengers at reduced fare. Children 12 and under are usually half price while young children are free. Single supplements are horrendous at 50%, or as high as 100% for deluxe rooms. Perhaps this is time to interest a friend in going with you.

Because of the variations involved, it is difficult to establish an average price for a cruise. Obviously a tour of New Zealand by cruise ship costs more than a party boat out of Miami, when you calculate in the price transportation to the departure port. Smaller ships which average 500 passengers are of course more expensive than the monster ships with 2,000 people stacked on six or seven accommodation decks.

Prices vary with cabin size and location. A rule of thumb is that a competitively-priced seven-day Caribbean cruise (including economy-class airfares, transfers, port charges and taxes from Toronto) will cost $1,400 to $1,700 per person in winter. A more upscale cruise to the same islands is about $1,500 to $3,000, while something truly luxurious would start at the top of this range.

Meals and snacks, entertainment and most on-board recreational facilities are free to passengers. Beauty parlour treatments, massages, personal shopping, skeet-shooting and your bar bill are paid separately, as are gratuities. While some cruise lines advertise that tipping is entirely optional, $10 to $13 per passenger per day is suggested on most ships. One half will be for the cabin steward and the remainder divided among dining-room staff. For a more personal touch you can write the recipient's name on each envelope and hand these out with a smile. But in reality these envelopes are turned in unopened to the purser's office, where contents are divided among the ship's hotel staff on a basis they have already arranged among themselves.

Shore excursions and car rentals can be arranged once you're on board, or sometimes prepaid before leaving home. When you sign up in advance for scuba diving, mountain biking, helicopter sightseeing and the like, transportation provided by the tour company will be waiting when you dock. Other tour companies may also have their representatives there to capture the undecided, and their prices can be very competitive.

As part of your pre-cruise homework I suggest you read about the places where you'll dock. Organized shore excursions may show you more than you'll see on your own. But, do you really need a three-hour drive in each direction to reach a famous landmark, when you have only eight hours in port? Often it is more enjoyable to walk, or hop a bus into town. Or take a cab to a nearby resort where a drink and lunch earns admission to the pool and the beach is free.

Experience has taught me to avoid bus tours in port. In consequence I've visited my last coconut factory, pineapple plant and clothing outlet. It means I miss out on the juice and nut samples in tiny paper cups, and I am learning to live without them. Instead I sometimes rent a car (in advance of arrival while small models are still to be had), or I find a taxi with an English-speaking driver. In either case I try to stay on reasonably well-travelled roads, where help isn't too far away should the vehicle break down.

SINGLES

Let's dispel the myth that cruises are only for romancing couples. A high proportion of passengers are older women travelling together or on their own. If you are overwhelmed by the thought of vacationing on your own after years of being half of a pair, a cruise is a very good place to start. Join a tour, a quality tour where you will be part of a small escorted group. You will meet other singles at a get-together arranged by the tour company ahead of departure and perhaps even a prospective cabin-mate to help share the rent. Older couples with different interests often split up for shore excursions, so you will have additional singles for company there. Others like to share the cost of a car rental or taxi for a day's outing. I have had some fine day-trips in rental cars, made all the more enjoyable because I invited another passenger along.

THEME AND CELEBRITY CRUISES

New and exciting theme cruises are introduced every season. Australia-bound ships will be gearing up for the Sydney Olympics any time now, probably with former champions on board. The fiftieth anniversary of D-Day saw performers from World War II brought out of retirement to entertain on cruise ships to Europe.

Movie and sports personalities on theme cruises are very popular with fans. These celebrities talk about their work, sign autographs, pose for pictures and generally mingle. An example is P. Lawson Travel's **Classic Movies Cruise** featuring TVO's movie host Elwy Yost aboard Celebrity Cruises modern ship *Meridian* in November. Evening entertainment will include some half dozen movie classics presented by Elwy, along with commentary from his vast fund of movie memorabilia. Sailing from San Juan, ports of call include St. Thomas, Martinique, Curacao and the San Blas Islands reached by way of the Panama Canal. Cost for the 11-day cruise, and air from Toronto or Montreal, is $2,900 to $3,700 per person, double occupancy.

Something a little different for sports fans is **Clipper Cruise Line**'s five-day cruise from northern Florida to Charleston, South Carolina. Passengers stop off for golf at St. Simons Island, Savannah, Hilton Head and two other islands along the coast.

Big bands, bridge, birdwatching, computer planning — whatever your interest, you can likely pursue it on board. It's a matter of asking around, then booking early, because themes suited to 50 plus travellers sell fast.

ADVENTURE CRUISES

If the above seem a tad tame, an adventure cruise will take you to exotic destinations without the hassle of humping your luggage through jungles or across ice flows. The choices are delicious: a 14-day **Antarctica** expedition from Argentina; a cruise in the **China seas**; a journey through the **Northwest Passage** from Greenland to Alaska in 28 days. Or you can explore the **Amazon**'s tributaries more than a thousand miles from the ocean, or cruise remote **Polynesian Islands** — these are just a few of the adventure cruises described in brochures on my travel agent's shelves.

EXPLORING THE WATERWAYS

If you would like to cruise but feel the need to keep land in sight, the world has some great inland waterways waiting for you.

Converted barges on Britain's canals and rivers provide a relaxed interlude during a busy tour, but their size prohibits spacious comfort. And don't expect to go far. A three-day **River Thames** cruise took me from Reading to Oxford, but then distance travel is not the object of this exercise. It is to tie up at historic pubs for a tipple with locals, to go antiquing or to a summer fair or for tea at a country mansion. Our pace was so slow the ducks overtook us, and I could walk alongside the boat all morning without losing it.

Travelling the **Nile** or the **Rhine** or the **Danube**, you will be in a huge floating hotel with air-conditioned accommodation, first-class diningrooms and good service. On both the Rhine and the Danube you can travel in one country or several, tailoring your cruise to fit into a longer vacation schedule. Danube cruises now include Romania and Bulgaria, and for music lovers several departing from Vienna focus entertainment around Mozart concerts.

France has some of the world's best gastronomic cruises. California has tours of its wine regions via the **Napa River**. In summer, a passenger ship travelling between St. Petersburg and Moscow is a grand opportunity to explore those two historic cities. A **Mississippi** sternwheeler provides a taste of the Old South. The *Canadian Empress* which replicates turn-of-the-century ships on the **St. Lawrence River** takes its passengers back to gentler times.

Toronto entrepreneur Sam Blyth (of Blyth & Company) usually recognizes a good travel idea when he sees one. He recently acquired a former Soviet icebreaker which used to sail for the KGB. Since then she has been exploring various parts of the world and 1994 was her first season on the **Great Lakes**, departing from Toronto for the Welland Canal, Georgian Bay and Sault-Ste.-Marie.

FREIGHTER CRUISES

Youthful dreams of running away to sea are not easily fulfilled these days. Containers, computerized systems and small unionized crews have replaced amateur ordinary seamen. But we have an alternative now, as paying passengers on a cargo ship.

Average or typical accommodation doesn't apply to cargo ships because each differs from the next. Some have only one luxurious apartment, designed for the ship's owner and rented out to a pair of passengers upon request. A few of the newer freighters are designed to carry both cargo and people.

Cargo-ship travel is not suitable for someone on a fixed two-week vacation. For this reason, most passengers are retirees, along with the occasional writer, who is there to work. Flexibility has to be the operative word, since cargo ships do not keep rigid schedules. They may be late leaving their departure port, and then make a detour to collect profitable cargo. Delays can occur through labour disputes dockside, or routes changed because of trade embargoes. Ports visited are seldom tourist attractions, and I should point out that cargo docks are rarely in the best part of town. None of which deters the avid freighter fan.

Mile for mile, freighter travel is relatively inexpensive, usually around $120 a person per day for all sea transportation, accommodation and meals, snacks and steward services. Drinks are paid for separately, at duty-free prices.

Daily living on a freighter is unlike the cruise-ship experience. Passengers eat with the ship's officers. A lounge, library and games room are shared with the crew. In the absence of organized entertainment there will be a collection of board games and videos and you will want to bring some books of your own.

Freighters are not fitted with stabilizers to keep them on an even keel, so you may take a few days to get your sea legs. Also, if there are fewer than 12 passengers, a doctor will not be on board. For this reason you may be asked for a medical certificate showing good health when you book your passage, and often there is an age restriction, commonly 79.

Vancouver and **Montreal** are the major Canadian ports used by cargo liners. In the United States, most sail from **California**'s coast, the **Gulf of Mexico** and the **New York** area. Shorter voyages are between the east coast of North America and Europe. Longer, more typical trips are from **Europe** to **East Africa** via Cape Town and return in 42 days. A return voyage from New Orleans to Japan, Hong Kong and Singapore is roughly 65 days. **Around-the-World** cargo voyages take close to three months, leaving from Europe or California. The cost is approximately $10,000 and here's one future passenger who has started saving.

If you like the idea of more than a handful of passengers on board, I can recommend two companies: Norway's **Ivaron Lines**, which operates ships with accommodation for 88 passengers and sails from the United States' east coast to South America. Another company to keep in mind is the **St. Helena Shipping Company** with a cargo liner equipped for 76 passengers. It sails between Britain and South Africa, with calls at the Atlantic islands of St. Helena, Ascension and sometimes Tristan da Cunha.

There are far more would-be passengers for freighters than there is space to accommodate them, especially during good weather seasons. Reserve early, and consult a travel agent who fully understands this market. One such agency is **The Cruise People** of Don Mills, Ontario and London, England. To put you in the mood for off-beat cruising, you should take a look at *Ford's Freighter Travel and Waterways of the World* (Northridge: Ford's Travel Guides, 1994), which is probably in your local library.

FERRIES

Ferry boat rides can't compare with cruises, but for a fraction of a cruise fare they can give you a pretty good experience at sea. Larger ferries have overnight cabins, on-board entertainment, dining-rooms and cafeterias. The newer ships are bright and comfortable, and often follow the routes taken by expensive cruise ships. In Europe, ferry travel is often included in your rail pass.

The large ferries plying the Baltic between such ports as Stockholm and Helsinki are very attractive and their voyages are actually mini-cruises. In Canada, **B.C. Ferries** has one of the best routes. Its *Queen of the North* sails through the west coast's Inside Passage from Vancouver Island to Prince Rupert in northern British Columbia on a 15-hour journey via one of the world's most scenic waterways. From Prince Rupert passengers often continue north on the State of Alaska Marine Highway ferries to Anchorage. Both will allow your car or motorhome on-board (be sure to book well ahead of your proposed departure), which allows you to drive back south at your leisure.

On our east coast, **Marine Atlantic** operates several ferry services, most popular being the route between New Brunswick and Prince Edward Island. For something approaching an ocean voyage, there's a 12 to 14 hours summer service between North Sydney, Nova Scotia and Argentia, Newfoundland. From Prince Edward Island, in the meantime, you can have a lovely few days in the French-speaking Magdalen Islands, approximately five hours by ferry from Souris — a trip I wholeheartedly recommend.

Organized Travel

One of my most memorable travel experiences was a Highlands and Islands tour of Scotland in a vintage coach named Janice, and one of my most successful travel articles was about it. (So many readers responded that the owner was able to restore a second coach, which he named Pamela after me!)

Small enough to travel the backroads prohibitive to bigger coaches, it was authentically restored to the 1950s by owner/driver David Dean of **Classique Tours** in Scotland. Whether it was because of the nostalgia evoked by this vehicle I don't know, but we had few passengers under the age of 60 and probably only two less than 50.

On the first day, Mr. Dean weighed our physical abilities carefully. More agile passengers were put in lodgings up the hill, while the rest slept in centrally-located inns and B & Bs close to where we met for dinner. On an island accessible only by small boat, there were pony traps at the arrival dock for anyone who couldn't comfortably handle the hilly terrain. There were frequent toilet stops. Wet weather saw us shepherded into tea rooms warmed by peat fires, and when the sun shyly peeped through the clouds we voted to detour from the planned itinerary for a couple of hours on a beach.

This kind of flexibility is not possible on larger coaches operated by megacompanies whose drivers must adhere to advertised schedules. And small outfits such as David Dean's are not in plentiful supply. Still, whatever your choice, there are great advantages to touring with a group. You can relax and let someone else do the driving. If the hotel is overbooked, you don't have to worry about finding another. When rough weather or clogged roads delay you to the point of missing a connection, it is not your problem. Most of your vacation is prepaid in Canadian dollars before you leave home, so there are no unexpected bites into your pocket. Here's how it works.

THE BIG TOUR

If you are touring Europe by coach your package will likely include return air fare from Canada, services of a full-time escort who accompanies you all the way, baggage handling, transportation, most meals and evening entertainment, chairlifts, admissions to attractions, boat and train excursions and all tips and gratuities. Some companies even provide limousine transportation between your home and the departure airport, or an overnight hotel room near the airport if you prefer. There may be pre-trip get-togethers to acquaint you with fellow travellers.

Fans of the group tour love it. They enjoy the company, not having to take care of details and watching the world slip by the coach windows. They are content to be four days into the tour without handling local currency, or interpreting a menu or striking a deal with the rickshaw or camel driver. These are considered hassles they can live without.

While every tour is different, most include a lot of coach travel in vehicles fitted with reclining seats, air-conditioning and, possibly, a toilet. (There will be frequent pit stops too.) Local guides come aboard for city tours and visits to featured landmarks.

How tiring is the tour you have in mind? Eight countries in 14 days with your luggage out for collection at seven each morning is not a leisurely vacation. Is there much walking involved? Some of those lovely old European towns have precious little space for residents' cars, let alone visiting coaches. In consequence, you could well be parked on the outskirts and may have to hike into the town core (or wait for a shuttle) where your walkabout begins.

Some of the most successful escorted tours are those with varied components. At a recent "Today's Seniors" travel show, I heard a new tour being discussed by P. Lawson's Allan Trollope and one of his regular clients. It begins in Calgary with a train ride through the Rocky Mountains, followed by a coach tour across southern British Columbia and a cruise to Alaska. The return journey is by coach south through British Columbia's **Gold Rush route** to Vancouver and air to Toronto. This tour was practically sold out by the time descriptive brochures hit travel-agency shelves.

In Canada, we have excellent tour companies catering solely to travellers in the 50 plus group, and also companies that attract us with leisurely yet exciting programs for all ages. If you tire easily, aim for a tour that puts you in cities or resort areas for several days. Then you can pass up an excursion to potter about on your own or take an afternoon nap, and rejoin the group with renewed enthusiasm later.

Read the Contract

Read the fine print on the brochure and you should know exactly what is included in the price. Some escorted tours cover everything except personal shopping and drinks. Others, regardless of the price, can have extras which are prohibitive unless you have budgeted for them in advance. I am thinking here about options such as hot air balloon rides in Africa. This may well be one of your safari highlights, but at $350 per person you won't be able to pay for it out of your loose change. On a two-week European tour you can pay as much as $500 to $750 for side excursions and meals not included in the tour price. As for taxes and surcharges, together these can add a further several hundred dollars to your bill.

? QUESTIONS TO ASK

? Ask your travel agent about the tour company's reputation, and try to talk to some of their clients. We have first-class companies whose marketing people work hard to put together attractive tours for the best possible prices. Many have sales representatives who cross the country giving film shows on their programs. Here's your opportunity to whip out your list of questions, and talk with clients who have come in anticipation of learning about new and different tours.

Check out those hotels that look so inviting. An artist's impression instead of a photograph may mean the property isn't quite finished. As for that old hotel undergoing a multi-million dollar refurbishing program it could be that your standard room has yet to benefit from the renovator's talents. How central is the centrally-located hotel? Are all meals buffet style? If so, can you pay a little extra and choose from the menu? It all sounds picky I know, but you don't need to settle on something you're not entirely happy with, because there are hundreds of tours to choose from.

Finally, do look at the tour company's business record. We have solid companies with impeccable reputations and sound backing. If your tour company declares bankruptcy, the least of your problems is that you won't be taking that vacation. How much of you money can be retrieved, and what happens if you are already on tour depends on the company concerned. This should be addressed when you make your reservations. (We discussed it earlier in connection with default insurance and compensation funds in Chapter 8.)

TOURS FOR 50 PLUSSERS

As travel companies recognize our growing numbers, more are creating programs specifically for 50 plus vacationers. CARP and AARP newsletters,

Today's Seniors and similar newspapers, Mature Traveller columns in weekend newspaper travel sections all tell of these. As well, some established programs successful with younger vacationers are now being reworked to attract us. One that comes to mind is **Club Med**, for so long linked with young singles. At certain locations these clubs offer discounts to guests 60 and over, along with recreational activities and entertainment beamed directly at us.

There are definite advantages to being with travellers your own age. We share the same humour and often the same memories. Music played on the coach is to our liking. The tour will be paced with lots of stops to stretch our limbs. And I find that together we laugh a lot.

I'm Proud To Be Me Travel Inc., **ElderTreks** and **Adventures in Travel** are just three of many Canadian 50 plus travel specialists. Although companies such as **Horizon Holidays** and **Wings of the World** of Toronto and **Adventures Abroad** of Vancouver don't specifically target this market, their well-planned itineraries, upmarket accommodations and attentive service are a magnet for older travellers. On a broader scale, the same can be said of the **P. Lawson Travel** and **Thomas Cook (Canada)** groups. **American Express** is CARP's official travel agency.

Saga Holidays of Britain, Australia and the United States are international leaders in 50 plus travel. Also in the United States are **Grand Circle Travel**, **Golden Age Travelers Club**, **The Over the Hill Gang International**, and the AARP **Travel Experience from American Express.**

MINI BREAKS

In the eighties brief getaways became very popular with stressed-out baby boomers. They were looking for a three or four-day escape from pressure on a nice warm beach in summer, and in winter sought quiet country inns where snow swirled around the windows and relaxation was a good book in front of a blazing hearth.

Now the rest of us are realizing the benefits of a mini-break, but our wishes are a little different. If I am going to Nassau I can stick around for more than three days, and in winter a good book by the fire is exactly what I'm leaving behind. Astute fellows that they are, the travel gurus realize this. Mini-vacations geared to our age group are for seminars, shopping sprees, summer theatre, festivals and special events where promoters are looking to fill seats at matinees and mid-week performances. Las Vegas and Atlantic City beckon with lights and a little flutter at the slots.

There is something deliciously wanton about abandoning everyday routine in this manner. Try it with a friend, a neighbour or as a stranger in a small group. It isn't terribly important that you know your travel companions well. You'll be back in your own world in less than a week. The options are many: river cruises, a tour of area antique markets, a winter resort at midweek with sleigh rides and cross-country skiing laid on. I know one country person who looks forward to semi-annual city visits, where she acts like a tourist although the city is only 40 km (25 mi.) from home.

Your provincial tourist office has brochures describing mini-breaks from your area, and names of tour companies who put them together. As I write this I'm reminded of some of our visitors from overseas who say it isn't worth their fare unless they come for a month. Two weeks into their visit we're fed up with them, and they have run out of ideas for day-trips from our home base. I realized the true value of these little breaks when I persuaded one couple to take an organized three-day tour of New York State, and another to join a rail excursion to Montreal. Since they enjoyed their mini-trips so much I started taking them myself. Three or four days away from home have seen me return home with renewed energy, as refreshed as if I'd had a full-fledged two-week vacation.

JOINING A TOUR OVERSEAS

Sometimes it is convenient to join a tour for a week as part of a longer itinerary, especially for a journey that could be complicated to do on your own. For example, David Dean's **Highlands and Islands** tour out of Glasgow saved me the vexation of dealing with delayed ferry services and searching out little inns and pubs he knows so well.

It's important to remember that on a tour originating in Britain, the majority of passengers will be from there, or will have come from Australia, New Zealand or North America. This makes for an interesting mix of cultures, while conversation is still chiefly in English. Joining a group in continental Europe you may find yourself short-changed on commentaries. In Belgium we once bought a tour of northern France. We were told our escort spoke excellent English. Maybe he did, but he used it so sparingly we didn't hear enough to judge. Ten minutes of dialogue in German for the majority of our passengers was followed by a few words of English for the four non-Germans on board. A big plus in booking this tour on the spot for departure next day was that we paid less than half the price it would have cost us at home. The saving more than paid for an English-language guidebook.

London's bucket shops list deeply discounted prices for imminent departures. If these vacations are with respected airlines and tour companies, and you are completely flexible about where you go, they can be very worthwhile. You will receive the same services, accommodation, aircraft seating — and whatever else is included — as clients who paid hundreds of pounds more when they booked three months earlier. For tours of Britain out of London within a day or two of booking, try The American Express Agency in British Tourist Authority's travel centre at 12 Lower Regent Street, off Piccadilly Circus (telephone: 071 839 2682). There you will find long and short tours of England, Wales and Scotland with reductions that can have budget-minded travellers going first class.

FOREIGN INDEPENDENT TOUR

This is the answer for me when I am on assignment and would like to extend my trip for pleasure. It is also the answer for vacationers who want to keep dry under a tour company umbrella but likens group travel to sheep herding. The Foreign Independent Tour takes worries out of your vacation, yet leaves you in control.

When planning an FIT I do the usual reading about my proposed destination, work loosely woven plans into my time frame and take them to a travel agent. She then calls a wholesaler, probably someone who specializes in that part of the world and has reliable contacts there. Together they are able to create a program to fit my exact needs.

Through such an arrangement you can be met at the arrival airport and driven to your hotel. (These are the meeters and greeters you see at an airport's arrival lounge, with name cards and hopeful smiles.) During your stay a guide may be provided for sightseeing and excursions, or you may be put on a coach or boat trip for a group tour. Your domestic flights, ferry-boat rides and train journeys are all booked for you. You will be taken to the departure point, transported to your new destination and someone will greet you upon your arrival. The local reps take care of all your vouchers, baggage handling, visas and other essential documents. It's like being on a tour without fellow passengers and is not as expensive as it sounds in countries where wages are modest.

SMALL-VEHICLE TOURING

For families, small groups of friends or like-minded strangers, the ultimate road tour is by mini-van with a driver/guide. In the autumn of 1992 I toured Britain's southwest coast with four travel writers. We drove in a small bus customized to seat eight passengers in comfort. Our driver/guide was a personable young woman called Julie of the **Back Roads Touring Company.**

Based in Britain, marketed in Canada by **I'm Proud To Be Me Travel, Inc.**, the company limits each group to 12 people travelling in various-sized vehicles adapted for touring. Scheduled tours are between 5 and 14 days long. Some focus on certain areas, others on themes such as King Arthur's Kingdom or Scotland's Whiskey Trail. Continental tours include the Heart of Charlemagne's Europe, and Gourmet France. Such programs include a full breakfast and dinner daily, accommodation, sightseeing and admissions. Like my vintage touring coach in Scotland, these little vehicles can travel even the smallest lane open to motorized traffic.

The company also customizes tours, so that if you and a few friends want to visit — say antique shops or auctions, literary shrines or golf courses, they will design an itinerary for your time frame and budget. And they are flexible. For the fun of it, we detoured from our World War II haunts to explore what, according to Julie, is the most haunted village in Britain. The only person we met was a salesclerk in a sweet shop. She said she knew nothing about ghosts, and then promptly disappeared at the back of the store, leaving us to serve ourselves with some humbugs. Two of the journalists vowed the shop had been empty all along....

TOUR COSTS

To give you an indication of tour costs, here is a sampling of various tours offered by Canadian travel agencies.

- ■ **SCOTLAND**. The Highlands and Islands tour out of Glasgow costs $700 for six days. It includes all transportation by restored vintage bus and ferry, accommodation, breakfasts, dinners and some afternoon teas, as well as sightseeing excursions and admission. Mr. Dean of **Classique Tours** will arrange discounts for your hotel accommodation before and after the tour.

- ■ **CENTRAL ENGLAND**. A tour originating at a Derbyshire dairy farm costs approximately $900 for six days. From London, it includes all transportation and accommodation with breakfasts and dinners, one day excursions to Staffordshire potteries, Peak District National park, Robin Hood's Nottingham, Chatsworth and two castle visits.

Organized by Back-Roads Touring Co., the Canadian contact is **I'm Proud To Be Me Travel Inc.**

■ **THE MEDITERRANEAN**. A 19-day tour departing from Toronto will taken you by air, land and sea to Sicily, Malta and Rome. Included are all meals and first-class accommodation, excursions, gratuities, etc., for a cost of $2,900. The organizers — **Senior Citizen's Tour and Travel** — also offer a 15-day tour of **CENTRAL EUROPE** in which you travel to Berlin, Warsaw, Budapest, Vienna and Munich from Toronto for $3,300, all expenses included.

■ **CALIFORNIA**. An Inside Hollywood Tour, organized by **P. Lawson Travel** and hosted by Elwy Yost, was so popular earlier this year, more are in the works. The tour (approximately $2,400) includes air from Toronto, 7 nights' hotel accommodation, cocktail parties, dinners and studio tours during which Elwy introduces celebrity friends to the group. Welcoming and farewell dinners are attended by movie people whose names are familiar to any filmgoer over 50. (On the last tour they had playwright Bernard Slade, screen composer David Raskin, actors Dick van Patten, Nina Foch and Jane Wyatt.)

■ **AUSTRALIA**. **Goway Travel** offers a 15-day tour for approximately $1,800, plus return air. (Fares from Toronto and Montreal are roughly $1,500; $1,000 from Vancouver.) Starting in Sydney, this tour includes farm stays and hotel accommodation, visits to Cairns and the Great Barrier Reef, Ayers Rock and Alice Springs, plus the cities of Canberra and Melbourne. Included is all domestic transportation, accommodation, excursions, some meals and admissions. A week-long add-on to Cairns and a Great Barrier Reef resort is approximately $900.

■ **NEW ZEALAND**. Also offered by **Goway Travel** is an 8-day tour to New Zealand for approximately $950, plus airfare to Auckland. Covering most highlights of both islands, it includes domestic flights, rail, coach and ferry travel, as well as sightseeing excursions, accommodation and some meals. A 15-day motor coach tour of the two islands costs $1,500.

■ **BANGKOK, BALI AND SINGAPORE**. **Horizon Holidays** offers a 20-day tour for $7,000, departure is from Toronto with adjustments for airfare from other locations. Designed for the carriage trade this includes luxury hotels and resorts, transportation, all accommodation, tours, meals and economy return fare.

Calling All Campers

Old campers never quit, they just trade up to a recreational vehicle. One hundred thousand motorhomes are sold annually in North America, where there are nine million currently on the road. If you are a veteran camper now electing for something sturdier than a canvas roof over your head, you may well see all of North America in your new motorhome before eventually hanging up your Good Sam cap. If you have never camped, or have only fond memories of ghost stories and marshmallows around the campfire as a child, I urge you to rent before making that heavy investment in your own self-contained motorhome.

We are old hands at the motorhome travel mode. Back in 1967 when we were all feeling sentimental about Canada's hundredth birthday, our family celebrated by crossing the country coast to coast. Our vehicle then was a Volkswagen Campmobile, the size of your average closet, with a pop-up roof and a tent that attached to the side door.

We were not experienced campers. We never graduated from Brownies or Scouts. Even our barbecues had little success. After our second day on the road I began fantasizing about the luxury of Holiday Inn rooms and their scrumptuous coffee shop meals. By the fourth, my aspirations saw me vacationing on my own, anywhere with a dry bed and a private shower. Then, somewhere around the beginning of the second week, I realized I enjoyed this gypsy life. I liked going shoeless and having the freedom of making spur-of-the-moment decisions to stay or move on. I liked passing up crowded fast-food places beside highways, and being able to change clothes halfway through the day as mood and weather dictated.

Within two years our little "travel bug" was replaced by a 7.3 m (24 ft.) motorhome, with a kitchen, full bathroom and — joy of joys — five beds indoors. More recently we have rented motorhomes and toured the country with visitors from overseas. And now, as thoughts turn to exploring Canada with our grandchildren, we are warmed to the idea of owning a motorhome again. Clearly, we are enthusiastic motorhome people. Still I must caution that this way of travel is not for everyone.

NEW TO THE GAME?

On even the shortest trip compatibility with your travelmates is essential. Remember this is a space roughly 2.4 m by 4.9 m (8 ft. x 16 ft.) and you are sharing it day and night. A sense of humour and the ability to give and take are mandatory. Whether you are two couples or four single adults, all aspects of your trip should be planned together beforehand. Are your interests similar when it comes to sightseeing? Will you take turns with driving? Who will be in charge of the food, admissions and gasoline money? Long ago when we travelled with our children, Michael did the driving and I took on all the housekeeping with help from the small fry. Travelling with another couple, we each put $100 in the kitty for food and admissions. I would shop for three days, and if someone else wanted to take over for the next three they could. If not, one person would visit the laundrette and another went to the liquor or hardware stores for essentials while I shopped for groceries. We have always been delighted with our travel mates on these trips, but I cringe to think of the consequences should incompatibility come into play.

YOUR HOME AWAY FROM HOME

Choose your motorhome with care. Experience has taught us to insist on a rental unit less than three years old. Twice we took out older vehicles when there was no alternative and regretted it after the first day. Your motorhome is more than transportation. It is your temporary home filled with your possessions, and you won't want to abandon it by the roadside in the event of a mechanical failure.

We broke down once at an intersection near Walt Disney World where we had a campsite booked and paid for at their Fort Wilderness Campground. After a tow to a garage we learned it would take three days to obtain and install a replacement part. There was nothing to do but rent a car. Every morning we arrived at Fort Wilderness' super-clean washrooms resembling delegates to a hygenists' convention: towels and toothbrushes, hair dryers, curling irons and make-up bags in hand. (The girls were teens at this time.) Each night we drove back to the garage to sleep in our motorhome because we didn't want to leave it on the lot unattended.

I have always reckoned that travellers who sleep well can cope with almost anything. In consequence we look for a vehicle with a double bed in the rear, preferably closed off with a curtain or door. This way our guests (or children) can nap in the daytime or retire early without disrupting anyone. After a long drive, and for an early morning start, Michael tucks himself into the bunk above the cab. This leaves the kitchen area free, so that the dinette can be converted to my comfortable double bed.

RENTAL UNITS

The monster 9 to 11 m (30 to 35 ft.) units sleep no more than their smaller siblings, but are infinitely more comfortable. So think it through. Talk to your neighbourhood dealers and motorhome owners. Go to the travel and leisure shows. Determine how many passengers you will carry most of the time and rent before you buy.

Most motorhomes are equipped with power steering and brakes. We try for cruise control too, and cab air-conditioning if warm weather is anticipated. (The roof-mounted unit functions only when the vehicle is stationary and hooked up to 240 V power at your campsite.) The cooking stove and heater are fueled by propane. The refrigerator usually operates on the vehicle's 12 V system as well as propane and 240 V power, but not at all unless you are on fairly level ground.

Motorhome dealerships have enticing brochures to describe their rental options and to illustrate the interior layouts of different-sized vehicles. Rental rates differ according to vehicle sizes and the seasons. For a fee some companies permit drop-off in other cities, to give you greater flexibility with your itinerary. Most companies rent for weekly periods only during the busy seasons; others offer daily rentals at any time of the year.

If you cannot find a suitable RV renter locally, two large RV rental companies with offices in various cities are:

■ **Go Vacations** of Rexdale, Ontario, near Toronto's Pearson International Airport, with branches in Montreal, Winnipeg, Edmonton, Calgary and Vancouver, and in the United States.

■ **Canada Campers Inc**. of Calgary with branches in Vancouver, Whitehorse and Toronto.

COSTS

In the summer of '92 we rented a mint condition 7. 3 m (24 ft.) fully-equipped motorhome for three weeks and drove 4,000 km (2,500 mi.). The total cost for rental, insurance, fuel, campground charges and taxes for three people was $5,000. Had the cost been split between four people (the unit was furnished to sleep four adults in comfort, six at a pinch) this would have worked out to be an inexpensive tour of the Atlantic provinces and parts of Maine from Toronto.

From time to time, Go Vacations advertises for drivers to move their vehicles around the continent, between such destinations as Montreal, Toronto, Calgary, Vancouver, Los Angeles, Denver, New York and Miami. In return for delivering their vehicles, the company offers up to 14 days of free use.

SETTING OFF

When you collect your rented vehicle it is vital that the dealer explains how everything works. (Impatient to get going we once told a dealer we knew how to convert sofas into beds and then couldn't get one of ours to work. We had a child sleeping on an air mattress on the floor until the second from last night, when she stumbled on the trick of opening up the bed.) Make sure you understand the propane system and how to hook up the water supply and sewage outlet.

With three, and more often four, teenage girls along we always had enough storage space in our 6.7 to 7.9 m (22 to 26 ft.) motorhomes. Plastic bags saved my sanity when the children were small. Each of us had an overhead cupboard in which to store socks and underwear in one plastic bag, T-shirts and shorts in another, jeans and sweaters in a third and so on. This way we weren't turning out an entire cupboard for a pair of socks. Another cupboard was set aside for our cameras and tape recorder and the girls' Walkmans and tapes. Two more cupboards contained groceries and dishes. Finally under the back seat we kept snorkelling gear, tennis rackets and swimsuits in plastic bread bags (if you saw someone in a Shake 'N Bake swimsuit a few years back it was me). "Good" clothes were hung in the wardrobe. Folding chairs and a portable barbecue went into an outside compartment, two or three bicycles on a rack at the rear. We carried enough clothes and food to last three days, then twice a week stopped in town at the laundrette and supermarket.

Even on new vehicles things are often shaken loose, so take along adhesive tape, screwdrivers and adjustable wrenches from your home toolbox. We also carry a flashlight and lantern, lengths of rope, clothes-line and pegs, folding chairs, board-games and lots of paperbacks. A pair of working gloves is useful for the messier jobs such as disconnecting the various life support hook-ups, including the sewage hose, when checking out of a campground. (The final chore before leaving a campground is to walk around your vehicle and see that it is not hooked up anywhere; and that there isn't a little person crouched down behind it.)

FLY/DRIVE PROGRAMS

These are very popular with Europeans visiting Canada and with Canadians touring this continent, Europe, Australia and New Zealand. Travel agencies will tell you of airlines, cruise lines and tour companies which offer such packages. Or you can create your own fly/drive program.

When we rented a motorhome in California I located the dealer in a San Francisco telephone directory. As do most dealers, he invited us to stay the first night on his lot, and gave us the option of renting sleeping bags, cookware and dishes from him. Instead of paying $30 per person for the six of us, we took our own sleeping bags, bought inexpensive cookware and dishes at a discount store and left them in the vehicle when we came home.

ORGANIZED TOURS

If RV travel appears daunting, but you would still like to try it, **Wagontrain Tours** of Vernon, Connecticut may be your answer. It offers two-week trips in a train of 9.7 m (32 ft.) vehicles stocked with everything except food, and led by a wagon master and wrangler/mechanic. Cost is around $2,000 per person. Routes travelled include one from Seattle, through Wyoming and British Columbia and Alberta. Others are in Florida, or the Oregon coast and the Sierras. Future plans include routes through Alaska and Mexico. Such tours don't give you the freedom of independent touring, but for novices they do provide a worry-free introduction to the motorhome travel mode.

CAMPGROUNDS

In Canada we are blessed with superb national and provincial parks, most of which have campgrounds and naturalist programs. They can be crowded in summer, particularly at weekends, and here again we are lucky in being free to travel outside school holidays. Late spring and early fall can be wonderful in these parks.

National park campsites are allotted on a first-come first-served basis. We find it best to arrive at the more popular campgrounds before 2 p.m. Don't be put off by the queue of campers ahead of you. It will move quickly, especially in late morning when an equally long line snakes out of the campgrounds. Most parks have overflow areas, and when you are in a self-contained vehicle it is no hardship to stay here for a day or two until a serviced campsite vacancy comes your way. You can still enjoy the scenery, the facilities and the park's townsite, which usually has restaurants and cafes, grocery stores, a laundrette, maybe even a movie house, riding trails, tennis courts, boat and bicycle rentals.

America's national and state parks and our provincial parks can be every bit as glorious as the nationals. After all, they too are established to preserve natural wonders and unique environments for posterity. Some accept campsite reservations, and some give discounts to visitors 60 or 65 and over. (Often these apply only to provincial or state residents.) Overnight fees vary according to the park's location and facilities. At the time of writing, a fully serviced campsite in a national park costs $10 to $18. In provincial parks (where sites may not be fully serviced) prices range from $7 to $15. In the U.S., state parks charge U.S. $8 to $18 (Can. $11 to $24) per night. Wilderness camping areas, often accessible to motorhomes but without designated lots and services, are usually free.

You might also look for a municipal campground. These often have attractive sites and are close to a town's centre.

In this highly competitive business most privately owned campgrounds are well maintained with tidy sites, and clean washrooms. If they are close to a city, or a major attraction, they may be little more than parking spaces but what commercial campgrounds lack in privacy and compelling scenery, they make up for with entertainment programs, swimming pools, on-site barbecues, recreation rooms, laundrettes and convenience stores.

Nowhere have I seen such commercial campgrounds as in Florida. Virtual vacation resorts on prime coastal land, their year-round operation makes them a viable proposition, able to support swimming pools, tennis courts, games rooms and evening entertainment which can include movies and square dancing. Most have bicycle rentals. Some operate shuttles to local malls. And except during school vacation periods, almost all of their happy campers are 55 plus.

Campsites are often just a short walk from the beach and each one usually has a concrete parking pad and patio, with a picnic table and barbecue. They are fully serviced, meaning you can connect your vehicle to hydro, sewage, water and air-conditioning. Air-conditioning? Hmmmm. I guess I should explain, in case you are as green as we were when we started out.

On our first trip to Florida in the Volkswagen, we checked into a campground one sultry August afternoon, thrilled with its ocean-front location,
paved roads for our bicycles, tropical shrubs separating the sites and very
large swimming pool nearby. At the check-in desk we were asked if we
wanted air-conditioning for an extra fifty cents. Did we ever! With dreams
of a good night's sleep we attached our tent to the camper, leaving as few
gaps as possible so the lovely cold air couldn't escape, then crawled about
on the ground searching for the magical hose which would pump some
frigid air into it. Eventually a neighbour came to ask what we had lost.
Turns out the 50¢ was for a site with a heavy-duty power outlet for our vehicle's air-conditioning unit which of course we didn't have.

Tourism authorities, automobile clubs and specialized publications are
all good sources of information on campgrounds. On the road, talk to
fellow campers. Tell them where you are heading and you will soon collect
a list of recommended campgrounds along your route.

Where to stay overnight when you can't find a campground? Not a
deserted lane or empty car park, and not a shopping mall where you will
be the only vehicle left once the stores close. Hospital parking lots are
good in that they are fairly busy through the night, and if you don't have
facilities on board you can sneak into the hospital washrooms. A couple
of times we have driven into dealers' lots, tucked ourselves in with the RVs
on sale and slept soundly.

Truck stops alongside highways are incredibly noisy. One place we decided would be quiet was beside the grass verge at a locked entrance to a
graveyard. There, pulling off a country lane we set up the tent and slept
well. Luckily we had put the tent away before the funeral procession
arrived next morning. Still it was embarassing to be sitting on the grass
eating our Cheerios, and Michael had to scramble to move the Volkswagen for the funeral cars to get by.

BUYING YOUR OWN MOTORHOME

By the end of a three-week trip you will have learned a few tricks about
motorhome travel and probably will know if you want to buy your own rig.
They come in many shapes and sizes, some costing hundreds of thousands
of dollars. A new 7.3 to 7.9 m (24 to 26 ft.) motorhome retails in the region of $50,000 to $60,000, fully equipped. A good used vehicle, four or
five years old, is around $20,000 to $30,000. If you buy a new vehicle from
a dealer who is prepared to rent it out for you, it can help pay for itself, and
as a business venture expenses are tax deductible.

In major cities, you may be able to buy from a dealer who rents motor-homes as dressing rooms to film companies in town to shoot a movie or television series. Its interior may be shabby when you get it back, but there won't be many miles on the motor and chassis.

CARAVAN CLUBS

As a motorhome owner you will meet members of clubs who go on marathon tours, across Canada, through the United States and down into Mexico. Perhaps as many as 40 vehicles travel more or less together, meeting at the same campgrounds each or every second night. It's a great way to go if you enjoy interesting people of a like mind, most of whom are in our age group. If you are still unfamiliar with all the mechanics of your vehicle, it is reassuring to be with people who can probably explain the source of those annoying thunks and rattles.

Some manufacturers sponsor clubs for purchasers of their equipment. There are many regional clubs, even one for women RV operators. Best known of the independent organizations is the **Good Sam Club** with head-quarters in Camarillo, California and chapters in many states and provinces. This organization publishes a campground directory; it offers insurance, a breakdown service and member discounts on other related goods and services.

Part Three
You've Arrived

$\mathcal{G}$etting Around

$\mathcal{I}$n Kyoto, the former capital of Japan, I wearily pushed my suitcase from one end of the vast railway station to the other, looking for an exit which I knew to be across from a tourist office. Half an hour later I struggled into that office, vowing never again to buy heavy souvenirs during the first few days of a trip. The woman behind the counter was all efficiency with her yellow crayon, marking a personalized map, telling me to get the No. 6 bus here and a train there, and to walk four blocks in this direction after turning off such-and-such a street. Three times I interrupted her to say I would like to hire a guide. Obviously, if it took me this long to reach her office, I wasn't up to navigating the city on my own. She was adamant, until I spotted a notice on the wall offering student guides for the price of lunch and bus fare.

That's how I met Masako, a demure 17-year-old English student from Osaka. With Masako I hopped on and off buses as directed on my map and then with time to spare visited a movie studio to watch samurai movies being filmed. Masako had an exam next day, but her friend took over for a trip by rail to Mikimoto Island, home of Japan's cultured pearl industry.

I learned a lot about Japanese culture from Masako and her friend. Moreover, what could have been a frustrating visit turned out to be all pleasure, simply because I made the tourist office my first stop.

TOURIST OFFICES

Totally unflappable personnel in local tourist offices have **up-to-the-minute** information you couldn't possibly glean from your guidebook. To fail to take advantage of their knowledge is to do yourself a disservice.

In Canada we have terrific tourist offices. I have crossed this country several times and written two travel books about it, but I still stop at the border tourist information centres as we cross from one province to another. If you arrive in Prince Edward Island by ferry, right there at the terminal is a tourist office crammed with mouth-watering pamphlets on everything from lobster suppers to regional theatre, casual farmhouse to elegant inn accommodation. The ferries between Nova Scotia and Newfoundland have both provinces' tourist offices on board. At the other end of the country, cruise passengers disembarking for a few hours in Victoria are met by residents in Victorian costume giving out flowers (symbolic of that city in summer) along with tourist information.

If asked to vote for the best tourist office, **British Tourist Authority**'s office on London's Lower Regent Street would have my nod. Here at separate counters are representatives of British Rail, American Express, tour companies, a theatre ticket agency, a Value Added Tax refund agency, and other travel-related services. This is one-stop shopping for travel in Britain. Videos, craft displays and books on different regions beckon you for a visit. Last-minute sell-offs for coach tours are often to be had at very reduced prices.

HIRING A PERSONAL GUIDE

Never accept the guide services of someone who approaches you on the street. Not even if they want to "be your friend" or "show you my beautiful city for no charge." However, in countries where wages are low, it can be ridiculously inexpensive to hire a **professional guide** with a car by the day or week, or a guide for two or three hours to show you the city highlights on foot. These guides can be arranged through travel agents before leaving Canada, in which case you will be met at the airport or railway station on arrival. But it costs less to make arrangements at your destination, through the tourist office or an agency they recommend.

If you are particularly interested in certain aspects of a place, its history or architectural treasures, a guide will enrich your visit tremendously. Often retired art gallery employees, teachers or senior students are available for little more than the price of a lunch.

I am still in touch with some of my former guides. Both of those Japanese girls have since visited us in Canada. For a while I corresponded with an Estonian teacher who showed me around Tallinn, then invited me home for tea from her meagre supply. An Indian guide who took me to his friend's wedding party in Jaipur sends photos of his young son. Then there is my guide in St. Petersburg, so Americanized in her speech I half wondered if she was a spy.

TRAVEL PASSES

Domestic air passes are wonderful for hopping around countries the size of sub-continents. Most are for a specified number of flights, so you will want to use them for long-distance travel only. Some require you to keep moving in the same direction, without backtracking. (Similar limitations can apply to passes for bus and rail travel.)

Many smaller or less-populated countries combine several transportation modes in one pass. An example of this is the **New Zealand Travel Pass** which combines train, ferry, highway and city buses in one pass, and even provides for air travel at extra cost as described in Chapter 13. Another is the **Swiss Pass** which includes travel on the entire national network of trains, boats, buses and street cars as well as discounts on privately-owned mountain lines. There are a number of variations, but to give an example, a first-class Swiss Pass costs $425 for 15 days of first-class travel and $295 second.

In many countries, **flexipasses** are an inexpensive alternative. These permit you to travel on a specified number of days during the length of your visit. Using Switzerland again for an example, a flexipass which allows three days of travel in any 15 day-period, costs $185 first class and $135 second. Even more savings are effected with the use of a two-person saver-pass such as the one described in Chapter 13.

Tips ·
 If you aren't familiar with the language, it's a good idea to purchase a **phrase-book**. Try to learn a few sentences or expressions, even if it is little more than "Good Morning," "Please," "Thank you" and "How much?" Said with a smile these few words will take you far. And, don't be shy of mispronouncing what you say. Believe me, your effort will be welcomed for its good intention. You can start practising with a simple expression or two during your flight, especially if you are flying with the national airline.

In tourist areas you are almost bound to find someone who speaks English. Hotel clerks and shopkeepers selling local souvenirs are always a good bet. In countries where I have run into language difficulties, I write my proposed destinations for the day in a notebook, then ask the hotel clerk or concierge to repeat them in their own language. Out on the street

I show the interpretation to a taxi driver who will get me there, or a shop-keeper who can usually point me in the right direction.

CITY TRANSPORTATION

Wait until the morning rush-hour has passed so you aren't swept along in that sea of humanity, and you will soon enjoy the advantages of **travelling underground** in traffic-clogged cities. Once again, study information on your tourist office map and write down the station where you plan to disembark. In most cities colour-coded maps of the underground system are available at ticket counters, along with information on reduced rates. Discounts are often given to riders 60 and over; in some places you must be over 65. All-day tickets are not only much cheaper than the cost of individual rides but allow you to ignore that impatient swarm around ticket booths.

Hong Kong has one of the most efficient and inexpensive subway systems I know, and offers special low rates to tourists. There, multi-journey tickets are stamped electronically as you go through the turnstile, so you know how many more rides you can take for one particular fare.

In Moscow some underground stations are remarkable for their mosaic ceilings, sculptures and chandeliers. (Train stations look like lobbies of five-star hotels, and modern hotels have lobbies as bleak and huge as other countries' rail terminals.)

So try them out. As well as getting from point A to point B, public transportation can give you an interesting experience. You know to carry your disembarkation station written in the local language don't you? Several years ago I was too shy to ask fellow bus passengers to tell me when I reached my stop. On my way to a St. Petersburg circus one dark night, I followed a bunch of excited children carrying balloons. Luckily they weren't going to McDonalds for a birthday bash.

A City Bus Tour

On arrival in an unfamiliar city, I always try to join a bus tour. The driver's English may be deplorable, but he knows his city and how to get around it and shows me what to look for when I begin exploring on my own.

$\mathcal{D}$ining Out

$\mathcal{F}$or me, fond memories of a successful trip almost always include a memorable meal or two. Not necessarily exotic or expensive, it might be a Bahamian lobster that slips so easily from the shell, fish and chips bought on Dublin's O'Connell Street, a well-matured steak grilled to perfection in Buenos Aires, chilli crab served at a Singapore cafe or a pair of succulent lamb cutlets eaten at an old Welsh pub. Even thoughts of ham and eggs with hash browns and fresh white toast can drive me off I-75 on our way south.

Don't be inhibited by your ignorance of the language or native dishes. Restauranteurs like to talk about their food. After all they want to sell it to you. In a small Hungarian town I had a waiter imitating barnyard noises by way of explaining the menu. (My spiced baa-aa-aa was delicious thanks very much.) In some countries plastic replicas of complete meals are displayed in restaurant windows. It's simple to order by number this way, but all too often your meal tastes as if you've been given the plastic replica by mistake. So be a bit adventurous and avoid the tourist bait.

As I get older my stomach rebels at large portions and at very rich or spicy foods. If your diet is fairly bland at home, I suggest you too take care not to vary it dramatically while away. And be cautious in developing countries, remembering the sanitary arrangements are not what you are used to at home.

TIME IT RIGHT

In American restaurants, especially in the southern states where older visitors stay for the winter, you will find impressive **Seniors Discounts** offered at mid-week. Also available are **Early Bird Specials** served before 6:30 p.m., which can cost up to 30% less than a similar meal ordered half an hour later.

In Latin countries restaurants seldom open for dinner before 9 p.m. and you may not get down to eating for an hour after that. Unless I am with a group, I am happier with a cooked meal towards the end of the lunch hour and a snack at a coffee shop or hotel lounge around seven. Lunch costs far less than dinner and won't lie on my stomach like a cannon-ball through the night.

GOOD VALUE

Unless you are going for *haute cuisine*, in which case the price may be considered too gauche to mention, you will find menus and prices posted outside most restaurants. A **fixed-price meal** is less exciting but far more affordable than à la carte. Today's Specials are items the chef would like to move but are not necessarily offered at a discounted price.

In many European countries restauranteurs work with local tourist boards to serve reasonably-priced fare to visitors. Using local produce they create traditional regional dishes which are nice and nutritious, but do warn your taste buds not to get wildly excited. Restaurants offering a **Tourist Menu** usually display pictograms outside — a fork with a camera slung across the tines or something similarly descriptive. Often these are first-class establishments where an à la carte lunch or dinner costs two or even three times as much as the tourist fare.

Meals in **British pubs** continue to be good value. One-dish meals served in a bar lounge — lasagna, steak and kidney pie, chilli and the like — cost around six dollars. Pub dining rooms, often providing a quiet oasis on the second floor, serve enormous three-course lunches for $20 – $30, even in central London.

TODAY'S SPECIALS

Medieval feasts in Britain, Hawaiian luaus and lobster suppers in a Prince Edward Island church basement can all be fun when you are with friends or a tour group. You will enjoy a laugh, play the fool when elected to participate and likely consider the evening well spent.

But such group jollies can leave you feeling flatter than the proverbial cow-patty when you are on your own or even one of a pair. For this reason, over the years I have kept note of unusual dining experiences to recommend to friends travelling independently.

In Britain

In the perfect English countryside of the Duke of Devonshire's Derbyshire estate, the **Cavendish Hotel** has a dining-room of high repute. It also has one table set with a pretty pink cloth, Wedgwood china and crystal in the corner of its kitchen. Anyone keen to watch top-notch chefs at work can sit here. They may order from the menu or ask for "a surprise" as I did. This is essentially small portions of everything being served to the other diners. All dishes taken to the dining-room are shown and explained, in passing. I felt like a cross between a food inspector and chief taster for a paranoid monarch, and was fascinated to watch as plain old produce was magically transformed into edible art.

In Hong Kong

What will happen after '97 is anyone's guess, but until then Hong Kong offers some of the world's most memorable dining experiences, from chicken baked in clay at a five-star hotel to a grubby cafe where patrons hang caged pet birds on rails above their seats and wash their own cups in cold tea. One dining experience I particularly enjoyed was in **Lei Yue Mein**, reached by metro from Kowloon and then by ferry boat to the fish market on its docks. (Wear solid shoes; it is wet underfoot.) Here you select your dinner, alive in fish tanks and pens, then take it to one of the restaurants on hand. Watching me flounder among the lobsters, crabs, octopus, eels and dozens of fish I couldn't recognize, a chef came to my rescue. We agreed on what should be grilled, steamed or fried and I was still on my first cup of green tea when the meal was served — cooked to order, accompanied by rice and steamed vegetables.

In Finland

In the heart of its Saimaa Lake district where ancient waterways and over-land trade routes met long ago, a settlement grew around a castle here at Savonlinna in the early 1600s. Now, **Olavinlinna Castle** is the haunting setting for a summer music and opera festival.

The opera starts at about nine each evening and ends around midnight. The temptation is to have dinner before the performance. A better idea is to settle on a waterfront snack so you will be famished enough in the wee hours for a supper of fried wendance (a small member of the salmon family caught locally) served with heavenly mashed potatoes. After three hours on a hard bench in a draughty old castle, trust me when I tell you this meal really hits the spot. Cafes and restaurants are filled to overflowing, talk is of the night's show and patrons include opera singers from all over Europe. With all the music, food and wine and general excitement of the festival, you will stroll back to your hotel warmed by the Finnish experience if not the early morning air.

In Ireland

Truly, hospitality is a way of life in the Emerald Isle, but never more so than in the fifteenth-century **Abbey Tavern** just outside Dublin. In the upstairs dining-room, we had a full dinner with wine, then followed with traditional entertainment in a downstairs barn. (You can come for the barn entertainment without having dinner.)

Songs range from humorous to haunting, and a rendition of Molly Malone brings the house down. You'll sit at long trestles, with more Dubliners than tourists present, every one of them drinking Irish coffee and bent on giving you a grand and friendly time.

Other Dining Specials

Here are a few more dining experiences I think you might enjoy:

- An informal lunch in one of Canada's produce markets: Saint John has Canada's oldest public market and offers terrific seafood lunches; the Byward Market in Ottawa, Toronto's St. Lawrence Market, The Forks in Winnipeg and Vancouver's Granville Island are also great;

- Game pie and claret, or tea and Maids of Honour tarts at Newnes, across from London's Kew Gardens;

- Sardines, freshly caught and grilled in coarse salt, eaten ocean-side in a fishing village of Portugal's Algarve;

- In Mexico, chicken simmered in a spicy chocolate sauce; also savory roast free-range chicken, that reminds you of times when it was a Sunday treat and not just the cheapest meat on supermarket shelves;

- Strawberries, huge, firm and sweet all the way through, with thick cream at a roadside cafe in Colombia's Andes;

- Afternoon tea at the Dorchester in London, The Empress in Victoria or the Richmond, a teashop not far from Harrods in Buenos Aires' La Florida;

- Sunday brunch at Patrick's overlooking Swansea Bay (South Wales). His Breakfast on a Mushroom is literally that: a giant mushroom on which eggs, bacon, sausages and tomatoes are served.

PICNICS

No, we aren't talking about warm lemonade and soggy sandwiches half eaten before you get to the site of your Sunday school outing. As vacationers looking for an alternative to restaurant meals, we deserve the best. This can be a hamper packed by a top-drawer hotel or restaurant or something you make up yourself with delicacies selected from a food emporium.

The Brits enjoy picnics so much you will see them beside motorways, sitting on camp stools and eating from the trunks of their cars. They also take wonderful spreads to outdoor concerts and royal parks and major sporting events.

I have enjoyed many a picnic packed by a resort for consumption at the end of the mountain trail. Summer theatre gives wonderful picnic opportunities. So do train journeys and ferry rides. In cities small restaurants often oblige with lunch to go. Find yourself a riverside seat or park bench (away from the pigeons). On a sunny day it's true joy.

DINING WITH A VIEW

Often the scenery or the passing parade fix a dining experience in memory. Some favourites include:

- The lounge bar of the Banff Springs hotel, with superb views of the surrounding Rockies;

- The Harbourside in Vancouver — try the Prow Restaurant at the seaward end of Canada Place for lunch;

- The patio restaurant at the Chateau Whistler Resort, from which you can view Whistler and Blackcombe Mountains;

- London's Hyde Park Hotel (which serves a scrumptious buffet breakfast) where you can watch early morning riders on Rotten Row;

- The Wank summit, about 1,780 m (5,840 ft). above Garmisch-Partenkirchen, Germany for morning coffee and cakes and glorious views of the surrounding Alps;

- Sunday lunch at the Mariskonea restaurant overlooking South Atlantic rollers in Uruguay's Punta del Este;

- A beachfront terrace in Goa, India, watching a fiery sun slip into the Arabian Sea;

- One of thousands of sidewalk cafes in the great cities of Europe.

Tips . . . .

Before handing back the menu note whether a **service charge** is included in the price of your meal. If so, it means you don't need to tip anything beyond the loose change. In Europe Value Added Tax is included in the amount quoted, which is far more palatable than in Canada where 20% or more in taxes are tacked onto your bill.

In most cities, Indian and Chinese meals cost less than Western, but only if you're not talked into a lot of extras.

Be wary of restaurants with few customers at times when others in the area are busy. Their food may not be fresh and, if you dine there, this might result in severe health problems. I know some of us grew up in times before in-house refrigeration and even enjoyed "strong tasting" meat smothered in thick gravies with no adverse effects. Still, it is better by far to settle on freshly-baked rolls and cheese than stale cooked food when you are travelling.

*O*n Stage

*A*s airfares become affordable, you really don't have to win a lottery to be able to fly off to London or New York for a few days of good theatre. Many people are now doing this, which is why show tours are so successful.

I get my main theatre fix in one shot during my annual visit to London. I arrive with one ticket for a top show bought in conjunction with my airline's program and add two or three more purchased from Leicester Square's same-day booth.

Anything I miss in London can often be caught in Toronto later. In Toronto I enjoy the luxury of attending matinees. They cost less than evening performances. And they are timed right, so I can meet a friend, have dinner afterwards and still be home at a reasonable hour. Mid-week performances, matinees and same-day discounts for anyone over 60 or 65 are all worth keeping in mind when you're not regimented by office or factory hours. (Does everyone feel guilty at afternoon shows, I wonder? Or is it just me, remembering when I played truant from school to see the latest James Mason/Margaret Lockwood films?)

Discussion on world theatre could easily fill a thick book. In our limited space I have focused on three theatre cities, all of which are frequented by 50 plus travellers, not necessarily for the shows alone, but also as the jump-off point for a tour.

Try to break up your journeys with an overnight stop and theatre visit. A flight to India or Israel via London, for example, is happily broken when you hop a bus or subway into town, have a good lunch, see a show and return to Heathrow the next morning. There's no need to haul your luggage with you; it can be stored at the airport. I have done the same in New York before boarding a cruise ship there. As for Toronto departures, it is far more exciting for out-of-towners to hop the bus downtown with theatre tickets in their pockets than to fritter away the hours in an airport hotel. If you agree, the following will steer you towards eventful stopovers or mini vacations in London, New York or Toronto.

LONDON

London's permanent theatre buildings date to the sixteenth century, although dramas performed largely in churches and outdoors have been flourishing since the tenth. **The Globe Theatre**, built in 1599, provided a stage for writers of the period. William Shakespeare, among others, presented his work here. I mention it now because it is being rebuilt on original foundations and in 1995 — for the first time in three centuries — you will be able to see the Bard's plays in all their Elizabethan glory.

There are close to 60 major theatres and concert halls in the two square miles that are central London. While the real oldies have gone, others constructed on their sites date to the early 1800s. To learn more about theatrical history here you can join a walking tour and go backstage in one of the old theatres. For atmosphere and a sense of great theatrical presence, you won't beat a visit to the **Drury Lane Theatre.** This is the fourth to stand on its Catherine Street site. Charles II granted its charter back in 1662 when he ordered a theatre built for the King's Company of Players. Every monarch since Charles II has used the royal box. "God Save the King" was first sung here in 1741, "Rule Britannia" in 1750.

Across the river at the South Bank, the **Old Vic** was bought by Toronto entrepreneur Ed Mirvish, sight unseen, and restored to an opulence which pleases even the most critical Brit outraged by its foreign ownership.

Dominating the South Bank alongside Waterloo Bridge, the **National Theatre** complex opened in 1976, and has tours most days except Sundays. Part of the complex is the **Royal Festival Hall**, the foundation of which was laid by Prime Minister Clement Attlee in 1949 and the opening concert was attended by King George VI and Queen Elizabeth.

South Bank theatres have wine bars, restaurants and cafeterias; to simply wander around the lobbies and outdoor squares is to be entertained. In the West End, where theatres are clustered around Leicester Square and Piccadilly Circus, all manner of intimate eateries are wedged in back alleys as well as main streets. They cater to theatregoers looking for pre- and post-performance meals or snacks. After the shows, taxis are virtually impossible to find and tube (subway) stations are packed, so unless you are walking home it can be a good idea to go for a snack or light meal while the traffic thins.

Time Out magazine and the *Evening Standard* newspaper sold on every London street corner list curtain times. Current shows are crammed with nostalgia for 50 plus audiences. Rekindling memories at this time is a new version of Rogers and Hammerstein's *Carousel*. George Gershwin's *Crazy for You* has music of the thirties. And do you remember the 1950s Billy Wilder movie *Sunset Boulevard*? It's the brightest new star in Andrew Lloyd Webber's musical galaxy. *Cats, Les Misérables, The Phantom of the Opera* and *Miss Saigon* continue to attract sell-out crowds even though similar productions can be seen in New York and Toronto. Agatha Christie's *The Mousetrap* has been playing in London for over 40 years and we are still asked not to divulge the ending!

Purchasing Tickets

Top musical extravaganzas command top prices, with the best seats in the house ranging from $70 to $100 each when purchased at the box office, more from agencies which often have them after the theatre has sold out. If your eyesight isn't quite what it used to be, I hope you will splurge on dress circle or orchestra stalls, from where you can clearly identify the performers. For the upper circle or gallery (also known as The Gods) you can pay as little as $20, but I don't really recommend it. Seats are uncomfortable and the pitch so steep you feel as if you are about to fall onto the stage. Also you have to climb the "stairway to heaven" to reach them. As a student I saw just about every new show from The Gods, and wouldn't have dreamed of paying for a more expensive seat. Recently I was so uncomfortable with the height I wanted to leave, but had to wait to the interval to see my way down.

Imagine you are in London and want desperately to see *Miss Saigon* or *Sunset Boulevard*, but there isn't a ticket to be had anywhere. Then this scalper comes along, probably when you are in line at the Half-Price Ticket Booth deciding to settle on a good play instead. His price is out of sight, but what the heck, you're on vacation. It's very tempting. Regrettably, this scenario doesn't always have a happy ending. The tickets could be forged or genuine except that the date has been changed. If you are bent on seeing a certain show, there are better ways....

You can write to the theatre direct or book through an agency well in advance of your visit. **London Theatre Land Ltd.**, of Toronto can provide tickets within 24 hours and charges the same commission you would pay to London ticket agencies.

British Tourist Authority's office on Lower Regent Street has a theatre ticket agency. The girl there smiled at my audacity when I asked about *Miss Saigon* tickets a week or so after the show opened to terrific reviews. Then to her surprise and mine half a dozen cancellations showed on her computer. I bought two for the box office price plus commission. Minutes later I passed the theatre where *Miss Saigon* was playing. A long queue of hopefuls waited for ticket cancellations to come in. Had they thought to call or drop by the BTA office (telephone 071 839 3952) some could have come in out of the cold.

If you are keen to see a specific show, check out your airline programs before deciding who will fly you across the Atlantic. Scheduled carriers offer **show tour packages** containing a choice of tickets. Or they will sell individual theatre tickets to anyone booking their flights to London. If you are flexible, and mustard keen, you can plan your London visit around availability of these tickets.

For example: **British Airways** passengers can buy good seats for the season's top musicals for about $90. Also, this airline's show tours allow for different permutations of air/hotel/theatre and car rental plans. In the winter of '93–'94 one of their programs provides three nights of hotel accommodation (including tax) and one theatre ticket for $69 per person, double occupancy. At this price you would be centrally located but not in London's best hotel. Upgrade to, say, the Park Lane Hotel and you pay $285 per person for three nights (double occupancy), plus a theatre ticket, and that's still a pretty good deal. These tickets are for plays such as *An Inspector Calls* or *Separate Tables*, or for musicals which include *Starlight Express* and *Five Guys Named Moe*. Combine this package cost with the winter Toronto-London return fare of around $490 and two people can have an exciting mini-break for less than $1,000 apiece. (Remember the discounts for travellers 55 and up and a travel mate of any age? See Chapter 11 for reductions major airlines will give you on air and land packages in Britain.) Whatever the price, it beats staying home to shovel snow, especially in early March when daffodils and hyacinths bloom in London's Royal parks.

One of my favourite places in London is the **Leicester Square** booth where I buy same-day half-price tickets. The booth opens at noon for matinees and at 2:30 p.m. for tickets to evening performances; it sells tickets for half price plus a $2 to $3 commission. A notice outside tells what shows are available, so you can make your choice while in line. Although not all theatres sell their tickets this way, I have seen excellent shows featuring the world's leading actors with tickets from this booth.

NEW YORK

This city's theatres are enjoying a revival, with new shows playing to full houses. The Andrew Lloyd Webber musicals inevitably open on Broadway following London successes. Currently *The Phantom of the Opera, Les Misérables* and *Miss Saigon* continue to do well. What I enjoy more is to see some of my favourite actors, who disappeared from the screen a while back, now turning up on New York stages. Willy Russell's *Blood Brothers* with Petula Clark in the lead role is one of the most poignant shows I've seen for a long time. *Shakespeare For My Father* starring Lynn Redgrave is another destined to be around for years.

Although New York has more than 250 legitimate theatres, visitors usually confine themselves to **Broadway**, which is between 42nd and 53rd Streets and 6th and 8th Avenues. Most of these theatres were built in the early 1900s. The city's oldest operating theatre is the **Lyceum**, which dates to 1903.

New Yorkers still tell that old chestnut about a tourist who stopped a young man carrying a violin case and asked him how to get to **Carnegie Hall**. His reply was "Practise, practise." Well some of the best did practise and found themselves on stage in the main auditorium which opened in 1891 with a concert conducted by Tchaikovsky.

Another tourist favourite is **Radio City Musical Hall**. It dates to 1932 and still features the acclaimed Rockettes chorus line. Conducted tours leave from the main lobby most days. Telephone (212) 632-4041 for details.

West of Broadway, between 62nd and 66th Streets, **The Lincoln Centre for the Performing Arts** houses the **Metropolitan Opera**, the **New York Philharmonic**, the **New York City Ballet** and the **Juillard School of Music**. Built in the 1960s on the site of a former ghetto, it is a glorious tribute to the arts. As with London's National Theatre complex it always has something going on by way of outdoor concerts, impromptu theatre and guided tours. Telephone (212) 877-1800 for details.

Purchasing Tickets

Ticket prices for New York's theatres have inched up in price during the past few years, but not quite so much as London's. Best seats in the house cost around $87 for both musicals and plays. Ticket agencies and theatre box office are the regular sources once you are there. Again, for the latest shows you are wise to book in advance.

Find out what's on from New York newspapers in your local library, then write the theatre box office. Or, using a credit card you can book tickets by calling Telecharge (telephone (212) 239-6200) or Chargit (telephone (212) 944-9300). Tickets may be picked up at the theatre on presentation of your credit card.

TKTS (**Times Square Ticket Center**) at Broadway and 47th Street sells tickets on the performance day for slightly over half price. It is open from noon to 2 p.m. for matinees, 3 p. m. to 8 p.m. for evening performances. The TKTS booths in the two World Trade Centre buildings handle tickets for evening shows only between 11:30 a.m. and 5:30 p.m. Mondays to Fridays and 11 a.m. to 3 p.m. on Saturdays. Line-ups are usually shorter here except at around 1 p.m. when office workers stream down from the towers for a lunch break.

For concerts and dance performances, same-day half-price tickets are sold at the **Bryant Park Ticket Booth** (42nd Street between 5th and 6th Avenues), open daily between noon and 7 p.m.

Holiday House, with offices in Toronto and Vancouver, has theatre packages to New York city. At the time of writing, these include round-trip air transportation from downtown Toronto (you fly out of the convenient Toronto Island Airport), hotel accommodation for two nights, a sightseeing tour and one theatre ticket for a matinee or evening performance of *Miss Saigon*, *The Phantom of the Opera*, *Les Misérables* or *Cats*. Prices range from $429 to $561 per person for double occupancy, depending on your hotel choice.

TORONTO

Anyone who lived in this city 40 years ago will be able to recall Sundays when thick curtains were drawn across Eaton's department store windows — so that we couldn't be entertained by the displays. To see a movie or buy a drink in a bar on Sundays we had to go to New York State. And I have to say the rest of the week wasn't a heap better. So now it's a little hard to believe that Toronto is taking a bite out of the Big Apple's tourism, largely because of our fabulous theatre. But 'tis true. Americans in border cities are booking show tours to Toronto, a city they consider clean and safe and as exciting as New York. With the current exchange rate, the price is right too.

At the time of going to press, Toronto's stages feature *Miss Saigon*, *The Phantom of the Opera*, and the Gershwin musical *Crazy for You*. *Carmen* performed by the Canadian Opera Company is in full swing at the O'Keefe

Centre. The National Ballet of Canada is rehearsing for four presentations. All this without straying far from the city's downtown core.

When we go a little further, we have *Forever Plaid*, forever successful with the 50 plus audience. **The Young People's Theatre** has delightful shows to draw grandparents with their small fry. **The Bayview Playhouse** and **Tarragon Theatre** both have their regulars who hardly miss a production. There are free lunchtime performances in **First Canadian Place** and **Harbourfront**'s theatrical potpourri is guaranteed to suit all of the people some of the time, if not all of the people all of the time.

At last count there were better than 100 theatres in Metropolitan Toronto. Grand old dame of Toronto's formal theatres is **Massey Hall**, 100 years old in 1994 and looking her age. Most of the world's greats performed here, until the 1960s when alternative venues with air-conditioning and modern accoustics lured them away.

In 1960, the then 50 plus **Royal Alexandra Theatre** was scheduled to meet with the wrecker's ball, until Honest Ed Mirvish of the wacky department store fame jumped to her rescue. Good business sense but never good taste was attributed to Ed for his garish store. In restoring the Royal Alex to its former glory he proved he had both.

When in 1960 the **O'Keefe Centre** opened on Front Street, we couldn't believe our luck — a modern theatre with seats for 3,000 plus. It hasn't the greatest accoustics, but for its capacity still attracts some of the world's brightest stars. A block or two east of the O'Keefe the **St. Lawrence Centre for the Arts** opened ten years later and hosts contemporary plays.

The building with a drum-like exterior (behind the CN Tower) is **Roy Thomson Hall** opened in 1982 to world applause for its architecture. Home of the Toronto Symphony Orchestra and Toronto Mendelssohn Choir, it features — among other musical groups — international orchestras and big bands of the fifties. (A recent show featured *Rosemary Clooney with the Spitfire Band*.) Unsold tickets are offered at reduced prices at the box office two hours before show time. Tours conducted Mondays to Saturdays at 12:30 p.m. are of particular interest to architecture and theatre buffs. Call (416) 872-4255 for details.

Across from their little gem known locally as The Alex (Royal Alexandra Theatre), the Mirvishes (Ed and son David) built the glamorous **Princess of Wales Theatre** which opened with *Miss Saigon* in the Spring of '93. The area also has good restaurants, including a couple owned by Ed in case you want to keep your spending in the family.

Recent restorations include the **Pantages Theatre,** just half a block south of the Eaton Centre, and the neighbouring **Elgin** and **Winter Garden Theatres** which are the world's only remaining stacked theatres and have decors as lavish as they were in the 1900s.

With little else to attract tourists North York (20 minutes from downtown) now has a stunning **Performing Arts Centre**. Although a controversial opening with *Showboat* in '93 brought protests, both the show and the theatre complex have received high acclaim.

Two theatres outside Toronto deserve a mention because they are seldom missed by theatre enthusiasts visiting the city. **The Shaw Festival** is at Niagara-on-the-Lake (90 minutes south-west of Toronto), one of Ontario's most historic communities. Its cultural fame emerged when plays by George Bernard Shaw were presented in a stifling little courthouse there. In 1962 a permanent theatre was built, and now plays by Shaw and his contemporaries bring visitors by the busloads. Try to stay overnight in one of the vintage inns, so you can enjoy a walkabout after the day-trippers have left. Tour packages include a show, dinner, hotel and bus from Toronto. The theatre season runs from early spring to late fall. For more information on the Shaw Festival call 1-800-267-4759.

Stratford (90 minutes north-west of Toronto) held its Shakespeare Festival in a capacious brown tent until the permanent theatre was built in 1957. Now its popularity is such that five or six buses and six trains leave Toronto daily for Stratford in its spring through fall season. Local restaurants pack hampers for picnics beside the River Avon. Character houses are converted to enchanting inns and B & Bs. For more information call the theatre at 1-800-567-1600.

Purchasing Tickets

Toronto's newspapers, including the free paper *Now* and *Toronto Life* magazine, have details of Toronto theatres. Seat prices range from $30 to $90 depending upon the theatre and production. Half-price tickets for same-day performance of some shows are available at the **Five Stars Ticket Booth** on Yonge Street at Dundas (outside the Eaton Centre) open Monday to Saturday, noon to 7:30 p.m. and Sundays between 11 a.m. and 3 p.m. A second booth in the **Royal Ontario Museum** (Bloor Street and Avenue Road) is open daily from noon to 6 p.m. and a little later some days.

Theatre packages in Toronto cost around $300 for a double room overnight and two tickets for either *Miss Saigon* or *The Phantom of the*

Opera. Travel agents can provide you with more details. But if you book far enough in advance to get tickets for these shows and ask for hotel discounts due to your 50 plus membership, you should be able to put together your own program for less.

SPECIAL THEATRES AROUND THE WORLD

The world has other great showplaces you will want to visit when in the neighbourhood. **The Sydney Opera House**, is one, the **Teatro Colon** in Buenos Aires another. Regardless of sky-rocketing seat prices in Moscow and St. Petersburg, you'll regret leaving either city without attending a ballet by the **Bolshoi** or **Kirov** dancers. (It isn't always possible because the companies tour overseas, but any presentation in these two theatres is an event.)

And let's not forget Canada. From Vancouver to St. John's we have excellent theatre, first-rate ballet companies and symphony orchestras and regional performers who focus on local culture often with wickedly funny humour.

Some special productions to look out for when planning your overseas tours are: the *Passion Play* in Bavaria's Oberammergau, staged every ten years and next presented in the year 2000. The Singer of the World contest, held in Cardiff's **St. David's Hall** every second year, next scheduled for the summer of '95.

Opera fans pour into Finland's little lakeside town of **Savonlinna** for its month-long summer festival which offers magical performances in a sixteenth century castle. **The Glyndebourne Festival of Opera** in England is an annual event, where tradition dictates that you bring a champagne picnic to eat on its velvety lawns. New England's summer stock, the Tanglewood Musical Festival in the Berkshires. Dylan Thomas' Under Milkwood in South Wales, Shakespearean theatre and Sunday concerts in London's Regent's Park, Pavarotti in Hyde Park are all worth a detour in your itinerary. Guidebooks and tourist pamphlets give details of these and other theatrical interludes to give you that quality time out during a busy tour.

*I*n Focus

*M*y walls at home are covered with photographs — black and white as well as colour, of people and places around the world. Most wouldn't win a prize. Certainly not the one of my daughter Liza feeding a monkey in Jaipur, or the one of her twin Susan laughing with a friend on the shores of Galilee. But, any one of our pictures brings instant recall of when, where and in what circumstances it was taken.

When shooting to illustrate a travel article, I must study the light in relation to my subject and general composition. If you can do this for personal shots, wonderful. But if the light's all wrong when the day's all right, my advice is that you capture the moment. The happy memories it will bring you far outweigh any artistic imperfections.

SELECTING A CAMERA

Never has photography been so easy. No more figuring out speeds and f-stops, because it is all done automatically. Aim and shoot is just about all you have to do with today's lightweight and compact cameras, some of which have a built-in flash. A good **automatic** camera can be bought for $200 or so. At this price you can probably get a replacement if it's lost or stolen, without spoiling the rest of your trip.

There are plenty of pocket-sized cameras which take full frames on 35 mm film, but because of their light weight require a steady hand to operate. Also they don't have interchangeable lenses. In this category, I use a **palm-sized Minox**. It is unobtrusive to work with and the resultant pictures are good enough for publication. Once a flash attachment is added it becomes less compact.

When buying a camera tell the sales person what you will be using it for. Serious photographers will be shown a Japanese-made **single-lens reflex camera** in which the picture is sighted through the lens. I find a 36 to 72 mm zoom lens useful. Its flash attachment is separate and quite bulky. Such a camera can cost from $500 to several thousands. If you buy a haze filter and keep it in place always, it will give you better pictures while protecting your lens against dirt and scratches. When travelling with expensive equipment remember that it is probably not adequately covered by your travel insurance. We have extra coverage under our homeowners policy.

USING YOUR CAMERA

That trip of a lifetime is not the place to familiarize yourself with a new camera. Examine and practise using it before leaving home. It will come with the manufacturer's instructions of course. There are also simple books such as Kodak's *Pocket Guide To 35 mm Photography* (Rochester: Kodak Corp., 1994) to tell you more. Some books focus on travel photography, so do some photography courses and workshops.

When borrowing a camera it too should become an old friend before you leave home. I remember a young woman on an African safari who stopped bringing her camera to our early morning wildlife hunts, although the photo opportunities were absolutely the best — lion cubs jumping all over their snoozing mothers, elephant families with youngsters hooked to the adults' tails so they wouldn't get left behind, baboons carefully grooming each other — the very shots we had come to Africa to capture. After one particularly exciting run the woman confided that her camera had just stopped working. When I asked if she had checked the batteries she replied that it didn't require them. It was her father's camera and he had said that everything was electronic. I replaced her battery with one of my spares, and she began shooting every wildebeest and warthog that trotted by our camp.

You should understand the purpose of film ASA **numbers** (the indicator which shows the film's speed or degree of sensitivity to light) and how to set your camera to use the film selected. Also, become familiar with the controls that double or halve exposure times when shooting in mixed light.

Use of a **flash** can be tricky at first. After a little practice it becomes obvious that it has only a limited range, effective when photographing close-up objects within the distance scales shown on the unit. Those shots of Niagara Falls at night, for example, are not improved by your flash. Don't be timid about using a flash outdoors in sunlight, to rid your subject of shadows.

PHOTOGRAPHY SUPPLIES

Buy at least twice as much **film** as you think you are going to need. Film may be sold where you are going, at prices to match any at home, but it's uncanny how often you arrive in town on early closing day or on a public holiday when stores are locked and shuttered.

Be prepared to "waste" film shooting at the same scene several times from different angles. If I know I am coming to a special scene or attraction I reload my camera, even when the film isn't quite finished. This sometimes enables me to take all the shots I want before we are doused by a rain shower, or the subjects stop dancing, or we have to get back on the bus.

Kodak Gold Plus 100 is a good all-round film for prints, Kodak Ektachrome Elite 100 for slides. With experience you may choose the tones and shades available from Fuji or some other manufacturer. Also, once you have read some photography books or taken a course, you will want to consider ASA 400 or higher speed films for use in poor light.

It's a good idea to stock up on extra camera and flash **batteries**, and make sure you have a sturdy shoulder strap. Also, a small soft brush for cleaning your camera and a micro-weave cloth or tissues for the lenses, can both be very helpful.

We have all seen signs telling travellers that X-ray machines will not damage film, but in fact they sometimes do. On one occasion my film became foggy after I had travelled through airports in several countries and the same rolls of film were subjected to these machines five or six times. While it used to be possible to have your camera bag hand-searched, I haven't come across such obliging personnel lately, except in Canada. In any case, this can be very time-consuming when you have 30 or 40 rolls of film. The answer is to pack both used and unexposed film into **lead foil bags** available from most professional camera stores. I even slip my camera containing a partially-used roll of film into such a bag.

CUSTOMS DECLARATIONS

Allow enough time at your Canadian departure airport to visit the customs office. Here, on a **green identification card**, the officer will note your camera and lens serial numbers as proof they were taken out of the country and not bought overseas. If you do purchase more equipment during your trip, keep the bills to show when you re-enter Canada, and have these recorded on your green card before leaving the country again.

DON'T SHOOT

Observe signs telling you not to photograph military installations, warships, airports, bridges and other security-sensitive areas. Ignore them and you can be arrested, even held overnight while your films are sent to a city for developing. You probably won't come to any harm physically, but it is unnerving to be held by people who speak a different language from yours and who make no attempt to understand your protestations. You really don't need those pictures anyway.

Photography is often forbidden in museums and art galleries, unless you have special permission. Some curators will tell you the flash damages ancient works of art, others that it is a matter of copyright or security. Whatever the reason, you will find plenty of good postcards pictures in the gift shop.

WHO, HOW AND WHAT TO SHOOT

When photographing strangers do so discreetly from a distance or ask their permission. Southern Belles at stately plantation houses in Georgia and the girls in national costume at Holland's Keukenhof gardens will gladly pose to enhance your picture. It's part of their job. But people wearing national costume in public squares and the like usually expect to be paid when posing for your camera. I know of travellers who complain about this custom, but I don't. These "subjects" spend the day providing us with colourful shots when they could be home or working somewhere else. In this regard they are really no different from street musicians. Few of us who stop to listen would fail to drop a coin or two into the musician's hat.

In some societies people simply dislike being photographed; in others, photography may offend them on religious grounds. For example, the reproduction of human images through photos or other visual arts offends some Muslims. You have to respect this, even though they may unwittingly present very photogenic scenes.

Tips

■ **Study guidebook pictures** and postcard scenes sold locally. Those photographers have had time to line up the very best shots. Figure out where they stood, and you have a good chance of capturing the scene yourself.

■ Beautiful landscapes and beach scenes may be too large to photograph effectively, but if you focus on an object close-up or on people shot against those scenes, you can create a good picture. Try to **compose your picture** so that your subject is part of the overall scene. Dark-skinned people are more difficult to photograph than light, so take the camera's light meter reading from their faces rather than from the surroundings. Lighting with a flash can also help.

■ **Night photography** for the amateur is a matter of experimentation and luck. Shots can be effective without a flash if you are prepared with a portable tripod for long exposures. Pictures with lights reflected on water — like those huge floating restaurants in Hong Kong for example — can be effective. A flash used in rooms with mirrored walls and chandeliers may give you dramatic results. On the other hand, your flash will not work well in a smoky cafe, where the light will be reflected off the smog to produce a milky effect.

■ **Heat and sand** are no friends of your camera. Never leave your camera in direct sunlight or in cars standing in the sun. Where possible keep both exposed and unexposed film in a refrigerator. Your hotel room's mini-bar is good for storing film. I stick a yellow adhesive note on the door reminding me they're in there. It makes me appear forgetful, but, hey, I've never left my films behind yet.

■ Unless you have good reason to be completely sure of local processors and have the time to wait for your photos to be developed, I suggest you **bring exposed film home** for developing. Professionals reckon if they get one saleable picture per roll they have done well, so don't be too hard on yourself when weeding out the throw-aways.

Photography, in particular travel photography, can be a very rewarding hobby for retirees. As you become more proficient you may consider joining the local photography club where you can exchange ideas and tips. Travel photography has the added advantage of providing — dare I say it — a special focus to your trip. And when you become really good at it, club members will be far more receptive to your slide shows than your children ever were.

Shopping Around

I don't know anyone who doesn't like to bring home souvenirs from their vacation, even if it is only a picture postcard or two. After decades of lugging huge carvings and wall hangings across continents, I have run out of house space and now confine myself to Christmas-tree decorations. If I can't find them I improvise with some other bauble representative of the country, such as the smallest babushka doll in the nest, a Ukrainian painted egg, a tiny outrigger canoe from Tahiti or a two-inch-high Chinese warrior.

Having reached the age and status when we are going into smaller homes, many of us have stopped buying traditional souvenirs. But habits are hard to break. Like dining on local foods, shopping overseas is something I enjoy. Birthday and Christmas gifts and clothes for myself are what I look for now.

WHERE HAVE ALL THE BARGAINS GONE?

If you are looking solely for bargains you might well come home empty-handed. The truth is that with so many sales, factory outlets and warehouse emporiums in Canada we don't have to go overseas for the good buys. But bargain hunting here is not as much fun is it? Memories of shopping beside 60-pack toilet rolls and boxes of detergent the size of a small car really don't compare with shopping en route home from a camel trek in the Negev with desert sand still in your shoes.

Shopping tours are popular with 50 plus travellers. Especially the two- or three-day forays into American malls. I know women who go twice a year without fail, returning loaded down with clothes for themselves and their grandchildren. They tell me these jaunts are cost-effective, that they pay for the gas or bus fare, hotel room and meals out of savings on purchases.

I have to admit to the same panting eagerness when I am near Staffordshire's Stoke-on-Trent, because I love to buy fine china. A blue and white bus will take you from one factory to the next (Wedgwood,

Royal Doulton, etc.). It travels a circular route, starting and finishing at the railway station, so is handy for day-trippers up from London. There are factory tours during which you can see your favourite figurines being hand painted, and every company has its sales outlet.

The only savings to be had at Stoke's manufacturers' outlets are in "seconds" and "ends of lines." For full sets of china, their prices are no different from local stores or other china shops throughout Britain. It is reckoned that the VAT refund will take care of shipping costs. I have had no breakages when carrying china in my luggage (separate each piece and wrap it in soft clothing), but, because china is quite heavy, I don't recommend you cart it around on tour, unless you are travelling by car.

London's **sales**, after Christmas and again towards the end of summer, bring shoppers from all over the world. Last fall at a Knightsbridge B & B around the corner from Harrods, I learned of three American women who book in for a week each January. They call it a Shop and Show tour, bargain hunting by day and attending theatres at night. Large department stores advertise their sales in London papers a few days ahead of the event. Harrods' sale is the biggest. Be there when its doors open each morning and you'll know know what the bulls feel like charging through the gates at a western stampede.

When looking for electronic goods overseas — cameras or watches which you believe cost less than at home — be sure to have the make and model number with you because appearances can be deceptive. If your purchase is something you have always wanted, and you later see it for less at home, don't give it a second thought. Memories of the time and place you bought it have some value too.

Crystal from Ireland, sweaters from Edinburgh, Thai silks, a teapot in warming basket from China, Bruges lace, Spanish Lladro figurines, Portugese tiles, a Japanese kimono — you can always find something to **buy at the source**, usually for less than you would pay elsewhere.

GIFTS

As an experienced gift buyer I can promise that the first rule is to keep it small. Work of local craftspeople is always happily received at home, especially unusual costume jewellery. And I don't confine myself to souvenir shops. Grocery stores have unusual jams and teas, nuts and herbs and spices. Soaps and pot-pourri made from local fragrances cost less in pharmacies than gift shops.

BUYER BEWARE

It's a well-worn phrase, but appropriate for travellers shopping overseas because we usually have no opportunity to return defective goods. Here are some cautions:

❑ When buying valuable items, avoid street dealers and deal only with **reputable merchants**. If in doubt consult with tourist boards and other government agencies. Hotel concierges and licensed guides are good sources of information, but indirectly you pay for their advice when they receive a commision from the merchant on anything you buy.

❑ If a price is much lower than in competitors' shops, look for defects, **check model number** and attachments to see nothing is missing.

❑ Recognize that **bargaining** is a way of life in many countries. The trick is to determine what the item is worth to you and go no higher. Start at 50% of the asking price, and move from there to your pre-determined limit.

❑ Make sure you get what you paid for and that the goods are not switched with something inferior. This applies especially to things like carpets and furniture which a shopkeeper will ship home for you. Sometimes it is wiser to arrange for transportation yourself.

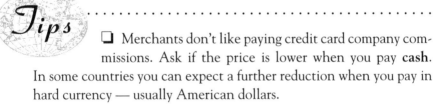

❑ Merchants don't like paying credit card company commissions. Ask if the price is lower when you pay **cash**. In some countries you can expect a further reduction when you pay in hard currency — usually American dollars.

❑ Some countries have **government-operated consignment stores** displaying national crafts at fixed prices. These are a joy for those of us who dislike bargaining. Nobody reaches for the wrapping paper when you stop to admire something, and you don't feel you are insulting the artist when you decide not to buy.

MARKETS

For anyone over 50, **flea markets** and fund-raising fairs are crammed with nostalgia. Handmade doll's clothes, crocheted tree decorations, antique jewellery and vintage cookbooks are all things I have snapped up at

bazaars. I also look for Hummel, Lladro and Royal Doulton figurines for collectors in my family. As welcome Christmas or birthday gifts, they are often more valuable than new editions and cost a great deal less.

Tourist offices have information on permanent antique and flea markets. London's markets are particularly entertaining. **Covent Garden,** where nothing much happens until noon, is one of the liveliest for its street entertainers, speciality shops, craft and general stalls guaranteed to put some fun into shopping.

AUCTIONS

An estate sale held by a leading auction house will introduce you to a slice of upper-crust British life you won't see elsewhere: champagne and salmon lunches are served in marquees and local pubs often do picnics. You may even pick up a bargain!

Estate sales are well-orchestrated affairs for leading auction houses, misery for owners putting their treasures on the block and enjoyable country outings for us. My most recent sale was in an Oxfordshire village, where contents of a seventeenth-century home were being sold. Prices astonished even the veteran auctioneer when gilt metal wall brackets valued at £700 ($1,400) sold for £18,000 ($36,000).

Sotheby's and **Christie**'s are two large international auction houses whose estate sales can be fun. Christie's alone has 72 offices in 27 countries. At the time I was in Oxfordshire, they were auctioning off antique cars in Monaco and estate jewellery in Toronto. In London I frequent their South Kensington showrooms to see what's being auctioned there. At one end of the showroom you can have your own treasures valued. It costs nothing, and if you decide to leave them for auction they will be put into appropriate future sales.

PROFESSIONAL ADVICE

Most **guide books** have a section on shopping, and **tourist offices** distribute pamphlets about traditional crafts and other good buys. If you are really keen, look to see if there's a *Born To Shop* guide (New York: Bantam Books) for the specific area you'll be visiting. This series of guides is honest, independent of advertising and should carry a label warning that it will incite you to buy all sorts of things you hadn't thought about before.

Beverly Rosenbloom of Mississauga, Ontario has written and published a *USA Factory Outlet Guide* (Mississauga: Beverly Rosenbloom, 1993);

it contains maps and store listings for close to 80 factory outlet malls in 22 states.

TAXES

Almost every country adds taxes to the price of goods and services. In Europe **sales taxes** (Value Added Taxes) are included in the listed price. Shoppers from overseas are advised they will have the tax refunded, but this is only if the stores cooperate, and only when you spend in excess of a certain amount — usually around $100 in Britain. All purchases in the same store can give you the elegible amount for refund of the 17.5% VAT. Even so, with the store's processing fee deducted, it isn't always worth queueing for.

Some countries make the rebate process easier than others. For example, in Ireland the shopkeeper often will make a separate charge card impression for the tax, and then tear it up once Irish customs informs him or her you have left the country.

In Britain shoppers claiming a tax refund are supposed to produce purchases at the customs desk of their departure airport. This doesn't make a lot of sense in view of restrictions on carry-on luggage. I simply show the bill, explain that bulky purchases are in my suitcase, and so far — touch wood — have had no trouble getting my forms stamped for rebates. (You will be given a form, and envelope addressed to the store for mailing it at the airport. Since few shops give free postage stamps any more, I suggest you buy your own sometime during the trip.) Your rebate cheque will arrive in the mail six to nine weeks later.

In excess of 60,000 retailers across Europe are plugged into **Europe Tax-Free Shopping**, a service which enables eligible shoppers to leave the store with a refund cheque in hand. Stamped by customs as you prepare to leave the country, they can be cashed at refund desks within airports and at border crossings.

DUTY FREE

Airports and some border crossing areas have duty-free stores where merchandise should cost less than in the country's interior, but airport rents are notoriously high and I seldom find real bargains there. Two exceptions are **Shannon in Ireland** and **Holland's Schiphol**. A recent survey of airport duty-free shops showed Schiphol to be number one in the world for the best selection and prices.

Duty-free ports in the Caribbean claim to have prices 30% to 50% lower than on the mainland. If you are hoping for bargains, it is important to check prices at home ahead of your trip.

Shopping in Asia isn't what it used to be when Hong Kong was one big discount mall. You can still have a decent suit made here for a very inviting price, but do leave enough time for two or three fittings.

Thailand has some remarkable buys in silks. Singapore, as a duty-free port is considered the best shopping centre in Asia for Chinese silk, Japanese electronic equipment, Swiss watches, jade and other imports. Shops bearing the red and white symbol belong to the Good Retailers Scheme, supported by the Singapore Tourist Promotion Board, and assure good value and quality.

HOME FREE

You are expected to declare everything purchased outside Canada. Some items carry no duty, and others do, so you may want to check with Customs before leaving Canada. **Duty-free allowances** for Canadian adults are $20 after 24 hours out of the country or $100 after 48 hours. An annual exemption of $300 is allowed after an absence of seven full days. Included in these allowances are 1.18 L (40 oz.) of spirits or wine or 48 x 355 mL (12 oz.) of beer. Tobacco products may include up to 200 cigarettes or 50 cigars or 1 kg (2.2 lb.) of tobacco.

Customs officers know more tricks than you do when it comes to smuggling undeclared goods. The duty payable averages 15% plus 7% GST, meaning that if you have overshopped by $300 you still only pay about $70. To avoid argument about items you have taken out of the country, check them at Customs before you leave. Items like cameras and jewellery will be listed on a green card which can be offered as proof of their origin if you are queried on your return home. Antiques bought overseas require a bill and certificate of antiquity when you re-enter Canada. Unlike us, artifacts 50 years and older are considered antique and as such will be admitted into Canada duty-free.

Certain goods are banned entry. Anything made from ivory or skins and furs of endangered species is prohibited. So are those cuttings from your friend's garden in Devon, for the very good reason they could introduce a new disease into Canada. Plants, seeds, bulbs and such may be imported under certain conditions. If you are likely to want some, check with Agriculture Canada in advance of your trip. Their number is listed in the blue pages of your telephone directory.

Firearms and weapons are not allowed into Canada. What, according to Customs Canada, constitutes a weapon, doesn't always make sense to me, especially since I had a papier-mâché blowgun from the Amazon confiscated at Toronto's airport.

Food smuggling is a real problem for airport officials. Travellers love to bring home Polish sausage, English back bacon or some other taste of home they can quite easily buy here. Many have no idea that in doing so they are breaking the law. This is where the dear little beagle wearing an Agriculture Canada jacket comes in. If you have a string of sausages up your jumper he knows it, and at your arrival airport he'll sit staring up at you with the most sorrowful brown eyes you have ever seen.

Playing It Safe

Keeping yourself and your belongings safe can be as much a question of good judgement and common sense on vacation as it is at home. There is no need to walk furtively around New York or Paris or Madrid hugging your purse in both hands, suspicious of everyone you see. Simply leave your valuables at home or in the hotel safety deposit box. Dress as if you are off to the supermarket. Know where you are going and move with confidence.

AIRPORT SAFETY

Airports are stressful places where travellers are particularly vulnerable to thieves. The same can be said of railway stations and bus terminals, although to me these generally appear safer.

Before leaving home I put my ticket, my passport and several two and five dollar bills in my jacket's inside pocket, where I can reach them quickly. My luggage labels have a flap covering the address, to thwart anyone who would like to know my home may be empty.

At check-in counters, thieves are known to bluster in with noisy questions, while clerks and passengers are distracted, and then to make away with passports lying on the counter. This is where I stand hunched over the counter, elbows guarding my space, and refuse to be distracted. My flight bag on the floor is between my legs, its shoulder strap looped around one foot. I probably look as inelegant as a pregnant giraffe, but I do get where I'm going without mishap.

You know, don't you, not to leave your luggage unattended? In a Tel Aviv airport security-check line-up one time I noticed that the man ahead of me had disappeared and that I was kicking his flight bag along with my own. I called a security guard who quickly carried it off. From the other side of the barrier I felt quite silly when its owner returned with a soft drink and frantically searched the queue for his bag. Even so, I would do the same thing again. Like our mothers used to tell us, better to be safe than sorry.

Finally, never, ever, carry someone else's bag or parcel of any description through airport security or customs on the way home.

HOTEL SAFETY

In my years of staying in hotels ranging from five-star palaces to sad little dumps so inhospitable even the roaches had moved out, I have been robbed only once in my lodgings — and the circumstances then were very unusual.

I have learned not to court danger. I do not flash my money or room key around in the hotel lobby. I seldom order from room service in huge impersonal hotels, though admittedly this is because delivery takes so long. If there is a knock on my door I let it go unheeded unless I am expecting visitors — and they are asked to call me from the hotel lobby. I don't advertise my absence by hanging a Please Make Up My Room notice on the doorknob. Like everyone else, I enjoy a room opening to the beach or patio, but such a room can be convenient for intruders so I ask for something higher up. Any prowler searching for a victim in my hotel can see I am no catch. My clothes are inexpensive and I wear practically no jewellery.

Travel shops sell inexpensive alarms and door locks, but I can't say I have ever considered them necessary.

THE STREET-WISE TOURIST

Dress for the occasion. I seldom carry a purse when out for the day. Over the years I have accumulated several cotton shirts with button-down pockets in which to keep a little cash, credit cards, a photocopy of my passport's pertinent information for identification, and anything else I need. By now you know about my jackets with pockets sewn into the lining? Sometimes I have a waterproof pouch hanging from my neck beneath my sweater too. With all those bulging pockets I look like a pack-horse I know, but I do enjoy having my hands free where possible, and consider the traditional handbag an unnecessary encumbrance. (Michael oftens wears a cloth belt-safe under his pants. It carries important items safely, but is difficult to get at in a public place.)

Tips

❑ If you carry a shoulder purse it's best to wear it across your body in the same style old-time bus conductors used to wear theirs. This way it's more difficult for somebody to cut the strap or yank your purse away. Thieves have become adept at slitting the waist straps of fanny packs.

❏ Walk as if you own the world but don't dress in a wealthy fashion. It amazes me that some women feel the need to wear diamonds on several fingers, and more dangling from their ears, when they are off to a souk to barter for souvenirs or to ride a camel through the desert. **"Dress Down"** as they say in the fashion mags. You may not be able to look like a native, but you can look as though you live there. To me this means dressing like anybody's mother off shopping for the family dinner, when in fact my nylon carry-all contains $2,500 worth of camera equipment.

❏ Men who can't break the habit of carrying a wallet in their pants' pocket should wrap a rubber band around it. This way, if someone tries to pick your pocket, you'll feel the friction of your wallet being lifted, and perhaps have time to retrieve it.

❏ Try not to behave like a tourist. Instead of standing on a street corner puzzling over a map or guide book, go into a quiet cafe and check your whereabouts with the waitress or cashier. I ask directions of my hotel's concierge, and if I forget his instructions before reaching my destination I consult an employee at another hotel.

❏ Ask at your hotel if it is safe at night to walk to your choice of restaurant or theatre. It is a good idea to carry your hotel's address on a card written in the language of the country, so you can show it to a cabbie should you decide to ride home.

❏ Recognize that **thieves** operate in crowded places. In European cities be aware of children swarming around you. These are professional pickpockets whose adult trainers bus them to tourist areas for work. Don't even begin to hesitate telling them to buzz off.

❏ Discourage polite strangers who volunteer to mind your bags while you nip over to the snack bar, or who want to clean off the back of your shirt. A favourite scam involves one person pointing out an offensive blob on your back (it is probably mustard, which he put there) and while you are distracted, his accomplice picks your pocket.

❏ Avoid taking valuables to the beach. It's far too tempting to leave them unattended while you go for a walk or swim.

$\mathcal{H}$elp!

$\mathcal{W}$ith all the pre-planning in the world, things can still go wrong. What you must remember is that seemingly hopeless situations can be happily resolved, often quickly, if you know where to go for help.

Here's where that all-important positive attitude comes in. And confidence. And knowing what to do next. And experience. Think about all those occasions when you've had to take over on the home front, in the workplace or on vacation with a sick child.

The point is that none of us has reached 50 plus without calling up resources and confidence we didn't know we had. Experience has taught us to turn a bad situation into a middling one because we know grumbling won't improve a thing.

You are stuck overnight in a jungle where mosquitoes are the size of toy helicopters. Your guide is with you and the float plane will pick you up the next day. Sure you would rather be back in your five-star hotel. But in the meantime the villagers are hospitable. As their guest you are given an unusual understanding of how they really live — not some show put on for tourists. And think how you can embellish the tale you'll tell your next door neighbour who won't leave her house on weekday afternoons because she has to watch Oprah.

With the **right attitude** you can make the best of any situation. Away from familiar surroundings even little problems can appear enlarged. Sometimes they crop up when you're about to leave home. A grandchild or travelmate is suddenly taken ill. I remember on my first extensive trip to Europe I had arranged to meet a former school friend from Britain in Amsterdam, and we were to tour together. On departure day, when I learned she was unable to join me, I felt utterly lost, and had I not been committed to writing about our tour I would have cancelled. Looking back, it really wasn't any big deal, simply a shock that my careful plans had been thrown for a loop. I went, enjoyed, and came home triumphant.

This sort of thing happens. Your travel companion is called home on urgent business or is delayed because of a lost passport. Do you go home, hang around for a few days and continue together, or arrange to meet up later? Knowing how to cope is very important, whether you are the one left behind, the one rushing home or the one continuing the trip on your own.

☎ USEFUL CONTACTS

☎ Before you leave home you should obtain from your travel agent, tour company or cruise line, the names of their **local representatives** in countries you are visiting.

Make sure you have copies of your travel insurance company claim forms, as well as their instructions for locating medical aid and their 24-hour help lines.

Add to these the addresses and telephone numbers of the **Canadian embassies,** high commissions or consulates (collectively known as missions) in the countries where you will be travelling. A complete listing of overseas missions, together with useful information about the role they play, is available in a booklet titled "Bon Voyage, But..." which describes our consular awareness program. You can get a copy from customs and passport offices or the Department of External Affairs and International Trade in Ottawa.

When renting a car, be sure to have a number you can call in case of breakdown or accident.

Carry all of this information in a safe place, with a copy of your itinerary, a list of your credit card numbers, including telephone numbers to call in case of loss, and airline telephone numbers and ticket details. In all likelihood none of this will be needed. But if so, it's easier on the nerves to pull out your list than to be fumbling around with telephone books in foreign languages.

CONSULAR OFFICES

When travelling independently in an area struck by political unrest or a natural disaster, make your first call to the mission to tell them where you are. (Before leaving home for areas where these events are a possibility, advise your family to contact External Affairs for news of your safety, *not* the hotel which may well have its communication lines disrupted.)

If you are arrested, consular officials can work to ensure you receive equitable treatment under local laws, but they cannot disregard these laws for your sake. They will not pay fines or legal bills, and they will not perform the functions of a travel agency, automobile club or bank. They cannot look after your belongings or search for lost property or provide transportation.

However, assisting citizens abroad is one of the consul's duties and they will do what they can within the law. In an emergency, they will contact your relatives in Canada or help you to have funds advanced. They will direct you to English- or French-speaking doctors, hospitals and lawyers.

Under an agreement with Australia, that country provides consular services to Canadians where it has representation and we do not. If neither country is represented and you need help, I suggest you contact another mission where your language is spoken — perhaps one representing Great Britain, the United States or France.

A lost or stolen passport should be reported first to the local police and then to the nearest Canadian mission. Before a replacement is issued you must complete an application form and produce evidence of Canadian citizenship. This is where a citizenship card, birth certificate, photocopy of pertinent data in your lost document and those extra passport photos are useful.

HOSPITAL CARE

How will you get home for a follow-up on emergency treatment? Do you have to pay the hospital bill up-front and apply for reimbursement from your insurance company later? You should understand exactly what your policy covers and if you have been given a 24-hour emergency help line, use it.

In a desperate situation, obviously you don't mess around making a lot of telephone calls, but if you telephone the Canadian mission, it will have access to someone who can provide medical assistance. And oh, how nice it is to hear that friendly Canadian accent in times of stress. Also, given time, a call to IAMAT will bring you the name of a doctor nearby who speaks English.

THEFT

I have said it before, but it bears repeating: leave your jewellery, extra cash, spare credit cards and important documents in your hotel safe. What you must carry keep on your body, preferably in some sort of pouch worn under your outer clothing or in fastened pockets. We all take chances now and again. I don't carry my cameras and attachments unless I am likely to use them. Nor do I trot them down to the hotel's office safe. I do put them out of sight in my room, and in its safe if there is one. Anything left lying around on bureaus and the like will probably not be covered by hotel insurance, or your own. If something of value is stolen, when the theft could have been avoided, try not to berate yourself for the rest of the trip.

The police may do no more than request you complete a form asking seemingly silly questions such as your mother's maiden name or grandparent's place of birth. Don't be impatient. They are simply trying to establish positive identity. Above all else stay calm. Be pleasant. It isn't the policeman's fault, and if you imply he should be out patrolling instead of lounging around the cop shop you'll only incite his ire. You want him on your side, after all. Although your goods probably never will be recovered, you will require a copy of his report for your insurance claim.

LOST CREDIT CARDS

- **Mastercard**: If you lose your Mastercard, call 1-800-826-2181, toll free from anywhere. The company will immediately block your account. If you need a replacement, after clearance from your bank, they will send a temporary card to you by courier. For example, if your Mastercard goes missing in Paris, a new one is approved by your bank and delivered from Cologne by United Parcel Service (UPS). An alternative is to ask the nearest Thomas Cook office to act on your behalf. In certain circumstances they can also obtain a cash advance for you.

- **Visa:** In the case of theft or loss of your Visa card, telephone 1-800-268-9460 from anywhere to block your account; ask for a replacement card to be sent to you from Canada by courier.

- **American Express**: Call the nearest American Express office if your card is lost or stolen. Your card will be cancelled and a replacement sent to you via the fastest route available.

USEFUL ORGANIZATIONS

Both American Express and Thomas Cook have overseas offices their clients can turn to for help. American Express cardholders have access to the company's Global Hotline (202-783-7474, call collect), which gives emergency assistance when you are more than 100 miles from home. It will provide the names of local physicians, health services, lawyers and translators. It will also notify your family or explain how to get emergency funds.

Automobile club membership has obvious advantages for drivers, especially when the club has affiliations in the countries you are touring.

Part Four
Travel Trends of the Nineties

$\mathcal{A}$dventure and Action

*I*t is virtually impossible to define adventure and action trips when a tour of a Napa Valley winery can be as much an adventure for some as a balloon ride over an African game park is for others.

At our stage in life almost any new experience can be termed an adventure. Sometimes the adventure is simply being there. Like when you're privy to unfamiliar lifestyles that show the sky won't fall if your dishes don't match and happiness isn't dependent on having indoor plumbing.

As for action, an afternoon's introduction to the back country on horseback was all the action I wanted at a holiday ranch, while other guests eagerly saddled up for a whole week in the bush.

The possibilities are endless as over 50s take to hang gliding, whitewater rafting, scuba diving, trekking and mountain climbing. But before you do so, know your limitations. Look for those experiences which involve others close to your own competence level, so you won't hold up the rest of the group. Programs organized by or for people over 60 (Elderhostel, for example) can be most rewarding of all.

ORGANIZED ADVENTURE

Unless you are very experienced in your chosen activity, go for something you can rest from as needed. When you set your own pace and are travelling independently this is easy. With a group, make sure the itinerary is flexible. If you have never ridden a horse, stay at a ranch where overnight camping is optional. This way you can return to a hot bath and comfortable bed at night if you wish. On a week's cycling or walking tour it can be reassuring to have a van escort. Ostensibly it is there to carry luggage and spare parts, but in a pinch can give you and your bike a lift.

At the beginning of the book I suggested you ask yourself "**What kind of traveller am I?**" Nowhere is this more important than in adventure and action travel. If you can't stand creepy-crawlies, take a luxury safari instead of one that has you sleeping under canvas. On the other hand, a veteran camper will find tenting in exotic destinations the ultimate camping experience. Are you fearful of being doused by driving water or of being tipped into it? If so, don't even consider a week of white-water rafting. There are gentle one-day rafting excursions you can try on for size. And if you dislike it altogether, no problem, because there are loads of dry adventures around.

ElderTreks of Toronto has the right idea with their "exotic adventures for the young at heart" tailored to fit 50 plus travellers. An example is their 21-day tour in Thailand: sightseeing in Bangkok and surrounds is followed by an overnight train ride to Chang Mai, with the week there highlighted by a bicycle trip into the countryside. From Chang Mai the group divides: some choose to go to the far north for three days; others opt to stay with the people living in the hills. The latter entails an elephant trek through the jungle and overnighting on bamboo floors of village houses. An experience of a lifetime for sure, but not for everyone, which is exactly why ElderTreks offers a less demanding alternative in the Golden Triangle. Here, in the northern area of Thailand bordering on Burma and Laos, you can visit villages and resorts, a national park and nature reserves. Cost for 21 days out of Bangkok is around $2,000 for accommodation, domestic transportation, guide services and 50% of the meals. International airfare is extra (Toronto to Bangkok return is approximately $1,500).

Another ElderTreks tour is to Borneo, with an optional adventure by way of white-water rafting on the Padas River. Pass up the rafting experience and you will still have an unforgettable adventure, highlighted by visits to an orangutan reserve and an island turtle sanctuary. Since the groups are small (12 to 18 people) everyone can stay in local homes and longhouses, allowing them a peek of life beneath the usual tourist veneer. This adventure is roughly $2,500 for all land costs, including 80% of meals and five domestic flights. Airfare from Toronto is approximately $1,800 round-trip.

Trek Holidays of Edmonton with branches in Calgary, Vancouver and Toronto gears its tours to all fit adults and attracts a fair number of 50 plus adventurers. Their 1994–95 catalogue includes a 15-day walking and camping tour in Tuscany. Another is for 15 days in the Alps (a little help is provided by cable cars and a support van to carry luggage.) Accommodation is under canvas tents and at small inns. Six rest days are scheduled, while the overall tour is described as "moderate to strenuous."

A tad more exotic, Trek Holidays' 16-day tour in Tibet and Nepal offers an introduction to what it calls "the complexities of Tibetan Buddhism, art, philosophy and history." Accommodation is in hotels and guest houses, and acclimatization is gradual so that altitude isn't a problem. (It's as well I'm nearing the end of this book, because just flipping through these brochures has me impatient to get up and go.) Land costs are roughly $1,000 for Tuscany, $1,200 for trekking in the Alps and $3,600 for the 16 days in Tibet and Nepal. In-country transportation, accommodation, guide services and some meals are included. International airfares are extra.

ACTIVE ADVENTURES

Often adventure and action go hand in glove, as in horseback safaris and scuba holidays, climbing Mount Kilimanjaro or tracking jaguars in Belize. Some involve skills you can acquire during a vacation, and that will continue to give pleasure in your leisure time at home.

If you're feeling the need to spice up your life, here are several fairly "soft" adventures to look for when planning your travels.

Water Adventures

Word is out about the extraordinary world beneath the sea. Little wonder since modern technology allows even non-swimmers to view coral reefs and their wildly exotic inhabitants.

Florida, the Bahamas and Mexico's Yucatan Peninsula are all surrounded by oceans rich in sea life. **Scuba-diving** and **snorkelling** instruction is provided by teachers so keen to introduce us to their world they display an indefatigable patience.

One of the best places I know for all levels of scuba competence is **Andros**, an island approximately 45km (28 mi.) west of Nassau in the Bahamas. Here at Small Hope Bay Lodge built by Canadian Dick Birch, the entire staff (most are members of the Birch's extended family) shares the enthusiasm of every beginner and applauds their progress. A favourite story concerns a guest who was 70 when they first taught him to swim, and the last I heard he was still returning annually to explore the reef. It is the reef that beckons divers from all over. Claimed as the largest and most exciting in the western hemisphere, it lies less than two kilometres from shore. If you cannot swim and have no wish to learn, you can be fixed up with a float and snorkelling gear.

Once you've discovered it, you will find yourself seeking out the undersea world whenever you travel. What scuba enthusiast, after all, could visit Australia without exploring the **Great Barrier Reef**? Or go to Israel and not plan on seeing the living treasures nurtured by the **Red Sea**?

You don't even have to get wet. Several countries have huge underwater glass-sided rooms from which visitors can view sea life in its natural habitat. The most remarkable sea creatures I have ever seen were around an underwater observatory in southern Israel's resort town of Eilat. Purple with green stripes and yellow spots, orange and blue, pink and black and mauve, the fish looked so comical they resembled plastic creations by Disney's Imagineers.

In the **Caribbean**, glass-bottomed boats and miniature submarines allow you to stay dry when looking at sea life and coral reefs. My most unusual experience of this kind was in French Polynesia. There, on the island of Moorea, our cottage on stilts at the end of a dock had a glass block embedded in the living-room floor. For after-dark entertainment, we would pull aside the rug and watch as psychedelic sea creatures attracted by the light swam over to see what we were about.

Air Adventures

Anyone who is physically fit and has reasonably good eyesight can take up flying. Sixty hours in the air and about the same at ground school can earn you a private **pilot's licence**. In Florida and Arizona, where predictable weather keeps costs down, you can complete your entire training in a three- or four-week vacation.

Classified advertisements in flying magazines will alert you to schools located in America's sunbelt regions. Instruction and accommodation are often packaged, to make the program affordable.

Gliding is one of the most exhilarating experiences I know of. It too can be learned during a vacation in Florida or Arizona. Once you get home, you can join a gliding club where members do the bulk of the work to keep expenses down to about a third of the cost of powered flight. Since retirees have more leisure time than most, many club members are in our age group.

Although it won't be just you and the birds up there, a couple of hours in a hot-air balloon can be the highlight of a tour. Especially when you float above the vineyards of southern France or Kenya's Masai Mara Game Reserve and end with a champagne breakfast cooked on the burners.

Walking and Cycling

Organized tours

Walking and cycling vacations have increased in popularity with 50 plus travellers, since enterprising organizers have taken the heavy work out of them.

Leaders of **walking tours** are always avid outdoors people themselves, escorting small groups on journeys of around 15 to 25 km (9 to 15 mi.) a day, returning to the same lodge each night or walking from one inn to another. A van carries luggage, lunches and snacks, and even tired walkers who aren't up to going the distance.

Walking tours are offered throughout Europe and North America. In Europe they are especially popular because there are so many historical landmarks and fascinating hamlets every few kilometres. Britain has over 160,000 km (100,000 mi.) of public pathways. Some run through privately-owned farmlands generously opened to the public. Many are in national parks where you can use hostels as your home base. In spring and fall, with youngsters back in school, you will find most walkers and hostellers are of our age.

Switzerland, Austria and Bavaria are great for walking. The countryside is criss-crossed with paths, the air is invigorating and the inns are welcoming. Take a train or cable car to a mountain top and start your walk from there. You will find yourself in another world.

Cycling tours are operated on the same principle as the walks in that you have a mini-van carrying your luggage. As with the walking tours, a nice aspect of these is that you aren't obliged to keep up with the group. You will be given a map and the name of the next inn and you can walk or cycle to the inn at your own pace.

The golden rules here are: wear thick-soled boots for walking any distance; make sure your bicycle is a comfortable fit; and if you have a bicycle at home and ride it often, consider taking it with you. (Check with your airline to determine costs and whether they want it disassembled.)

Advertisements in newspaper travel sections are a good source of information on walking and cycling tours. Tourist office people can tell you about tours in their region. Know your limits, especially if you are attracted to cycling through countries like India, Japan and China, where traffic is so dense I myself have hesitated to cross city roads on foot, and would only join the hordes of cyclists in my worst dream.

Independent adventures
The nice thing about these particular adventures is that they don't have to present a great challenge. I know a woman in her sixties who works in an office five days a week and walks her dogs in the country at weekends. Yet two years ago she and a friend trekked through the mountains of Nepal for ten arduous days; now they can hardly wait to go back. My leisurely

walk up Mount Snowdon seems puny by comparison (seven- and eight-year-olds overtook me!) But sitting up there with a picnic lunch, my elation was no less than Sir Edmund Hillary's when he conquered Mount Everest.

Books are written about the world's more famous walking trails. Canada has several. To mention just two, Ontario's 720 km (448 mi.) **Bruce Trail** takes well over a month to cover should you choose to hike it all in one trip, and British Columbia's **West Coast Trail** in Pacific Rim National Park is a five or six days hike for practised walkers.

In the United States the **Appalachian Trail** wanders through 3,380 km (2,100 mi.) of wilderness between the state of Maine's Baxter Peak and Georgia's Mount Springer. New Zealand's **Milford Track** is claimed the most beautiful foot trail on earth. Its 52 km (32 mi.) route usually takes five days to walk, allowing for one rest day along the way. (The midges are fierce. You require a permit and must book ahead.)

As far back as I can remember, I have loved to ride a bicycle. To me it has meant freedom — to gobble up the miles, to travel in solitude on quiet lanes, to get me to where I want to go.

In Europe, **Holland** is my favourite cycling country because of its flat yet interesting countryside. It has **bicycle paths** on major streets and roads to eliminate the hazards of crowded cities and highways. In Canada, **Prince Edward Island** is ideal for cycling; its flat, uncongested inland roads are flanked by fields of potatoes growing in the rich red soil; closer to the water the highway skirts beaches in the national park.

When cycling overseas choose a country where bicycles are an important means of transportation. In Europe this usually means bicycle paths are provided alongside major highways and city roads. Organizers of cycle tours say cycling is very rewarding in **China** because it is one of the few ways to get close to the people.

Mountain biking is a thrill requiring no special skills. I first joined a one-day excursion to ride down the side of a volcano in Hawaii and have since loved similar rides in Alberta and British Columbia. It's downhill all the way, with a support van, group leader and picnic lunch, and is as close to flying as you can get without leaving the ground.

Horseback Riding

All of us who saw the movie *City Slickers* shared the excitement of Billy Crystal's challenge to meet the rigors of a cattle drive. A travel writer I know, who qualified for 50 plus membership at least a decade ago, wrote glowingly of a similar round-up he joined. But whoa, boy. Don't rush off for a seven-day adventure on horseback if you are in the upper range of our age bracket, have a weak back and don't know which end of a horse is up. Start instead with a few days at a guest ranch. You can dress like a cowboy, join in cook-outs and square dances and ride the trail for an hour or so at a time. Then, if you're still keen and have the stamina, a *City Slickers* type of vacation could be the really big one for you.

Western Canada's guest ranches are among the best. Europeans and Asians love them, hardly able to believe we have all that empty space. You don't have to stay for an entire vacation. Even a couple of days at a ranch allows city slickers to experience that traditional western hospitality.

Close up, do those horses look bigger than you thought? Maybe you'll be happier with pony trekking in Wales, or on an elephant in India with a nice little seat on his back. Camels aren't my favourite beasts but at least they are polite enough to kneel down for you to mount, and that's less embarassing than having to ask for steps when climbing onto a great big horse. Travel agents and tourist boards can tell you of more adventure rides.

Back to Nature

Almost everyone over the age of 50 has a natural concern for wildlife and the environment. After all, our generation caused much of the destruction, or at least stood by and allowed it to happen. We are of an age to remember when rivers ran clear and the fish we caught in them were edible. We can recall forests no longer here, and wildlife that's all but vanished, and a time when the sun's rays were considered healthful.

Now retirement affords us the time to get closer to nature. **Bird-watching**, it is said, has become the fastest growing hobby of the nineties. **Walking clubs**, which provide companionship and much needed exercise are also popular these days. These can be especially enjoyable when the weekly walk is in a local park or conservation area.

As I get older my general appreciation of nature heightens. There's really nothing to match it. Man walks on the moon, researchers are closer to curing deadly diseases, a touch of a button brings world events in progress to our living rooms. But nature beats all.

More than ever before I find myself marvelling at the intricacy of a flower growing wild, the unmatched beauty of an iceberg off Newfoundland's **Viking Trail**, the serenity of a forest on a crisp autumn day or the cunning survival tactics of tiny creatures.

A remarkable sight for me last September was that of Monarch butterflies, thousands of them, gathered for take-off from southern Ontario's **Point Pelee** to winter in Mexico. This is a journey of about 3,500 km (2,200 mi.). No luggage. No boarding card. No fuss. A breeze in the right direction is all they need and they are off across Lake Erie. Witnessing such feats now, I feel as if I have had my eyes closed for much of my first 50 years.

As retirement or semi-retirement frees up our time, the opportunities for enjoying nature become more apparent and these opportunities aren't necessarily expensive. If you like to walk or cycle, day-trips can be the price of a packed lunch. Longer excursions need cost no more than the gas in your car.

And then there are the big ones: the **African safari**, cruises to

Antarctica or the **Galapagos Islands**, a trip down the **Amazon** river. Should one of these head your wish list, I urge you to find a way to go now. Be warned though that safaris are not restful holidays and for this reason you should buy the best tour package you can afford.

A tour operator who specializes in Africa told me of families who forgo new cars and the latest electronics, and even spend savings put by for children's education, so that they can go to Africa before species becoming rare in our lifetime vanish. An acquaintance of mine recently telephoned to say she and two friends had met for lunch, where they commiserated over dwindling interest rates on investments and increased taxes nibbling at savings. They decided to "blow a bundle" on one big trip, and now she wanted my thoughts on African safaris. I told her to start packing. Certainly I would sacrifice a new car or a few thousand sitting in my savings account for such an adventure.

CANADA'S OUTDOORS

Here at home we are only now taking maximum advantage of our outdoor resources and creating programs so exciting they bring visitors from the United States, Europe and Japan.

In Canada we can practically reach out and touch the whales. We can camp in preserves of mountain goats, elk and deer. Black bear still wander by the roadside in our parks; polar bears are the focus of tundra buggy tours in Churchill, Manitoba. And remember those cuddly white seal pups, the fat little guys with expressive eyes who used to be clubbed to death on the iceflows off our Atlantic coast? You can visit them now, photograph and pet them, on excursions from the mainland towards the end of winter.

A lasting memory for me was to be awakened on a summer's night in a cottage just three hours by road from Toronto to listen to the wolves howl. On previous visits to **Algonquin Provincial Park** I had joined organized "howls" but was never sure whether our replies were from wolves or human imitators. This time there was no mistaking the sound. Wolf packs were definitely howling to each other on that starry Algonquin night.

National Parks

Canada has 35 national parks covering 180,000 sq. km (69,500 sq. mi.). Every province has at least one park, and with the exception of those in the far north, they can be reached via the Trans-Canada or other major highways. The park chain's first link was forged back in 1885 when squabbles arose over ownership of newly-discovered sulphur springs in the Rockies. These arguments were resolved with the creation of what we now know as **Banff National Park**, enlarged over the years to embrace 6,640 sq. km (2,564 sq. mi.).

Most national parks are open year-round, with reduced facilities between October and May. Modern visitor centres present slide shows on park ecology and wildlife. Interpretive staff give out information, maps, descriptive brochures on self-guided tours and educational programs.

Tragically, some of our favourite parks have become over-developed in and around their townsite hubs, where summer crowds can detract from the region's natural beauty. But, even then, it is no more than a brief drive to walking trails leading to wilderness beaches, quiet coves, mountain spectacles and the unique environment which caused the park to be so designated in the first place.

Admission to our national and provincial parks varies between $5 and $8 per car. **Annual passes** are worthwhile if you will be using the parks for more than a few days. Discounts for persons over 60, 62 or 65 are posted at entrances. Many parks have very affordable lodges and cottage accommodation. A call or postcard to provincial tourist offices will bring wads of information about these natural treasures, guaranteed to provide balm for the soul of every visitor.

Across the border you will find American national and state parks offering many similar opportunities. More information about these is readily available from state tourism authorities.

SPECIAL WILDLIFE ADVENTURES
Whale-watching

A travel experience I often take from my memory bank is a one-day whale-watching excursion off New Brunswick's **Grand Manan Island**. Organized by a company called Ocean Search, it took us aboard a 13.5 m (44 ft.) motor launch to look for the rare Right Whales. From this mother boat a marine biologist escorted two or three passengers at a time in a Zodiac inflatable boat for a close-up look at these gentle giants. For a full 15 minutes I watched three whales, so close I could have reached out and touched them. Weighing about 50 tonnes (tons) apiece and measuring 20 m (66 ft.) they could have tipped us with a single flick of their huge tails. Instead, for our pleasure and seemingly their own, they performed a graceful ballet of sorts. I have since watched whales from cruise ships off Canada's east and west coasts and in California, but nothing compared with my Grand Manan experience.

Ocean Search now has five-day packages which include hotel, meals and the whale-watching and lecture programs for around $540 per person.

Or, on a suitably clear day, you can book a one-day excursion (current cost is $69 per person), as I did. I suggest you stay on the island for several days. Accommodation is in small inns and B & Bs. Scenery is so haunting artists have been known to come for a visit and stay for ever. Coastal walks are heaven. Birders come in search of some of the 275 bird species known to inhabit Grand Manan.

Bird-watching

For this outdoor activity all you need is time, binoculars and all-weather clothing. Little wonder so many retirees name birding as their favourite pastime. An estimated 3.5 million Canadians are birders, spending their leisure hours seeking out, recording and photographing some of the world's 9,000 species.

A trip to your local conservation area will get you started on Canada's 600 bird species. Once hooked you can attend classes on identification, buy guidebooks on the subject and notebooks to record your sightings. Join a club today!

Bird-watching is a very relaxing hobby. It has you tramping about the woods, unmindful of inclement weather, and enjoying all aspects of nature. Local naturalist associations can tell you about mini-tours of two to three days, leaving from towns near your home. Most cost between $150 and $200 per person, for transportation, accommodation, a naturalist escort and some meals.

Preferring to tour independently you can still be in touch with fellow birders. *The Birder's Guide to Bed and Breakfast: United States and Canada* (Santa Fe: John Muir Publications, 1994) lists 250 B & Bs scattered throughout North America's finest bird-watching regions. Your hosts are keen birders with first-hand knowledge of local species. They keep logs and sightings by guests, and dinner-time conversation invariably turns to the lives and habitats of feathered friends.

Seabird Specials

At seabird colonies in our coastal areas you don't have to search for the in-habitants, because they number in the hundreds of thousands. Most are best viewed on boat excursions. Some of these can last a couple of hours, others drop you ashore and pick you up towards the end of the day.

My favourite is **Bonaventure Island** off Percé, on Quebec's Gaspé Peninsula. Here a shuttle service will give you a close-up view of cliff-side seabird colonies before landing you on the island. An escorted walk takes you through the woods to colonies of gannets wedged on the cliffs. You will hear them, and smell them, long before you reach a plateau covered by birds who leave hardly an inch or two to spare. On-site plaques explain the habits and gestures of the gannets, who return each spring to the same ledge they occupied a year before.

You can buy snacks on the island. A better idea is to bring a picnic and find a spot where wildflowers colour the landscape in pastels and the tiny coves are idyllic.

SOME EXOTIC WILDLIFE EXPERIENCES

By now you may have decided that wildlife watching is definitely for you. Adventure specialists and tour companies operate nature tours, led by zoologists, botanists and other scientists to shorelines, jungles and mountain ranges across the world.

African Safari

Several Canadian tour companies offer first-class safaris to east Africa. They put you in air-conditioned lodges with ensuite facilities. Your food will be well-prepared, your escorts knowledgeable. The only time you carry your luggage is when you put it outside your room. Although there is concern that Africa's animals are becoming extinct, at this time you are likely to see all of the **Big Five**: lion, cheetah, rhino, elephant and buffalo. Spotting the big game is only half the thrill. Staying around to watch them care for their young, to witness the affection between adults and mutual respect of different species, to accept the sometimes harsh rules of nature by which these animals survive, this is the great fascination. A few days at a coastal resort before flying home is the perfect conclusion to a safari program because it gives you time to rest and reflect.

Safaris are tiring. Travelling between game parks you will be bumped along unpaved roads for hours on end. There you will be awakened at dawn for early morning wildlife viewing. A second run is at dusk, and there may be other outings in between. At **The Ark** or **Treetops**, you aren't expected to sleep at all. The whole point of being there is to see animals at night as they drink from the waterhole, so you are awakened by a buzzer sounding in your room at each sighting.

Another word of caution. Civilized as they seem, these and similar environments are hostile to strangers. Every so often some clown leaps from the viewing van for a closer shot, or goes off for a walk on his own when told to keep with the group, or thinks he knows better than the guide requesting guests to keep their distance from a grumpy looking beast who's having a bad day. If a tourist is injured, the safari company suffers and the guide may lose his job. And for what reason? Even the simplest camera gives you photographs so perfect your friends back home will think they were taken in a zoo. There is no need to flirt with danger for anything more.

Sadly this is only one aspect of the overuse that is killing the African safari. Another is the garbage left behind by thoughtless tourists. At a televised press conference a couple of years ago, the famous naturalist Richard Leakey emptied a bag of dried elephant dung onto a table. It contained, among other goodies, a soft drink can, film containers and two plastic bags.

Jungle Safaris

I am the first to agree that a trip down the **Amazon** is a vacation of a lifetime, but I must also point out that the heat and humidity can be debilitating, the food may not be all you could wish for and the insects are the size of small cats. (Well, almost.) Sleep can be patchy since jungle noises seem louder than city traffic at rush hour. Day excursions are usually in large motorized canoes, and often you will find yourself clambering up muddy river banks.

Then again, isn't this part of the adventure you came for? In addition, you'll have the opportunity to visit the people living in the jungle much as their ancestors did centuries before. You'll see brilliant birds, butterflies as big as your hand, monkeys gossiping furiously about your unannounced arrival and always the muddy, mysterious Amazon River.

Ecuador's Galapagos Islands

The birds and animals of the Galapagos Islands seem oblivious to the boatloads of visitors who come to see them. They allow themselves to be photographed at close range and some will even smile into your camera! During your stay your cruise ship will be comfortable, though not luxurious. Entertainment will consist of slide shows and talks by naturalists who accompany you on land excursions. You don't need a lot of stamina, but should know that Zodiac inflatables (*pangas*) take you from ship to shore, often in less than perfect weather. Some landings are "wet" meaning you have to wade ashore. On land you will be scrambling over slippery rocks.

Your reward? Fur seals and sea lions, pelicans, prehistoric-looking iguanas, giant turtles and birds so humorous in appearance it is almost as if they stepped out of a comic book.

If The Idea Appeals

Travel agents will put you in touch with tour companies specializing in exotic nature tours. To give you some idea of costs at the time of writing: **Quest Nature Tours** is offering 12 days in the Galapagos Islands and Andes Mountains for around $4,000 including airfare. **Horizon Holidays**, with a reputation for high-quality tours, has a 20-day safari in Kenya and Tanzania for around $7,500, everything included. This company also has an Amazon tour to tack onto its Galapagos tour, a combination that tops most other wildlife safaris for approximately $6,500.

ECOTOURISM

Ecotourism is the buzzword of the nineties. Basically it brings nature and tourists together, in harmony and without damage to the environment. Close to home our national parks have practised fairly strict damage control for a hundred years.

In countries where ignorance, disinterest or the pursuit of short-term profits have destroyed scenic beauty and decimated wildlife, tourism has now fallen off because little remains to be enjoyed there. Other nations are learning from their neighbours' mistakes. Costa Rica for one. A land with long stretches of tropical beaches on two oceans, rain forests, rivers, volcanoes, exotic orchids and brilliant birds, it has put more than 10% of its land under environmental protection. Belize is another country to adopt sound ecological practices as a national policy. Travellers concerned with the environment should be happy in either of these countries.

An example of what's being offered is a tour by **Wings of the World Travel Inc.** of Toronto. This eight-day Caribbean eco-safari in the Caribbean coast zone of Costa Rica costs approximately $1,400 per person, airfare extra. **Questers**, based in the United States and Britain, specializes in luxury worldwide nature tours. The company's 15-day tour of Costa Rica is $4,000 plus airfare, while its 22-day expedition to Chile and Easter island is $7,465, airfare to South America extra. To read more about ecotourism vacations, I recommend Evelyn Kaye's *Eco Vacations: Enjoy Yourself and Save the Earth* (Leona: Blue Penguin Publications, 1991), which can be found in libraries and travel bookstores.

FOR MORE INFORMATION

There are several Canadian associations and tour companies involved in adventure and nature travel that can provide you with more information. You'll find their addresses and telephone numbers listed in Appendices A and B.

- Canadian Parks and Wilderness Society
- Federation of Ontario Naturalists
- Sierra Club of Western Canada
- Sierra Club of Eastern Canada
- Club Aventure
- Riding Mountain Nature Tours
- World Expeditions

Spa Vacations

*W*hen our children were very small, I wondered if I would ever again enjoy a bath without urgent bangings on the door or listening to one child tell another "Hey, just you wait 'til she sees what you've done...." Never in my wildest dreams did I envision the luxury of Brenner's Park Hotel in Baden-Baden, Germany, where in an over-sized marble bathroom I could lie in perfumed splendour with French doors open to a balcony and gardens below. The only sounds, I recall, were of birdsongs above the gurgling River Oos and rustling leaves on its far banks. It came to me then that you don't have to believe in the therapeutic powers of their waters to find relaxation at a spa. A few days out of a busy tour amid such tranquillity is guaranteed to restore you body and soul.

In ancient China and Japan, they recognized the benefits of bathing in **hot springs** loaded with minerals. Two thousand years ago Romans directed such springs into thermal baths which they considered essential to daily life. When the Roman Empire went the way of all empires, European towns with therapeutic hot springs continued to profit from their resources. In the middle ages, Spa — the Belgian town to give health resorts their name — was attracting royalty, aristocrats and wealthy merchants. Two hundred years ago hotels and leisure centres sprang up around the hot springs, while physicians established clinics nearby for the believers who came to be healed.

Spas differ considerably from one part of the world to another. So does the mineral content of the waters used for their medicinal powers. If you are looking for a cure or respite from serious ailments or even minor aches and pains, it is essential to check with your family doctor about spa treatment before going ahead with it. You are likely to require a letter from your physician in Canada before treatment can begin at an overseas spa, anyway, so it's best to arrive prepared.

On the other hand, for a few days **rest and relaxation** you can simply check in and enjoy. Many Europeans return to a favourite spa annually for their vacations; at these spas they study nutrition, exercise daily and relax in beautiful, natural surroundings.

Europe's spas are usually located in picturesque little towns. They offer clean air and sunshine, leisurely exercise, fine food and accommodation and a nightlife that won't interfere with your beauty sleep.

SWITZERLAND

Some of my favourite spas are in Switzerland. As a sickly child I remember a pompous doctor telling my mother I needed a month in Switzerland, where, he said, I would become strong simply by living like a cow: eating and sleeping well and inhaling that precious mountain air. Since we had raided the gas meter for the bus fare to his clinic and had a long, wet walk home, his prescription became something of a joke between my mother and me. But thirty years later I understood what he meant.

There are approximately 250 medicinal springs bubbling from Switzerland's earth. When selecting a spa here for its curative possibilities, you should check out the various properties contained in them. Also, climatic conditions and altitude must be taken into account.

The highest and probably most famous hot springs are at **St. Moritz**. At an altitude of 1,830 m (6,000 ft.), their baths are favoured by people with heart and circulatory disorders and by victims of accidents. The bonus for summer visitors is exquisite scenery, 110 km (68 mi.) of walking paths, a golf course, swimming and fishing opportunities and all that bracing alpine air.

Switzerland's most productive spring emerges from the **Tamina Gorge** on the country's eastern boundary. A thirteenth-century English duke discovered it. He told some neighbouring monks about it and together they established a spa that continued in operation for 600 years. In 1850 these waters were persuaded down the mountain to **Bad Ragaz**, where today there is a modern medical facility as well as public baths. Special diets are catered to in local hotels, and in town nice little patisseries beckon when the need to indulge is urgent. What with the afternoon tea dances and concerts, summer recitals in a wooded setting beside a pond, half-day excursions by bus — who could feel anything but one hundred percent in such a place?

Perched on a mountain top in the Alps, **Leukerbad** is a delightful little community with no fewer than 22 thermal springs containing the highest percentage of calcium and sulphur in the country. The town can accommodate more than a thousand visitors in private homes as well as in hotels, some of which have their own thermal baths and treatment rooms. There are public pools too. The hotels often cater to long-term spa patients. Some come to the dining room in housecoats and slippers, giving a hospital atmosphere not wholly upbeat for vacationers. In clear weather lifts take visitors to dizzying heights for spectacular views and alpine walks.

Gateway to the Bernese Oberland, prettily set between lakes Thum and Brienz **Interlaken** has no thermal springs, but is a climatic resort because of its sheltered location and moderate weather. Here visitors sip coffee at sidewalk cafes or in a casino while listening to a palm-court type orchestra. At Beau Rivage, a luxury hotel in grand old European style, every guest is treated like royalty. Its fitness centre offers facials and peeling, massages and keep-fit programs. Golf, tennis, sailing and horseback riding are available. Candlelight dinners, horse-drawn carriages, afternoon teas and an excursion up the mighty Jungfrau from the town's centre, all warm your heart and lift your spirits to heights where usually only birds soar.

GERMANY

This country's spas have been around since time began, or pretty soon after. In A.D. 70 Roman soldiers stopped off to soak in **Baden-Baden's** 26 thermal springs following a tortuous march across the Alps. By the early 1800s this had become the fashionable summer place of the continent's rich and royal. To accommodate them in style, grand hotels and spas, in addition to leisure and cultural facilities, were built in town. The Lichentaler Allee, a seventeenth-century avenue of oak trees beside the River Oos was developed into a park planted with exotic trees, flowering shrubs and rose gardens. The Kurhaus became the place for glittering functions. Gambling was introduced in a casino with decor so lavish it is distracting. A Pump Room enabled visitors to drink the mineral waters in high style while Friedrichsbad allowed them to soak away aches and pains in a public spa resembling a Roman palace. Now, hotels along the banks of the Oos come in all price ranges. Some have medicinal clinics attached. If you are in the market for a few nips and tucks, you can have plastic surgery before embarking on a beauty program; clinics have specialists in residence to treat the seriously ill.

Do no more than wander into town each day, listen to a concert, luxuriate in the Roman baths and have a massage or two, and you will be rejuvenated. Super little art galleries and antique shops make for fascinating browsing. Cafes tempt with tables and chairs on the sidewalk when it's warm. Day-trips into the Black Forest will have you home in time for tea.

CZECH REPUBLIC

As part of the **West Bohemian Spa Triangle** this country's spas were enormously popular with aristocrats of the nineteenth-century. They flocked to elegant towns like Karlovy Vary (which they knew as Carlsbad) and nearby Marianske Lazne (Marienbad) where facilities as luxurious as palaces were built for them.

One of the republic's loveliest cities, **Marianske Lazne** exudes an atmosphere of inborn gentility. Its 40 hot springs service spa hotels, sanatoriums and a public facility. A century ago, doctors advised their patients to soak in the water for 48 hours and drink 12 L (2.6 gal.) of water a day. Now "sip and stroll" is a pastime for many who believe in its curative powers. First they fill their cups (equipped with narrow spouts) at public drinking fountains in the handsome colonnade. From there they walk in the parks and on riverside paths, sipping and talking, listening to outdoor concerts and watching all the people. Diseases of the kidneys, urinary and respiratory tracts as well as nervous disorders are treated here.

Karlovy Vary has a dozen of its 100 hot springs channelled into health facilities, several hotels restored to original majesty and the modern Thermal Hotel complex. Accident victims, post-operative patients and those with digestive and arthritic ailments are sent by physicians to Karlovy Vary for a regime that includes drinking gallons of bitter-tasting water. This elegant town is a little over two hours by road from Prague, which makes it an ideal rest stop following a tour of the Czech capital.

HUNGARY

Some of Hungary's wonderful old spas raise the word *ornate* to exalted levels. **Budapest** is the only capital in the world with spa hotels and thermal springs (72 of them) spurting from the ground within city limits. Rheumatism, arthritis and circulatory problems are treated with the aid of the waters. Dental surgery is performed here too because the waters are said to help the gums heal.

Two spas I particularly like are on **Margaret Island**, smack in the middle of the Danube where it flows through the city. The entire island is a park, free of motorized vehicles (other than cars going to the two hotels). Transport is by horse-drawn carriages and bicycles, or better still your own two feet on paths that wind through flower gardens and open parklands. On this little island you can sit and watch the Danube traffic, listen to the birds, dine on patios and terraces or in sumptuous hotel restaurants, sleep like the drugged, and be totally unaware of city traffic and its attendant fumes just across the river in the city's core.

A change of plans brought me to Margaret Island unprepared for the spa experience. Once here, I couldn't resist it and so followed one of life's little embarrassing moments. The terry robe provided by the hotel was made for someone half my size, the flip-flop sandals so large I had to imitate a moon-walker to keep them on my feet. Waiting for an elevator I decided on a nonchalant approach and undid the restricting robe. It didn't work. The swimsuit borrowed from the pool mistress' limited supply drooped almost to my knees, and did nothing for my confidence when I emerged to what I thought would be the baths. It was in fact the hotel lobby where a group of Budapest's beautiful people were gathered for Sunday lunch! Next time, I wore my poacher's style raincoat and didn't put the plastic shower cap on 'til I sighted steam ahead. Still, I urge you to bring your own gear if you want to feel at home among the satin-robed and slippered regulars familiar with the spa scene in Hungary.

After three days you could become restless on Margaret Island unless you were truly immersed in spa treatments. No matter. Across the bridge is downtown Budapest with its riverside walk and museums, sidewalk cafes and patisseries, excellent shopping, theatres, casinos and opera houses. Packages to Eastern Europe's spas are very inexpensive. In winter you may pay approximately $80 a day for accommodation, treatments and two meals a day, or around $2,500 for three weeks including airfare from Toronto.

ISRAEL

Spas here are as varied as everything else in this country. I don't suppose anyone will ever ask what I have in common with King Solomon, Cleopatra and Lawrence of Arabia, but if they did I could say that like them I have succumbed to Israel's soothing mineral baths. Known to banish or reduce aches and pains since time began, the ancient waters are experiencing renewed popularity now through attractive facilities, modern technology and supervision by top medical personnel. Notables as far apart as Aristotle and King Herod were familiar with these hot springs. Roman armies bathed in them following battle. Now, 2,000 years later, battle casualties are sent for post-operative treatment to Israel's spas.

The largest aggregation of this country's spas is centred around two seas linked by the River Jordan: the **Dead Sea** and **Sea of Galilee**. Each of these regions is blessed with mineral-rich hot springs, a warm and sunny climate and first-rate accommodation. This makes them inviting to vacationers as well as the chronically ill.

Medical treatment will be administered only after the spa doctor has examined you and your health records from home. People with skin diseases, rheumatic and arthritic complaints, or post-operative and digestive problems are reputedly helped by treatment here. Documented results are so impressive that in many European countries the national health and insurance programs will cover patients' expenses. For the rest, there is clean air and constant sunshine in this Shangri-la where flowers bloom all year and roadside trees are heavy with fruit.

In the Dead Sea region there's a saying that you will be cured of your ills but die of boredom, which isn't quite true if you settle for total relaxation and a profound sense of well-being. Four hundred metres (1,300 ft.) below sea level, the Dead Sea is at the bottom of the world. In consequence atmospheric pressure and quality of oxygen are very high. There is no pollution, humidity is low and the annual rainfall is 5 cm (2 in.). The sun shines 350 days a year. Better still, the destructive ultra-violet rays cannot reach this low, so you aren't risking skin disease or sunburn by staying outside for hours on end.

The Dead Sea contains a staggering concentration of minerals. Its high magnesium content is said to be an effective cure of skin diseases, the bromide content supposedly relaxes nervous systems and the iodine content is believed to influence certain glands. Generally, bathing in the Dead Sea twice daily will do wonders for your disposition. Cleopatra relied on local mud for cosmetic purposes. In addition to rejuvenating properties it penetrates heat deeply into your body to reach aching muscles and joints. Several health centres on the Dead Sea's shores are suited to vacationers as well as the infirm.

The country's most popular kibbutz is **En Gedi**, with a health facility on the shores of the Dead Sea. At the southern end of the lake a five-star resort spa has everything, including private baths and resting rooms and eucalyptus sessions to clear sinuses. Another is **En Bokek**, less inviting for vacationers, but apparently valuable to psoriasis sufferers. Sightseeing in the area is easily arranged, with excursions to the fortress Masada, the Qumram Caves where the Dead Sea scrolls were found, and Jericho, the oldest continuously inhabited city in the world.

In the Galilee region you will hear how King Solomon, in need of a hot bath to ease his weary bones, sent a group of devils to the bottom of the earth to heat up the water. So many people came to use the baths and benefited from them, he was concerned that the heat might be turned off when he died. And so he caused the devils to be deaf. They have yet to hear of his death and continue to heat the water for us down below....

Tiberius on the lake's western shore is well below sea level. Hence its climate is sub-tropical and the atmospheric pressure is high. No less than 17 underground springs have been trapped by the Tiberius Hot Springs Company for use in their modern facility.

Beneficial in treatment of muscular and joint diseases, post-operative problems and disorders of the upper respiratory tract, most of the springs are so hot when leaving the ground they are cooled for use at the spa. Several big hotels are within walking distance of the health facility. The Galilee is great for water sports, whether you choose to swim, water ski, fish or watch the action from beaches and outdoor cafes. This is a holiday town with nightclubs and discos and souvenir shops. Also available are full and half-day tours of surrounding regions.

UNITED STATES

While America's spas of the 1980s leaned towards cosmetic and weight loss programs, now more are promoting "wellness" with emphasis on natural foods and exercise. Holistic health resorts are, like the European spas of old, established in beautiful settings. Often balance is restored to the body by alternative therapies and herbal preparations, homeopathy and similar treatments. Some guests are here strictly for the rest, long leisurely walks and good nutrition, complemented by energizing massages and aerobics. Others are serious about learning to cope with the stress, which for older guests often comes with retirement from a demanding profession or loss of a partner.

Pritikin Centers in California, Florida and Pennsylvania are among the most expensive of these. According to Pritikin philosophy, middle age can be extended to age 80. (You don't have to be a rocket scientist to figure out that a lot of their guests are 50 plus!) For a fee of roughly $6,000 for two weeks, you receive room and board plus programs designed to help you reach your ideal weight, reduce stress and hypertension and start on the road to a healthier lifestyle. I hear there are people who frequent these centres regularly and swear by them. Mind you, a $6,000 vacation in Hawaii will do wonders for stress and hypertension too.

Not all such spas are this expensive. Dispense with the pampering of the Golden Door in California and you can have a stint at Lake Geneva's Wooden Door for approximately one fifth of the top spa's fee. Most American spas offer exercise programs to match your ability, classes on nutrition and low-cal meal preparation, as well as sports and leisure activities. Florida has terrific spa resorts, just what you need for a week or two during your winter of doing-nothing-much in the Sunshine State. Arizona's spas are also very popular with Canadians because of this state's warm dry climate.

CANADA

Canada's retreats and spas are resorts rather than medical facilities. **Banff** is our most famous, for its hot mineral springs discovered by railroad workers hacking their way through the Rockies in the 1880s. To celebrate its centennial the original public pool fed by those hot springs was restored, and allows you to indulge in a glorious soak surrounded by snow-draped mountains.

Miette Hot Springs, 60 km (37 mi.) north of Jasper, feeds into another pool, less attractive but just as soothing as Banff's.

British Columbia has **Radium Hot Springs Resort** at the southern end of Kootenay National Park offering a superb respite from the rigors of touring, and **Harrison Hot Springs**, just 130 km (81 mi.) from Vancouver. Harrison is an appealing little community on the shores of Harrison Lake. It has a private spa facility in the Harrison Hot Springs Hotel, a public pool fed by the hot springs and lots of small hotels and motels. For excitement you can go looking for Sasquatch, the giant ape-like creature said to inhabit these hills.

Long before the arrival of Europeans, the Plains Indians were bringing their sick to the "Lake of the Healing Waters." Now known as **Little Manitou Lake**, this resort, 90 km (56 mi.) south-east of Saskatoon, Saskatchewan is well known for the healing qualities of its rich mineral waters. Most visitors to the lake stay at the fairly new Manitou Springs Mineral Spa, a complex where the program includes massage therapy and use of indoor and outdoor mineral pools.

In Ontario's scenic Georgian Bay region on the shores of Lake Manitouwabing, the **Inn at Manitou** is perhaps Canada's most luxurious small resort. Certainly it is Canada's only Relais et Chateaux member awarded a "gold." Originally a tennis camp, it has gradually added full resort facilities and earned a reputation for superb French and Canadian cuisine. Their spa menu is so tasty you won't believe it is also good for you. European mud is imported for spa treatments, which can include hydrotherapy baths, body wraps and similar procedures. Have no more than a shiatsu massage and you will become more energized than the little pink bunny on TV. Take a walk in the woods or a boat on the lake on an autumnal afternoon, and you will know there is a heaven.

For many a traveller these spas provide an oasis during a busy tour. I enjoy them so much I go out of my way to stay at one for a few days when travelling.

Information on spas is available from tourist authorities and from travel agencies. The travel and health sections of most large bookstores and libraries have books on spas and spa resorts.

$\mathcal{L}$earning Vacations

$\mathcal{L}$ast summer while having tea in an English garden with the owner of a country hotel, a van pulled up and six or seven travellers piled out, laughing over a joke, or perhaps excited by the lovely setting. In any event they were a little noisy. Frowning over the interruption, my host asked her sister who had come to meet them, "Who are these people, Grace. What are they up to?" Grace replied that it was her art group — Americans, here for five days. Returning her attention to me, the innkeeper commented that not one of them was under 65. "I don't know why it surprises me," she added, "they all seem to be on the move these days, the retirees, or pensioners as we call them. And as you can see, they are jolly keen to do things." In that couple of sentences she said it all. We are definitely on the move and yes, we are "jolly keen to do things."

Learning vacations have been around a long time, but they really took off when **Elderhostel** came into being two decades ago. A century before that two enterprising gentlemen in New York State started a program combining educational, religious, recreational and social activities. Their **Chautauqua Institution** is still going strong, and last year over 3,000 people participated in its courses of one day to nine weeks' duration.

If your interests lie mainly in the outdoors, you may want to look at another veteran institution: the **Sierra Club**. It celebrated its centennial in 1992 with over 350,000 members belonging to 57 chapters, including two in Canada. This club offers something like 300 excursions a year to the United States, Canada and Mexico, as well as some to countries further from home, for periods generally of one or two weeks. Programs feature nature walks and hikes, fishing trips, cycling, rafting, skiing, photography and environmental education.

Worldwide educational and cultural institutions organize tours led by experts in their fields. Similarly, some experts align themselves with hotels and resorts to create all-inclusive packages. Here instruction can be on topics as varied as garden design, photography, the basics of Mediterranean cooking, travel writing, regional theatre and history.

There is something quite exhilarating in studying for the sake of gaining knowledge, rather than to earn a school credit or enhance a career. On literary tours I have learned intimate details about my favourite authors. I once spent the best part of three days sloshing around Scottish islands in heavy rain on the trail of Bonny Prince Charlie. In search of knowledge, virtually as useless as yesterday's boarding card, I have followed the haunts of royalty and ghosts and toured the world below ground to see what makes Walt Disney's kingdom work. (Mickey Mouse with his "head" under his arm, having a quick drag on a cigarette is not a happy sight.) I learned all I could possibly want to know about Peking Duck at a cooking class in Hong Kong, and how to grow better roses in an Irish country inn. Actually gardening can be tricky, unless you attend classes where soil and climatic conditions are comparable to yours at home.

None of the information gained has made me more interesting or even enlightened in anyone else's eyes, but these were things I wanted to do at the time.

Recognizing that 50 plus travellers are keen to learn and free to travel in off-peak times, organizations and tour companies are constantly expanding these options for us. If all this is news to you, and you would like to seize the day, here are some ideas to steer you in the right direction.

ELDERHOSTEL

Elderhostel is the biggest success story in the world of affordable learning vacations for anyone 60 and over. An accompanying companion can be 50 plus. In 1975, during this organization's first year, it housed 200 members in five New Hampshire colleges. By the end of 1992, it was catering to an annual 300,000 who were lodged in 1,800 institutions and resorts in 60 countries. Utilizing campus accommodation during school vacations, hotels and resorts outside prime times, it has host countries as far apart as Greenland, Bermuda and Australia. Subjects studied are as diverse as local history and ecology, photography, Renaissance art, Nepalese culture, astronomy and bee-keeping. There are bird-watching expeditions, bicycle tours, white-water rafting excursions and African safaris, all with study periods to complement field trips.

Anyone of qualifying age is welcome, regardless of formal education. There are no membership fees, no examinations and no credits on completion of the course. Only the most intensive programs require homework.

To give you an idea of trip costs, an average week in North America is

$300 per person for accommodation, meals, tuition excursions and use of on-site recreational facilities. Overseas programs, usually for three weeks average $3,600 including airfare. More specifically, a recent catalogue shows an all-inclusive three-week program at three different universities in Scotland, Wales and England, departing New York City, for around $3,000. Similarly, three weeks at three different universities in Brazil, leaving from Los Angeles, is approximately $4,000, while two weeks at an environmental centre in Costa Rica, out of Miami, is roughly $2,000.

Elderhostel Canada was founded in 1986 and has grown rapidly through its infancy. In addition to a domestic calendar, it offers international programs in settings ranging from universities and field centres to homestays.

In spite of stated age limits, some popular inter-generational programs cater to accompanying grandchildren. Physically impaired members are offered schedules designed to match their abilities. And if you have a recreational vehicle, you can attend selected programs at American and Canadian university campuses, using your camper as accommodation.

INTERHOSTEL

An alternative to Elderhostel is Interhostel, open to anyone who's active and 50 plus. Established in 1980 it is operated by the University of New Hampshire and co-operating institutions overseas. Interhostel provides two-week programs as part of a co-operative arrangement between American and primarily European institutions. Accommodation is in residence halls or hotels. Lectures, seminars, field trips and excursions are led by professors and local experts, while host institutions arrange for social outings and entertainment. A typical two weeks with Interhostel costs around $1,200 plus airfare.

UNIVERSITY STUDIES

Isn't it funny how schoolwork becomes a pleasure when every course we sign up for is optional? If in your salad days you had dreams of attending a prestigious university but plans were thwarted by inadequate resources or academic standing, now you have a second chance, because some of our finest learning institutions have summer programs for students 50 and over.

I know a man in his sixties who is retired from the business world where he earned an enviable track record despite the fact he never finished high school. Last time I met him he boasted of studying fifteenth-century English history at **Oxford**. Well, he did, for two weeks a couple of summers ago. He was taught by an Oxford don, studied for five mornings during the first week, ate in the "halls" and even rented a bicycle to get him around town just like the younger students.

In class he wrestled with the argument that perhaps Henry Tudor and not the much-maligned Richard III had the two young princes murdered in London's Tower. For his second week he and his group went to Bosworth where Richard died in battle. Then they followed the route of Henry's march from the Welsh coast to London, and ended with two days of touring historic landmarks and attending evening theatre. With travel in a luxury motorcoach, most meals and accommodation at either the university or first-class hotels, this chap's fortnight cost him $6,000 plus airfare. Not cheap, even for fulfillment of a dream, but oh, how he loves talking about his "schooldays as a senior at Oxford."

Dispense with the organized tour and you pay far less. In the summer of 1994 a three weeks' session at Oxford's Exeter College cost £1,125 ($2,250) for accommodation, all meals and tuition. Non-residents paid £575 ($1,150) for three weeks, £970 ($1,940) for six weeks. The subject was Victorian and British Literature. Of particular appeal to graduate students these courses are open to adults of all ages with serious interest in study at a senior level, and you can be sure many applicants are in their 50 plus years. For brochures and application forms write to British Universities Summer Schools at Oxford University (address in Appendix A).

Other educational opportunities overseas include: studying Polynesian culture at a Hawaiian university, building a log house in British Columbia, flower arranging in Japan and stir-fry cooking in Hong Kong. The possibilities for learning vacations are endless.

LONG-TERM STUDIES

As snow creeps up my office window and the squirrels have disappeared to shelter from Arctic winds, I am thinking how very nice it would be to have a winter's lease. My choice is a cheery apartment in Spain or Mexico, preferably for three months. I would shop in the market, experiment in cooking local dishes and take excursions to historic and cultural sites, either on my own or with school friends. School friends? Yes, for three or four hours a day, five days a week, I would be learning Spanish. Not only is this possible, it has become a reality for many North Americans who choose to replace their treacherously cold winters at home with immersion in a new culture and language in a place where it is warm. Some prefer homestays, living with a neighbourhood family with whom they can converse in Spanish after school. They probably learn the language faster than I do in my self-catering flat, but there are also advantages to living independently in a foreign land.

Spain, Portugal, Italy, the Greek Islands and southern France are particularly favoured for long-term stays because their winter climate is temperate, yet visitor accommodation is priced at off-season rates. Restaurant prices reflect what locals are prepared to pay. The language spoken is what you are here to learn not English from hordes of visiting tourists.

Airlines and hoteliers work in tandem to package very affordable two- and three-month **winter stays** in **southern Europe** and **Mexico**, aimed directly of course at retirees. Your travel agent should be able to tell you of classes conducted in English by institutions such as the Alliance Française. Tourist offices also have descriptive brochures.

CULTURAL TOURS

Escorted tours sponsored by museums and art galleries are among the most expensive learning vacations, but they can also be the most rewarding. I once took a self-guided tour to the haunts of Charles Dickens. I wandered the Kentish countryside he so loved, tramped about the London he knew as man and boy, visited museums devoted to his work and pubs and restaurants featured in his novels. When I was through I felt I knew the author intimately. But later a three-hour ($10) guided walk through Dickens' London, escorted by a witty and highly entertaining literary student, showed me the value of an accompanying expert. Now if I decide to follow the steps of Mozart in Austria, Van Gogh in France or Dylan Thomas in Wales, I shall look for a tour led by an authority on the subject.

A NEW HOBBY OR SPORT

The gaining of any knowledge, however trivial or useless it may seem to be, is better than doing nothing because it keeps the old grey matter working. If you are not academically inclined, you may choose a vacation in which you can learn a new sport or hobby or perfect skills you already have.

In my work as a travel writer I have come across retirees learning to scuba dive in the clear waters of Bahamian and Caribbean islands. At a central Ontario tennis resort I was told that one week's concentrated instruction, followed by a week or two of practice, is enough to get any able-bodied adult to a proficient level. (Their tournament for 60 plus players held each autumn was won last year by a 70-year-old.) South Carolina's golf weeks are immensely popular with 50 plus golfers. Novice and veteran alike can enjoy the camaraderie, the tips and instruction from pros and evening classroom sessions.

This brings me back to our amateur artists arriving at that English country hotel last summer. While it has been sold now to become one family's holiday home, others with similar programs are listed with the British Tourist Authority in Toronto, and you'll see more advertised occasionally in the *Globe and Mail*.

To give two other examples of learning vacations: Mrs. Myrtle Allen of Ballymaloe House, Shangarry, Midleton, Co. Cork (20 km or 12 mi. west of Cork) Ireland, is well known for the **cooking lessons** she gives at her bed and breakfast establishment. **Country House Garden** weekends in Northampton are led by its head gardener, Joanne Miles. This weekend features instruction and practical workshops on traditional and modern gardening techniques, based mainly in the Victorian Glass Houses. Accommodation is at the Falcon Inn on Lord Northampton's estate. Just bring your gardening gloves; all other equipment is supplied. The Irish Tourist Board and British Tourist Board in Toronto can provide details on the above and other vacations where you can learn a little something extra.

Author, travel journalist and lecturer Helga Loverseed conducts **travel writing** and **photography workshops** across Canada, through either the Elderhostel Canada program or her own Visual and Verbal Workshops. Her students, she says, return time and again to different locales. Few expect to earn a living with their newfound skills, but they are keen to document their travels more interestingly for family and friends. They enjoy the company of fellow students, the good food and lodgings and the field trips into the countryside. And they have a sense of achievement when they're through. I wonder, can any traveller ask for more? A typical program of this type is a two-day travel writing and photography workshop in Niagara-on-the-Lake for $175 per person; the cost for accommodation and breakfast is $60 per day. **Visual and Verbal Workshops'** address is in Appendix B.

FURTHER READING

Not all learning travel opportunities are available through the organizations I have mentioned, or through travel agents. Therefore you may like to read:

- *The Canadian Guide to Learning Vacations Around the World* (Athabasca: Athabasca University, 1994)

- *Learning Vacations* by Gerson G. Eisenberg (Princeton: Peterson's Guides, 1989)

- *Travel and Learn* by Evelyn Kaye (Leona: Blue Penguin Publications, 1990)

*W*orking Vacations

*W*hen my 60-year-old friend Ida returned from a month's vacation in Israel with blistered hands, her son was aghast. Had he raised his head and seen the sparkle in her eyes his frown might have vanished. I saw the same glow in the face of a woman on television, who had volunteered to instruct prospective hotel staff in Jamaica. And I remember the *joie de vivre* of four elderly Americans we almost ran down on a remote Pacific island, where they were working as surveyors on a new road.

If your expertise is in a field that could improve living conditions overseas — teaching, farming, carpentry, medicine or small business management, to name a few — you can embark on a volunteer experience for two years or more and probably change your life forever. An alternative is the **short-term volunteer project**, for which you likely have to contribute to your room and board and pay your own airfare to overseas sites. Either way, you won't live in luxury, or feel joyful *all* the time. Veteran volunteers say there are times of defeat and despair and frustrations they never dreamed of, yet most agree they can't wait to get back to the field. In addition, they will tell you they gained far more than they gave.

It is difficult to quit working after 30 years or so on the job, which is why so many of us are busier now than ever before. And you know, you don't have to be a famous eye surgeon or a mining engineer — or even a member of their teams — to make a difference. True, it's less dramatic to watch over pre-schoolers in a playground or hospital ward, to dust off shards at a dig site or to plant baby trees, but these are all jobs for volunteers. So, if the months ahead are shaping up as a great big yawn, you might want to give volunteering a thought, either as an extension to your vacation or as a whole new dimension to your travels.

VACATION DIGS

In 1963 a small advertisement in a London newspaper requested volunteers for Israel to help excavate the site of King Herod's palace high above the Dead Sea. The result was overwhelming. They came from all walks of life and dozens of countries to join the dig. Some chose to spend their two-week vacation this way, but many were students and retirees who worked for months from a camp in that scorching desert. Physical discomfort was of no importance to them. They believed in what they were doing, which was to resurrect Masada, claimed by wind-swept winds almost 2,000 years before.

Some of the world's more important historic sites would be buried still if it weren't for volunteers. Some call for workers to be under 35 years and in top physical condition. Others have a minimum age limit of 16 or 18 but no upper limit.

A few years ago in Jerusalem I met former Chicago caterer Bernie Alpert whose passion for archaeology caused him to team up with noted archaeologist Schlomo Margaht. Margaht was desperate to search for the 2,000 years old Essene Gate on the southern slopes of Mount Zion, but lacked the required funding. Ideally he wanted volunteers who could stay two or three weeks and be trained for the work with infinite care. Instead he settled for vacationers who came to him for the day.

The **Dig for a Day** program proved useful for everyone concerned. Two thousand volunteers worked on the dig in its first year. According to Bernie this brief initiation can be the start of a lifelong addiction. "Something like playing bingo," he said. "One small win and you have to keep trying for a bigger prize." He has tourists who abandon travel plans so they can return a second, third then fourth day with his program. Others go home, read all the archaeology books in sight, and return a year later to work on one of Israel's numerous other digs.

A list of some 30 digs requiring volunteers is distributed by the Israel Government Tourist Office in Toronto. Cost of participation varies from one site to the next. If hotel or tent accommodation is provided, you may pay no more than a small registration fee. Bear in mind that it's gruelling to crouch in the dirt scratching away for hours beneath a fierce sun. But there are other things to do. Shards have to be carefully dusted and numbered and the workers have to be fed — whatever your assignment, everyone shares the elation when an important artifact is uncovered.

Israel is practically one great buried treasure site. **Egypt** is another, with ongoing digs in and around Luxor and across the Nile in the Valley of the Kings. **Britain** has volunteers unearthing Roman, Viking and Medieval communities. **Italy** and **France** also have digs. And across **North America** fascinating evidence of early settlements is being uncovered — all with the aid of volunteers.

The Archeological Institute of America publishes a list of fieldwork opportunities worldwide, currently available for $8. If you have a particular country in mind, you could also contact its tourist office.

BUILDING OLD AND NEW

Faster rewards for your labours are achieved when you assist in the rebuilding of historic communities in Europe or forts and trading posts in North America. It's also well worth working as a member of a **Habitat for Humanity group**. The most prominent members of the Habitat program are Jimmy and Rosalynn Carter. Their first involvement was to work as carpenters for a week on a tenement in New York's Lower East Side. The resultant publicity generated so many volunteers this organization built in excess of 2,000 houses in 1990, at some 400 locations around the world. If you can stay for months rather than weeks you can volunteer for their overseas projects. Working alongside families who, because of your help, will know the dignity of living in a proper home must be a real high.

The **Frontiers Foundation of Toronto** is a Canadian organization in which volunteers work in housing construction and recreation projects in northern Canada and in South America.

GIVING THE ENVIRONMENT A HAND

In northern British Columbia last summer we pulled off the highway to watch enormous salmon leaping upstream. On a rock nearby, a woman about my age sat writing on a clipboard. According to a chap who sold us some of his fish, she was one of several volunteers from Toronto there for a three-week working vacation. Just last week I heard of a group of environmentalists from England who spent their annual vacation repairing segments of Ontario's famed Bruce Trail.

For sure, in summer, ours is a beautiful country to be useful in. In winter, when warmer climes beckon, your help could be needed for two or three weeks in jungles, under water or in remote forest areas. Self-reliance is important. Nobody is going to hold your hand as you brave those jungle noises to answer nature's call. You should feel at home tenting in primitive terrain and be prepared to walk for miles to get to your work site each day.

Would-be environmental volunteers should contact tourism authorities or organizations such as the Canadian Parks and Wilderness Society, Sierra Club, The Cousteau Society and Earthwatch. See Appendix A for the addresses and telephone numbers.

LONGER STAYS

Long-term commitments of two years or more are mostly for volunteers with skills required in developing nations. Many a retiree has gained a new lease on life from renting out his expertise for minimal wages, accommodation and travel expenses. Some act as advisors and consultants.

Couples are welcomed in certain circumstances. Typically they will have years of practical experience in skilled trades, or in areas such as agriculture, fisheries, forestry, teaching, computer science, public health, business management and community development.

Don't be discouraged if you have to tick off "none of the above." Compassion and a little knowledge of the language are important assets, and there are all kinds of volunteer jobs out there. You may be suited to counting flowers or wildlife species or to accompanying mentally challenged adults on vacation. Become a camp cook. Help clean up a river or build a river bank. Fill in for a resident of a kibbutz who's off on military duty. Not what you're used to? Of course not. That's the fun of it. The advancement of human knowledge owes a lot to volunteers at every level.

FOR MORE INFORMATION

Tourist offices have brochures on volunteer projects in their countries. In addition, there are several volunteer organizations in Canada that have international networks:

- **CUSO**, with its head office in Ottawa and regional offices or local committees in many major Canadian cities;
- **Canadian Bureau of International Education**, which is part of an international work camp organization;
- **Canadian Executive Service Organization** (CESO), which looks for former executives to act as consultants;
- **Canadian Foundation for World Development**, which works within the existing social framework in developing countries rather than creating a whole new service.

FURTHER READING

For more information on international volunteering, read Bill McMillon's *Volunteer Vacations: A Directory of Short-Term Adventures That Will Benefit You and Others* (Chicago: Chicago Review Press, 1987).

$\mathcal{G}$randparent Specials

$\mathcal{I}$ look forward to a time when my grandchildren can handle *National Geographic* magazine without trying to eat it, and when we can go farther than the local mall without a diaper bag. I see it often — little girls in frilly dresses taken for Afternoon Tea in posh London hotels — being tucked in with Teddy on an overnight train — learning to fish from a friend's dock in Muskoka. (Who but a doting Grandpa would get up that early?)

My dream these days is to give each grandchild a very special trip, one for which we spend weeks of learning and planning together before savouring the event. In reality they may not want to accompany me beyond the nearest Toys R Us store. Only time will tell. But here and now it seems like a great opportunity, in this era of cash-strapped parents and stressed-out small fry. Many grandparents have told me the bonding during such a trip lasts a lifetime, and I like to believe them.

I figure we'll be ready in five or six years. Meantime my **Granny File** includes the following possibilities.

CLUB MED

For years Club Med villages conjured up an image of partying young singles, when in fact they reached out to all age groups. The secret is to know which property is right for you. Some are best suited for the swingers, some for couples and families with young children, and now at last some are focused on the 50 plus generation.

At certain times children under five can stay free of charge in the room of a parent or legal guardian. (One child per adult, land arrangements only.) Others make a bid for older children by having special programs for them. Some Club Med villages give members 60 and over $150 discounts on a one-week package.

Remembering the cost of hot dogs and ice-cream cones, uneaten restaurant meals ("we didn't think it would look like this") and $5 admission fees for alligator farms displaying tourist-weary creatures, I am all for an all-inclusive club when accompanied by children under ten.

More importantly, programs are planned specifically for us and our little friends. For example: a Club Med village in St. Lucia currently offers children 4 to 12 years old scuba diving in the pool, carriage and pony rides, a go-cart racetrack and kids-only circus school. For tots there are different shows and activities and a supervised wading pool.

A nice aspect of these clubs is that adults and children can do things with vacationers their own age as well as with each other. Flights, airport transfers, meals, use of recreational equipment, some sports instruction and organized activities are all included in the rent. Usually the only extras are souvenirs and bar drinks, and assuming junior isn't into the hard stuff yet he can probably pay for his own.

BRITISH HOLIDAY CAMPS

An enterprising Canadian named Billy Butlin became king of the all-inclusive family vacation in Britain when he created holiday camps there in the 1930s. As an alternative to seaside boarding houses, camp accommodation was somewhat spartan, but nobody minded because there was always something going on, for all ages, in all weather. In the immediate post-war period, these and other holiday camps flourished throughout Britain. To keep them filled four decades later, accommodation is in chalets with ensuite baths, and evening entertainment is a trifle more sophisticated. But it's the original concept of round-the-clock organized activities that brings loyal fans back year after year. In spring and fall lowered rates attract large numbers of 50 plus vacationers, many with their grandchildren.

Holiday camps, clubs or any other all-inclusive resorts are great for a gathering of the clans, where the grandchildren can join overseas relatives on vacation. If my family can get it together we shall be from three continents and number 25 to 30, which would be far too many to fit into any of our homes. And, anyway, who wants to be stuck washing all those dishes.

CRUISES

A very exciting prospect is the cruise. Again, everything is included in one price, except for land excursions which we can select carefully during our planning stage. A cruise affords independent school-age children the freedom to be with us, yet allows them to go off on their own without getting terribly lost. For a cruise that particularly caters to children, you might look into either of the following.

- A three-day cruise from Florida to the Bahamas aboard one of Premier Cruise Line's **Big Red Boats** is understandably popular, for its Disney characters and themed parties on board. Seven-day packages can include the cruise, a stay at Walt Disney World with accommodations and park admissions, car rentals and breakfast with Disney characters.

- Carnival Cruise Lines **Fun Ships** won Family Circle magazine's Best Cruise for Families award in 1991 and 1992. Their three to seven-day cruises are to the Bahamas, the Caribbean and the Mexican Riviera. The programs are for all ages, even for tots two to four years old who want to be creative with finger paints and puppets. Talent shows, swimming under the stars and deck parties keep older-young passengers happy. There is a pediatrician on board in case the pizza pig-outs and ice-cream eating contests have after-effects. Cabins are fitted to sleep five or six. Seventy thousand lucky youngsters vacationed on these Fun Ships last year, so Carnival must be doing something right.

SPECIALTY TOURS

A dozen or more companies in North America specialize in trips for grandparents travelling with their grandchildren. Your travel agent can steer you towards those with tours for destinations of interest to you and your young sprout. You might want to check prices at the outset. Some are quite expensive.

Saga International Holidays of Boston (see page 13) has grandparent-child tours, going into different regions of North America during school vacation periods. **Elderhostel** (see page 186) has what it calls inter-generational programs for grandparents and children.

Catering to the carriage trade is a company called **Grandtravel** of Chevy Chase, Maryland. I drool just reading their booklet (free on request). Each itinerary is created to appeal to both generations, with special attention given to natural attractions. Sensibly, children are put into different age groups, so you can't bring along a four-year-old sister on a tour suited to your eight to eleven-year-old.

A number of Grandtravel's tours are in the United States. Others are once-in-a-lifetime trips such as the two weeks in Italy, a Kenya Adventure safari, a tour of Australia's outback and an Alaska Wilderness Adventure. They sure beat my gran's treat of a double-decker bus ride along the seafront, followed by an ice cream and Punch and Judy show on the beach. Still, the intimacy of those outings has stayed with me to this day, which is why I am impatient to fill in some granny trips on my calendar.

DO IT YOURSELF TRAVEL

■ **A city experience**. For me, a long weekend in a city close to home will be a good starter to see how we get along. We will stay in a central hotel, plan our time in advance and with care. And hopefully graduate to London and Paris sometime later.

■ A **train ride** will be among my priorities for a long-distance trip in Canada. Preferably it will take us west to the Rockies then on to the coast. We will have our own private room for overnights on board, and stop off at fairy-tale resorts and maybe a farm or dude ranch along the way. A ferry boat will take us to Vancouver Island, and an airplane will bring us home. All in all, I reckon we will chalk this up as a winner.

■ **Motorhoming** is ideal with grandchildren if you are so inclined. Junior can bring his toys, even a pet or friend at no extra cost. Very young children love the cosiness of sharing such close quarters, particularly at night. Hopefully our national parks will still have enough wildlife to make it exciting: private campgrounds can provide commercial entertainment when nature begins to pall.

■ **Cycling.** This may be stretching it a bit, but if I can catch one of mine at the right age — meaning he or she is around 10 or 12 and I am still in reasonable shape — I would love such company on a bicycle tour. Nothing too demanding. The gentle terrain of Prince Edward Island, Denmark or Holland sounds about right, provided my young companion can follow a map.

■ **Tripping into the Past**. For an adventure into the past, Colonial Williamsburg is hard to beat. Accommodation can be an historic house. We will eat in nineteenth-century taverns and pursue the day-to-day lives of children who lived here when this was the capital of the Colony of Virginia.

■ **Walt Disney World** in Florida is a natural for grandparents. Selecting the right accommodation is important. We will try for something within "the World," preferably connected with the Magic Kingdom by monorail. Hotel rooms are huge, furnished to sleep four comfortably. Self-catering units provide even more space in townhouses and treehouses where peacocks come to visit on the deck.

For a camping experience, Walt Disney World has on-site trailers in Fort Wilderness. Furnished to sleep four to six and equipped for self-catering, each one has a picnic table and barbecue outside. Fort Wilderness has its own beach and a convenient water shuttle to the Magic Kingdom. Campsites are carved from a forest, giving no hint of crowds milling around the theme park just across the bay.

Tips

❏ Remember that in most cases two generations are company, **three's a crowd**. Family vacations can be terrific, but for special bonding leave the middle generation at home, along with the other children.

❏ Be sure to have a **letter of consent** from your grandchild's parents that permits you to take him or her out of the country and gives you the power of attorney to obtain emergency medical treatment (see also page 50).

❏ Keep an eye out for special promotions. As more travel organizations realize our growing numbers, you can safely bet your last dollar they will increase their **Grandparent Specials**.

❏ When driving long distances, get an **early start**. With pillows in the rear seat our children used to doze until 9 a.m., at which time we stopped for breakfast with three hours driving already behind us.

❏ Remember how much active children can eat? Be prepared to **stop often** or carry snacks and drinks in a cooler. When they tell you they're hot or thirsty they probably are, because little people overheat quickly. Use your air-conditioner.

❏ **Be flexible.** If Junior has made new friends or is having a particularly good time, consider staying a day or two longer even though you had planned to move on.

❏ Children are great mimics and they pick up foreign languages easily. Encourage them and explain cultures which differ from yours. It could be the start of something good.

❏ If you don't have a grandchild, substitute a great niece or nephew, or child of a close family friend.

Associations and Government Departments

AMERICAN ASSOCIATION OF DISTRICT OF COLUMBIA, RETIRED PERSONS (AARP) Head Office 601 E. Street N.W. Washington, District of Columbia, 20049, telephone 1-800-424-3410. Membership processing, 3200 E. Carson Street, Lakewood, California, 90712.

AMERICAN YOUTH HOSTEL ASSOCIATION 733–15th Street N.W., #840, Washington, District of Columbia, 20005, telephone (202) 783-6161.

ARCHAEOLOGICAL INSTITUTE OF AMERICA 675 Commonwealth Avenue, Boston, Massachusetts, 02215, telephone (617) 353-9361.

ARP OVER 50 Greencoat House, Francis Street, London SW1P 1DZ, England, telephone 071 828 0500.

BRITISH UNIVERSITIES SUMMER SCHOOLS Department of Continuing Education, University of Oxford, 1 Wellington Square, Oxford OX1 2JA, England.

CANADIAN ASSOCIATION OF RETIRED PERSONS (CARP) 27 Queen Street E., Suite 1304, Toronto, Ontario, M5C 2M6, telephone (416) 363-8748.

CANADIAN AUTOMOBILE ASSOCIATION 60 Commerce Valley Drive E., Thornhill, Ontario, L3T 7P9, telephone (905) 771-3120.

CANADIAN BUREAU OF INTERNATIONAL EDUCATION 85 Albert Street, Ottawa, Ontario, K1P 6A4, telephone (613) 237-4820.

CANADIAN EXECUTIVE SERVICE ORGANIZATION (CESO) 415 Yonge Street, Toronto, Ontario, M5B 2E7, telephone (416) 596-2376.

CANADIAN FOUNDATION FOR WORLD DEVELOPMENT (CFWD) 2441 Bayview Avenue, Willowdale, Ontario, M2L 1A5, telephone (416) 445-4740.

CANADIAN HOSTELLING ASSOCIATION 1600 James Naismith Drive, Suite 608, Gloucester, Ontario, K1B 5N4, telephone (613) 748-5638.

CANADIAN PARKS AND WILDERNESS SOCIETY 160 Bloor Street E., Suite 1335, Toronto, Ontario, M4W 1B9, telephone (416) 972-0868. Also chapters in Vancouver, Yukon, Calgary, Edmonton, Saskatoon, Winnipeg, Ottawa and Dartmouth.

CHAUTAUQUA INSTITUTION Chautauqua, New York, 14722, telephone 1-800-836-ARTS.

COUSTEAU SOCIETY 930 West 21st Street, Norfolk, Virginia, 23517, telephone (804) 627-1144.

CUSO 135 Rideau Street, Ottawa, Ontario, K1N 9K7, telephone (613) 563-1242. Also has regional offices and local committees in Victoria, Vancouver, Calgary, Edmonton, Regina, Saskatoon, Winnipeg, Guelph, Toronto, Kingston, Ottawa, Montreal, Fredericton and Halifax.

DEPARTMENT OF EXTERNAL AFFAIRS AND INTERNATIONAL TRADE 125 Sussex Drive, Ottawa, Ontario, K1A 0G2, telephone (613) 996-9134 (1-800-567-6868 for passport inquiries).

EARTHWATCH P.O. Box 127, Belmont, Massachusetts, 02178, telephone (617) 487-3030.

ELDERHOSTEL 75 Federal Street, Boston, Massachusetts, 02110–1941, telephone (617) 426-8056.

ELDERHOSTEL CANADA 308 Wellington Street, Kingston, Ontario, K7K 7A7, telephone (613) 530-2222.

FEDERATION OF ONTARIO NATURALISTS 355 Lesmill Road, Don Mills, Ontario, M3B 2W8, telephone (416) 444-8419.

FRONTIERS FOUNDATION 2615 Danforth Avenue, Toronto, Ontario, M4C 1L6, telephone (416) 690-3930.

GLOBETROTTERS CLUB BCM/Roving, London, WC1N 3XX, England.

GOOD SAM CLUB P.O. Box 6060, Camarillo, California, 93011, telephone (805) 389-0300.

HABITAT FOR HUMANITY 121 Habitat Street, Americus Georgia, 31709, telephone (912) 924-6935.

INTERHOSTEL University of New Hampshire, Division of Continuing Education, 6 Garrison Street, Durham New Hampshire, 03824, telephone (603) 862-1088.

INTERNATIONAL ASSOCIATION FOR MEDICAL ASSISTANCE (IAMAT) 40 Regal Road, Guelph, Ontario, N1K 1B5, telephone (519) 836-0102.

ONTARIO MARCH OF DIMES, THE 60 Overlea Boulevard, Toronto, Ontario, M4H 1B6, telephone (416) 425-0501.

OVER THE HILL GANG INTERNATIONAL, THE 3310 Cedar Heights Drive, Colorado Springs, Colorado, 80904, telephone (719) 685-4656.

SIERRA CLUB OF EASTERN CANADA Suite 303, 517 College Street, Toronto, Ontario, M6G 4A2, telephone (416) 960-9606.

SIERRA CLUB OF WESTERN CANADA 1525 Amelia Street, Victoria, British Columbia, V8W 2K1, telephone (604) 386-5255.

TRAVELIN' TALK P.O. Box 3534, Clarksville, Tennessee, 37034, telephone (615) 552-6670.

Travel Agencies, Tour Companies and Suppliers

ADVENTURES ABROAD Suite 202, 1037 West Broadway, Vancouver, British Columbia, V6H 1E3, telephone (604) 732-9922, 1-800-665-3998.

ADVENTURES IN TRAVEL 3630 Lawrence Avenue E., Suite 34, Scarborough, Ontario, M1G 1P6, telephone (416) 439-7326.

AMERICAN EXPRESS CANADA, INC. 101 McNabb Street, Markham, Ontario, L3R 4H8, telephone (905) 474-8000.

AMTRAK CUSTOMER RELATIONS, Washington Union Station, 60 Massachusetts Avenue, Washington D.C., 20001. Marketing Distribution, P.O. Box 7717, 1549 W. Glenlake Avenue, Itasca, Illinois, 60143–7717, telephone 1-800-USA-RAIL.

BC FERRIES 1112 Fort Street, Victoria, British Columbia, V8V 4V2, telephone (604) 386-3431 and (604) 669-1211.

BACK-ROADS TOURING CO. Leeland House, 8a Leeland Terrace, London W13 9HA, England, telephone 081 566 5312.

BLYTH & COMPANY 13 Hazelton Avenue, Toronto, Ontario, M5R 2E1, telephone 1-800-263-9147.

BRITRAIL TRAVEL INTERNATIONAL INC. P.O. Box 89510, 250 Eglinton Avenue E., Toronto, Ontario, M4P 3E1, telephone (416) 482-1777.

BULLDOG CLUB, THE 35 The Chase, London SW4 0NP, England, telephone 071 622 6935. In Canada: 6 Kittredge Court, Richmond Hill, Ontario, L4C 7X3, telephone (905) 737-2798.

CANADA CAMPERS INC. Suite 510, 1212, 31 Avenue N.E., Calgary, Alberta T2E 7S8, telephone (403) 250-3209. Branches in Vancouver, Whitehorse and Toronto.

CLASSIQUE TOURS (David Dean) 8 Underwood Road, Paisley, Renfrewshire PA3 1TD, Scotland, telephone 041 889 4050.

CLUB AVENTURE 1221 St. Hubert, Montreal, Quebec, H2L 3Y8, telephone (514) 286-9290. Also 115 Avenue Parent, Ottawa, Ontario, K1N 7B5, telephone (613) 236-5006 and 935 Chemin Ste-Foy, Quebec City, Quebec, G1S 2L3, telephone (418) 687-9043.

CLUB MED 2 Place Alexis Nihon, Suite 1800, Montreal, Quebec, H3Z 3C1, telephone (514) 937-1428. Also 162 Cumberland Street, Toronto, Ontario, M5R 1A8, telephone (416) 960-3279 and P.O. Box 1005, Station A, Vancouver, British Columbia, V6C 1A0, telephone (604) 687-8433.

CRUISE PEOPLE, THE 1252 Lawrence Avenue E., Don Mills, Ontario, M3A 1C3, telephone (416) 444-2410 or 1-800-268-6523. Also 106 Seymour Place, London W1H 5DG, England, telephone 071 723 2450.

ELDERTREKS 597 Markham Street, Toronto, Ontario, M6G 2L7, telephone (416) 588-9839.

EUROPE BOUND Catalogue orders and store 49 Front Street E., Toronto, Ontario, M5E 1B3, telephone (416) 601-9875, 1-800-363-3427. (Two other stores in Toronto and one in London.)

GO VACATIONS 129 Carlingview Drive, Rexdale, Ontario, M9W 5E7, telephone (416) 674-1880. Branches in Montreal, Winnipeg, Edmonton, Calgary and Vancouver.

GOLDEN AGE TRAVELLERS CLUB Pier 27, The Embarcadero, San Francisco, California, 94111, telephone 1-800-258-8880.

GOWAY TRAVEL Box 2331, Suite 2001, 2300 Yonge Street, Toronto, Ontario, M4P 1E4, telephone (416) 322-1034 and Suite 456, 409 Granville Street, Vancouver, British Columbia, V6C 1T2, telephone (604) 687-4004.

GRAND CIRCLE TRAVEL 347 Congress Street, Boston, Massachusetts, 02210, telephone (617) 350-7500.

GRANDTRAVEL The Ticket Counter, 6900 Wisconsin Avenue, Suite 706, Chevy Chase, Maryland, 20815, telephone 1-800-247-7651.

GREYHOUND BUS LINES P.O. Box 660-362, Dallas, Texas, 75266– 0362, telephone 1-800-752-4841.

GREYHOUND LINES OF CANADA 877 Greyhound Way S.W., Calgary, Alberta, T3C 3V8, telephone 1-800-661-8747.

GULLIVER'S TRAVEL BOOK SHOP 609 Bloor Street W., Toronto, Ontario, M6G 1K5, telephone (416) 537-7700.

HARI-WORLD TRAVEL 1 Financial Place, 1 Adelaide Street E., Toronto, Ontario, M5C 2V8, telephone (416) 366-2000.

HARRISON HOT SPRINGS HOTEL 100 Esplanade Avenue, Harrison Hot Springs, British Columbia, telephone (604) 796-2244.

Holiday House 110 Richmond Street, Toronto, Ontario, M5C 1P1,
   telephone (416) 367-5860, 900 W. Georgia Street, Suite 108, Vancouver,
   British Columbia, telephone (604) 687-0380.

Horizon Holidays 160 John Street, Toronto, Ontario, M5V 2X8, telephone
   (416) 585-9922 or 1-800-387-2977.

I'm Proud To Be Me Travel Inc. 75 The Donway S., Suite 910, Don
   Mills, Ontario, M3C 2E9, telephone (416) 447-7683.

Inn at Manitou McKeller Centre Road, McKeller, Ontario, P0G 1C0,
   telephone (705) 389-2171.

London Theatre Land, Ltd. 385 The West Mall, Suite 257, Etobicoke,
   Ontario, M9C 1E7, telephone (416) 695-8759.

Manitou Springs Mineral Spa P.O. Box 967, Watrous, Saskatchewan,
   S0K 4T0, telephone (306) 946-3949.

Marine Atlantic 100 Cameron Street, Moncton, New Brunswick,
   E1C 5Y6, telephone (506) 851-3600.

Mountain Equipment Co-Op Catalogue orders 1655 W. 3rd Avenue,
   Vancouver, British Columbia, V6J 1K1, telephone (604) 732-1537, 1-800-
   663-2667. (Stores in Vancouver, Calgary, Toronto and Ottawa.)

Ocean Search P.O. Box 129, North Head, Grand Manan Island, New
   Brunswick, E0G 2M0, telephone (506) 662-8144.

P. Lawson Travel Suite 1200, Centre Tower, 3300 Bloor Street W.,
   Toronto, Ontario, M8X 2Y2, telephone (416) 236-1921. Also includes
   Voyages Bel-Air Inc. and **Harvey's Travel Ltd.**

Quest Nature Tours 36 Finch Avenue W., North York, Ontario,
   M2N 2G9, telephone (416) 221-3000, 1-800-387-1483.

Questers Worldwide Nature Tours 257 Park Avenue S., New York,
   New York, 10010, telephone 1-800-468-8668.

Questers U.K. 1 St. Petersburgh Mews, London W24 JT, England, telephone
   071 221 7815.

Rail Europe 2087 Dundas Street E., Suite 105, Mississauga, Ontario,
   L4X 1M2, telephone 1-800-361-RAIL.

Riding Mountain Nature Tours Box 429, Erickson, Manitoba, R0J 0P0,
   telephone (204) 636-2968.

SAGA HOLIDAYS The Saga Building, Middelburg Square, Folkestone CT20 1A2, England, telephone 0800 300500.

SAGA INTERNATIONAL HOLIDAYS LTD. 222 Berkeley Street, Boston, Massachusetts, 02116–9489, telephone 1-800-343-0273.

SENIOR CITIZENS TOUR & TRAVEL 225 Eglinton Avenue W., Toronto, Ontario, M4R 1A9, telephone (416) 322-1500 or 1-800-268-3492. (Offices also in London, Ottawa, Hamilton.)

SMALL HOPE BAY LODGE P.O. Box N1131, Nassau, Bahamas, telephone (809) 368-2014 or 1-800-223-6961.

THOMAS COOK GROUP (CANADA) LTD. 110 Yonge Street, 14th Floor, Toronto, Ontario, M5C 2W1, telephone (416) 359-3700.

TILLEY ENDURABLES INC. 900 Don Mills Road, Don Mills, Ontario, M3C 1V8, telephone (416) 441-6141 or 1-800-387-0110. (Stores in Toronto, Montreal, Vancouver.)

TRAFALGAR TOURS 21 E. 26th Street, New York, New York, 10010, telephone (212) 689-8977.

TRAFALGAR TOURS 15 Grosvenor Place, London SW1X 7HH, England, telephone 071 235 7090. Tour operator: Trafalgar Travel, 9 Bressenden Place, London SW1E 5DD, England, telephone 071 828 8143.

TRAVEL HELPERS LTD. 156 Duncan Mill Road, Suite 5, Don Mills, Ontario, M3B 3N2, telephone (416) 443-0583.

TREK HOLIDAYS 8412 109 Street, Edmonton, Alberta, T6G 1E2, telephone (403) 439-0024 also 336 14th Street, Calgary, Alberta, T2N 1Z7, telephone (403) 283-6115 and 1965 W. 4th Avenue, Vancouver, British Columbia, V6J 1M8, telephone (604) 734-1066 and 25 Bellair Street, Toronto, Ontario, M5R 3L3, telephone (416) 922-7584.

ULYSSES TRAVEL BOOKSHOP 4176 Saint-Denis, Montreal, Quebec, telephone (514) 843-9447 and 101 Yorkville Avenue, Toronto, Ontario, telephone (416) 323-3609.

UPTOWN RESERVATIONS 50 Christchurch Street, Chelsea, London SW3 4AR England, telephone 071 351 3445.

VIA RAIL Customer Service Department, 2 Place Ville Marie, Montreal, Quebec, H3C 3N3, telephone 1-800-561-3952 in the Maritime provinces, 1-800-561-3926 in Newfoundland, 1-800-361-5390 in Quebec, 1-800-361-1235 in Ontario and 1-800-561-8630 in the prairie and western provinces and the Territories.

Visual & Verbal Workshops (Helga Loverseed), 3086 Don Mills Road, Suite 8, Willowdale, Ontario, M2J 3C3, telephone (416) 493-8967 and 2123 rue des Aulnes, RR 2, Magog, Quebec, J1X 3W3, telephone (819) 868-1833.

Voyageur Colonial Bus Lines 265 Catherine Street, Ottawa, Ontario, K1R 7S5, telephone (613) 238-5900.

Wagontrain Tours 520 Hartford Turnpike, Vernon, Connecticut, 06066, telephone 1-800-875-7978.

Way to Go 118 Cumberland Street, Toronto, Ontario, M5R 1A6, telephone (416) 928-9166, 1-800-668-1929.

Wings of the World Inc. 653 Mt. Pleasant Road, Toronto, Ontario, M4S 2N2, telephone (416) 482-1223.

Wolsey Lodges 17 Chapel Street, Bildeston, Ipswich, Suffolk IP7 7EP, telephone 0449 741297.

World Expeditions 2050 St. Denis, Montreal, Quebec, H2X 3K7, telephone (514) 844-6364 and 78 George Street, Suite 4, Ottawa, Ontario, K1N 5W1, telephone (613) 230-8676.

Tourist Information Sources

NOTE: *It will save time to use a postcard when writing for tourism information.*

CANADA

CANADA Tourism Canada, 880 Place Victoria, Suite 3800, P.O. Box 247, Montreal, Quebec, H4Z 1E8, telephone (514) 283-8823.

ALBERTA Travel Alberta, 10155 102nd Street, Edmonton, Alberta, T5J 4L6, telephone (403) 427-4321 or 1-800-661-8888.

BRITISH COLUMBIA Tourism British Columbia, 1117 Wharf Street, Victoria, British Columbia, V8W 2Z2, telephone (604) 685-0032 or 1-800-663-6000.

MANITOBA Travel Manitoba, 155 Carlton Street, Winnipeg, Manitoba, R3C 3H8, telephone (204) 945-3777 or 1-800-665-0040.

NEW BRUNSWICK Tourism New Brunswick, P.O. Box 6000, Fredericton, New Brunswick, E3B 5H1, telephone (506) 453-3984 or 1-800-561-0123.

NEWFOUNDLAND AND LABRADOR Department of Tourism and Culture, P.O. Box 8730, St. John's, Newfoundland, A1B 4K2, telephone (709) 729-2830 or 1-800-563-6353.

NORTHWEST TERRITORIES Northwest Territories Tourism, P.O. Box 1320, Yellowknife, Northwest Territories, X1A 2L9, telephone (403) 873-7200 or 1-800-661-0788.

NOVA SCOTIA Nova Scotia Tourism, Suite 515, 1800 Argyle Street, Halifax, Nova Scotia, B3J 3N8, telephone (902) 425-5781 or in Canada 1-800-565-0000, from U.S. 1-800-341-6096.

ONTARIO Ontario Travel, Queen's Park, Toronto, Ontario, M7A 2R9, telephone (416) 314-0944 or 1-800-ONTARIO.

PRINCE EDWARD ISLAND Visitor Services, P.O. Box 940, Charlottetown, Prince Edward Island, C1A 7M5, telephone (902) 368-4444 or 1-800-565-0267.

QUEBEC Tourisme Quebec, P.O. Box 20,000, Quebec City, Quebec. G1K 7X2, telephone (514) 873-2015 or 1-800-363-7777.

SASKATCHEWAN Tourism Saskatchewan, 1919 Saskatchewan Drive, Regina, Saskatchewan, S4P 3V7, Telephone (306) 787-2300 or 1-800-667-7191.

YUKON Tourism Yukon, P.O. Box 2703, Whitehorse, Yukon, Y1A 2C6, telephone (403) 667-5340.

UNITED STATES

(Toll-free numbers may not apply in every calling area).

UNITED STATES Travel and Tourism Administration 480 University Avenue, Suite 602, Toronto, Ontario, M5G 1V2, telephone (416) 595-5082, and P.O. Box 5000, Station "B", Montreal, Quebec, H3B 4B5, telephone (514) 861-5036. Also 1-900-451-4050 (charge: $2 per minute).

ALABAMA Bureau of Tourism and Travel, P.O. Box 4309, Montgomery, Alabama, 36103, telephone (205) 242-4169 or 1-800-252-2262.

ALASKA Division of Tourism, P.O. Box 110801, Juneau, Alaska, 99811, telephone (907) 465-2010.

ARIZONA Office of Tourism, 1100 W. Washington Street, Phoenix, Arizona, 85007, telephone (602) 542-8687 or 1-800-842-8257.

ARKANSAS Tourism Office, 1 Capitol Mall, Little Rock, Arkansas, 72201, telephone (501) 682-7777 or 1-800-628-8725.

CALIFORNIA Office of Tourism, Box 1499, Sacramento, California, 95812, telephone 1-800-862-2543.

COLORADO Tourism Board, 1625 Broadway, Suite 1700, Denver, Colorado, 80202, telephone 1-800-433-2656.

CONNECTICUT Department of Economic Development, 865 Brook Street, Rocky Hill, Connecticut, 06067, telephone (203) 258-4355 or 1-800-282-6863.

DELAWARE Tourism Office, 99 Kings Highway, P.O. Box 1401, Dover, Delaware, 19903, telephone (302) 739-4271 or 1-800-441-8846.

DISTRICT OF COLUMBIA Convention and Visitors Association, 1212 New York Avenue N.W., Washington, D.C. 20005, telephone (202) 789-7000.

FLORIDA Division of Tourism, 126 W. Van Duren Street, Tallahassee, Florida, 32399-2000, telephone (904) 487-1462, and 121 Bloor Street E., Suite 1003, Toronto, Ontario, M4W 3M5, telephone (416) 928-3139 or 1-800-268-3791.

GEORGIA Department of Industry and Trade, 233 Peachtree Street, P.O. Box 1776, Atlanta, Georgia, 30301, telephone (404) 656-3590 or 1-800-847-4842.

HAWAII Department of Tourism, 2270 Kalakaua Avenue, Suite 801, Honolulu, Hawaii, 96815, telephone (808) 923-1811 or 1-800-257-2999.

IDAHO Department of Commerce, 700 W. State Street, Boise, Idaho, 83720, telephone (208) 334-2470 or 1-800-635-7820.

ILLINOIS Bureau of Tourism, 100 W. Randolph, Suite 3-400, Chicago, Illinois, 60601, telephone (312) 814-4732 or 1-800-223-0121.

INDIANA Division of Tourism, 1 North Capitol, Suite 700, Indianapolis, Indiana, 46204-2288, telephone (317) 232-8860 or 1-800-782-3775.

IOWA Department of Tourism, 200 E. Grand, Des Moines, Iowa, 50309, telephone (515) 242-4705 or 1-800-345-4692.

KANSAS Travel and Tourism Division, 400 S.W. 8th Street, 5th Floor, Topeka, Kansas, 66603-3450, telephone (913) 296-2009 or 1-800-296-2009.

KENTUCKY Department of Travel Develoment, 2200 Capital Plaza Tower, Frankfort, Kentucky, 40601, telephone (502) 564-4930 or 1-800-225-8747.

LOUISIANA Office of Tourism, 1051 Riverside Street N., P.O. Box 94291, L.O.T. Baton Rouge, Louisiana, 70804-9291, telephone (504) 342-8119 or 1-800-334-8626.

MAINE Office of Tourism, 189 State House Station 59, Augusta, Maine, 04333, telephone (207) 287-5711.

MARYLAND Office of Tourism Development, 219 E. Redwood Street, Baltimore, Maryland, 21202, telephone (410) 333-6611 or 1-800-543-1036.

MASSACHUSETTS Office of Travel and Tourism, 100 Cambridge Street, 13th Floor, Boston, Massachusetts, 02202, telephone (617) 727-3201 or 1-800-447-6277.

MICHIGAN Travel Bureau, P.O. Box 3393, Livonia, Michigan, 48151-3393, telephone (517) 373-0670 or 1-800-543-2937.

MINNESOTA Office of Tourism, 375 Jackson Street, 250 Skyway Level, St. Paul, Minnesota, 55101, telephone (612) 296-5029, 1-800-657-3700.

MISSISSIPPI Department of Tourism, 1201 Walter Sillers Building, P.O. Box 849, Jackson, Mississippi, 39205, telephone (601) 359-3259.

MISSOURI Division of Tourism, Truman State Office Building, P.O. Box 1055, Jefferson City, Missouri, 65102, telephone (314) 751-4133 or 1-800-877-1234.

MONTANA Travel Montana, 1424 9th Avenue, Helena, Montana, 59620, telephone 1-800-541-1447.

NEBRASKA Division of Travel and Tourism, 301 Centennial Mall S., Room 88937, Lincoln, Nebraska, 68509-4666, telephone (402) 471-3796 or 1-800-228-4307.

NEVADA Commission on Tourism, Capitol Complex, Carson City, Nevada, 89710, telephone (702) 687-4322 or 1-800-237-0774.

NEW HAMPSHIRE Office of Travel and Tourist Development, P.O. Box 1856, Concord, New Hampshire, 03302-1856, telephone (603) 271-2665.

NEW JERSEY Division of Travel and Tourism, 20 W. State Street, C.N. 826, Trenton, New Jersey, 08625-0826, telephone (609) 292-2470 or 1-800-537-7397.

NEW MEXICO Tourism and Travel Division, Joseph Montoya Building, 110 St. Francis Drive, Santa Fe, New Mexico, 87503, telephone 1-800-545-2040.

NEW YORK State of New York Division of Tourism, 1 Commerce Plaza Complex, 1515 Broadway, New York, 10036, telephone 1-800-456-8369.

NORTH CAROLINA Division of Travel and Tourism, 430 N. Salisbury Street, Raleigh, North Carolina, 27611, telephone (919) 733-4171 or 1-800-847-4862.

NORTH DAKOTA Parks and Tourism Department, Capital Grounds, Bismark, North Dakota, 58505, telephone (701) 224-2525 or 1-800-437-2077.

OHIO Division of Travel and Tourism, 30 E. Broad Street, P.O. Box 1001, Columbus, Ohio, 43266-0101, telephone (614) 466-8844 or 1-800-282-5393.

OKLAHOMA Tourism and Recreation Department, 500 Will Rogers Building, Oklahoma City, Oklahoma, 73105-4492, telephone (405) 521-3981 or 1-800-652-6552.

OREGON Tourism Division, 775 Summer Street N.E., Salem, Oregon, 97310, telephone (503) 373-1270 or 1-800-547-7842.

PENNSYLVANIA Bureau of Travel Marketing, 453 Forum Building, Harrisburg, Pennsylvania, 17120, telephone 1-800-VISIT-PA.

PUERTO RICO Puerto Rico Tourism Company, 2 Bloor Street W., Suite 700, Toronto, Ontario, M4W 2R1, telephone (416) 969-9025.

RHODE ISLAND Tourism Division, 7 Jackson Walkway, Providence, Rhode Island, 02903, telephone (401) 277-2601 or 1-800-556-2484.

SOUTH CAROLINA Division of Tourism, Edgar A. Brown Building 1205 Pendleton Street, Suite 106, Columbia, South Carolina, 29201, telephone (803) 734-0122 or 1-800-346-3634.

SOUTH DAKOTA Department of Tourism, Capital Lake Plaza, 711 Wells Avenue, Pierre, South Dakota, 57501, telephone (605) 773-3301 or 1-800-843-1930.

TENNESSEE Department of Tourism Development, 320 6th Avenue N., 5th Floor, P.O. Box 23170 Nashville, Tennessee, 37243, telephone (615) 741-2158.

TEXAS Department of Commerce, Tourism Division, P.O. Box 12728, Austin, Texas, 78711, telephone (512) 462-9191 or 1-800-888-8839.

U.S. VIRGIN ISLANDS USVI Division of Tourism, 33 Niagara Street, Toronto, Ontario, M5V 1C2, telephone 1-800-465-8784.

UTAH Travel Council, Council Hall, Capitol Hill, Salt Lake City, Utah, 84114, telephone (801) 538-1030.

VERMONT Travel Division, 134 State Street, Montpelier, Vermont, 05602, telephone (802) 828-3236.

VIRGINIA Division of Tourism, 1021 E. Cary Street, Richmond, Virginia, 23219, telephone (804) 786-4484 or 1-800-527-6517.

WASHINGTON State Tourism and Development Division, 101 General Administration Building AX-13, Olympia, Washington, 98504-0613, telephone (206) 586-2088 or 1-800-544-1800.

WEST VIRGINIA Division of Tourism and Parks, 2101 Washington Street E., Charleston, West Virginia, 25305, telephone (304) 345-2286 or 1-800-225-5982.

WISCONSIN Division of Tourism Development, 123 W. Washington Avenue, P.O. Box 7606, Madison, Wisconsin, 53707, telephone (608) 266-2161 or 1-800-432-8747.

WYOMING Division of Tourism, Frank Norris Jr. Travel Centre Cheyenne, Wyoming, 82002, telephone (307) 777-7777 or 1-800-225-5996.

FOREIGN TOURISM OFFICES

ANTIGUA Antigua Department of Tourism & Trade, 60 St. Clair Avenue E., Suite 304, Toronto, Ontario, M4T 1N5, telephone (416) 961-3085.

ARGENTINA Embassy of the Argentine Republic, Suite 620, 90 Sparks Street, Ottawa, Ontario, K1P 5B4, telephone (613) 236-2351.

ARUBA Aruba Tourism Authority, 86 Bloor Street W., Toronto, Ontario, M5S 1M5, telephone (416) 975-1950 or 1-800-268-3042.

AUSTRIA Austrian National Tourist Office, 2 Bloor Street E., Suite 3330, Toronto, Ontario, M4W 1A8, telephone (416) 967-3381 and 1010 Sherbrooke Street W., Suite 1410, Montreal, Quebec, H3A 2R7, telephone (514) 849-3709.

AUSTRALIA Australian Tourist Commission, 489 5th Avenue, New York, New York, 10017, telephone 1-800-677-5213.

BAHAMAS Bahamas Tourist Office, 121 Bloor Street E., Suite 1101, Toronto, Ontario, M4W 3M5, telephone (416) 968-2999.

BARBADOS Barbados Tourism Authority, 5160 Yonge Street, Suite 1800, North York, Ontario, M2N 6L9, telephone (416) 512-6569 or 1-800-268-9122; and 615 Rene Levesque Boulevard W., Suite 960, Montreal, Quebec, H3B 1P5, telephone (514) 861-0085.

BELIZE Belize Tourist Board, 15 Penn Plaza, 415 7th Avenue, New York, New York, 10001, telephone 1-800-624-0686.

BERMUDA Bermuda Department of Tourism, 1200 Bay Street, Suite 1004, Toronto, Ontario, M5R 2A5, telephone (416) 923-9600 or 1-800-387-1304.

BONAIRE Bonaire Tourist Information Office, 512 Duplex Avenue, Toronto, Ontario, M4R 2E3, telephone (416) 485-8724.

CAYMAN ISLANDS Cayman Islands Department of Tourism, 234 Eglinton Avenue E., Suite 306, Toronto, Ontario, M4P 1K5, telephone (416) 485-1550.

CHINA China Travel Service (Canada) Inc., 438 University Avenue, Suite 306, Toronto, Ontario, M5G 2K8, telephone 1-800-387-6622.

COSTA RICA Costa Rica Tourist Board, P.O. Box 777-1000, San Jose, Costa Rica, telephone 1-800-327-7033.

CUBA Cuba Tourist Board, 55 Queen Street E., Suite 705, Toronto, Ontario, M5C 1R5, telephone (416) 362-0700 and 440 Rene Levesque Boulevard W., Suite 1402, Montreal, Quebec, H2Z 1V7, telephone (514) 875-8004.

CZECH REPUBLIC Embassy of the Czech Republic, 50 Rideau Terrace, Ottawa, Ontario, K1M 2A1, telephone (613) 749-0033.

DENMARK Danish Tourist Board, P.O. Box 636, Mississauga, Ontario, L5M 2C2, telephone (519) 576-6213 or (905) 820-8984.

DOMINICAN REPUBLIC Dominican Republic Tourist Office, 2080 Crescent, Montreal, Quebec, H3G 2B8, telephone 1-800-563-1611.

ECUADOR Ecuador Tourism Information Office, AET Building, 7270, N.W. 12th Street, Miami, Florida, 33126, telephone (305) 593-9955.

EGYPT Egyptian Tourist Authority, 1253 McGill College Avenue, Suite 250, Montreal, Quebec, H3B 2Y5, telephone (514) 861-4420.

FIJI Fiji Visitors Bureau, 1275 W. 6th Avenue, Vancouver, British Columbia, V6H 1A6, telephone (604) 731-3454.

FINLAND Finnish Tourist Board, P.O. Box 246, Station "Q", Toronto, Ontario, M4T 2M1, telephone 1-800-346-4636.

FRANCE 1981 McGill College Avenue, Suite 490, Montreal, Quebec, H3A 2W9, telephone (514) 288-4264 and 30 St. Patrick Street, Suite 700, Toronto, Ontario, M5T 3A3, telephone (416) 593-4723.

GERMANY German National Tourist Office, 175 Bloor Street E., North Tower, Suite 604, Toronto, Ontario, M4W 3R8, telephone (416) 968-1570.

GREAT BRITAIN British Tourist Authority, 111 Avenue Road, Suite 450, Toronto, Ontario, M5R 3J8, telephone (416) 925-6326.

GREECE Greek National Tourist Organization, 1300 Bay Street, Main Level, Toronto, Ontario, M5R 3K8, telephone (416) 968-2220 and 1233 de la Montagne, Montreal, Quebec, H3G 1Z2, telephone (514) 871-1535.

GRENADA Grenada Board of Tourism, 439 University Avenue, Suite 820, Toronto, Ontario, M5G 1Y8, telephone (416) 595-1339.

HONG KONG Hong Kong Tourist Association, 347 Bay Street, Suite 909, Toronto, Ontario, M5H 2R7, telephone (416) 366-2389.

HUNGARY Malev Hungarian Airlines, 175 Bloor Street E., Suite 712, Toronto, Ontario, M4W 3R8, telephone (416) 944-0093.

INDIA India Government Tourist Office, 60 Bloor Street W., Suite 1003, Toronto, Ontario, M4W 3B8, telephone (416) 962-3787.

INDONESIA Embassy of the Republic of Indonesia, 287 LacLaren Avenue, Ottawa, Ontario, K2P 0L9, telephone (613) 236-7403.

IRELAND Irish Tourist Board, 160 Bloor Street E., Suite 1150, Toronto, Ontario, M4W 1B9, telephone (416) 929-2777.

ISRAEL Israel Government Tourist Office, 180 Bloor Street W., Suite 700, Toronto, Ontario, M5S 2V6, telephone (416) 964-3784.

ITALY Italian Government Tourist Office, 1 Place Ville Marie, Suite 1914, Montreal, Quebec, H3B 3M9, telephone (514) 866-7667.

JAMAICA Jamaica Tourist Board, 1 Eglinton Avenue E., Suite 616, Toronto, Ontario, M4P 3A1, telephone (416) 482-7850.

JAPAN Japan National Tourist Organization, 165 University Avenue, Toronto, Ontario, M5H 3B8, telephone (416) 366-7140.

KENYA Kenya Tourist Office, 424 Madison Avenue, New York, New York, 10017, telephone (212) 486-1300.

KOREA Korea National Tourism Corporation, 480 University Avenue, Suite 406, Toronto, Ontario, M5G 1V2, telephone (416) 348-9056.

MACAU Macau Tourist Information Bureau, 13 Mountalan Avenue, Toronto, Ontario, M4J 1H3, telephone (416) 466-6552.

MARTINIQUE Martinique Tourist Board, 1981 McGill College Avenue, Suite 480, Montreal, Quebec, H3A 2W9, telephone 1-800-361-9099.

MEXICO Mexican Government Tourist Office, 2 Bloor Street W., Suite 1801, Toronto, Ontario, M4W 3E2, telephone (416) 925-0704 and 1 Place Ville Marie, Suite 1526, Montreal, Quebec, H3B 2B5, telephone (514) 871-1052.

MOROCCO Moroccan National Tourist Office, 2001 University Avenue, Suite 1460, Montreal, Quebec, H3A 2A6, telephone (514) 842-8111.

NETHERLANDS Netherlands Board of Tourism, 25 Adelaide Street E., Suite 710, Toronto, Ontario, M5C 1Y2, telephone (416) 363-1577.

NEW ZEALAND New Zealand Tourism Board, 888 Dunsmuir Street, Suite 1200, Vancouver, British Columbia, V6C 3K4, telephone (604) 684-2117 or 1-800-888-5494.

NORTHERN IRELAND Northern Ireland Tourist Board, 111 Avenue Road, Suite 450, Toronto, Ontario, M5R 3J8, telephone (416) 925-6368.

Peru Embassy of the Republic of Peru, 130 Albert Street, Suite 1901, Ottawa, Ontario, K1P 5G4, telephone (613) 238-1777.

Portugal Portugese Tourist Office, 60 Bloor Street W., Suite 1005, Toronto, Ontario, M4W 3B8, telephone (416) 921-7376.

Russia Russian Intourist Information Office, 1801 McGill College Avenue, Suite 630, Montreal, Quebec, H3A 2N4, telephone (514) 849-6394.

St. Kitts & Nevis St. Kitts & Nevis Tourist Office, 11 Yorkville Avenue, Suite 508, Toronto, Ontario, M4W 1L3, telephone (416) 921-7717.

St. Lucia St. Lucia Tourist Board, 4975 Dundas Street W., Suite 457, Etobicoke "D", Islington, Ontario, M9A 4X4, telephone 1-800-456-3984.

St. Vincent & Grenadines St. Vincent & Grenadines Tourism Office, 32 Park Road, Toronto, Ontario, M4W 2N4, telephone (416) 924-5796.

Singapore Singapore Tourist Promotion Board, 121 King Street W., Suite 1000, Toronto, Ontario, M5H 3T9, telephone (416) 363-8898.

South Africa South African Tourism Board, 4117 Lawrence Avenue, Suite 2, Scarborough, Ontario, M1E 2S2, telephone (416) 283-0563.

Spain Spanish Tourist Office, 102 Bloor Street W., Suite 1400, Toronto, Ontario, M5S 1M8, telephone (416) 961-3131.

Switzerland Swiss National Tourist Office, 154 University Avenue, Suite 610, Toronto, Ontario, M5H 3Y9, telephone (416) 971-9734.

Taiwan Tourism Bureau Taiwan R.O.C., 222 Spadina Avenue, Suite 820, Toronto, Ontario, M5T 3A2, telephone (416) 971-6912.

Thailand Tourism Authority of Thailand, 250 St. Clair Avenue W., Suite 306, Toronto, Ontario, M4V 1R6, telephone (416) 925-9329.

Hotel/Motel Chains Offering Discounts

Following is a listing of major Canadian and American hotel, motel and resort chains that offer incentives to older travellers. Discounts may not apply at all locations. Some internatonal chains offer discounts worldwide.

Symbols indicate discounts available to association members: (A) = AARP and (C) = CARP. Where no symbol is shown, discounts are available to people showing proof of age, over 50 in some cases, 60 or 62 in others. Approximate cost of accommodation before taxes or discount is indicated by $ = less than $70 per night for two, $$ = $70 – $100, $$$ over $100. Toll-free numbers usually apply continent-wide.

- Best Western (some) (C eastern Canada) $$ 1-800-528-1234
- Bristol Group (C) $$ 1-800-268-4927
- Budgetel $ 1-800-428-3438
- Canadian Pacific Hotels & Resorts (A) $$$ 1-800-441-1414
- Chimo (C) $ 1-800-387-9779
- Choice Hotels (A) (C) $ – $$ U.S. 1-800-424-6423, Can. 1-800-221-2222 (worldwide group including: Calinda, Clarion, Comfort, Courtyard, Econo Lodges, Friendship, Quality, Rodeway and associated also with Journey's End)
- Colony (A) $ 1-800-777-1700
- Days Inns (A) $ 1-800-325-2525
- Doubletree (some) $$–$$$ 1-800-441-1414
- Drury Inns $ 1-800-325-8300
- Economy Inns $ 1-800-826-0778
- Fairfield (A) $ 1-800-228-2800
- Forte, Travelodge, Viscount (A) (C) $–$$ 1-800-255-3050
- Hilton (by membership) $$–$$$ 1-800-HILTONS
- Holiday Inns (A) $$ 1-800-HOLIDAY
- Howard Johnson (C) $$ 1-800-634-3464
- Hyatt (some) $$$ 1-800-228-9000

- Journey's End (C) $ 1-800-668-4200 (Associated also with Choice)
- La Quinta $ 1-800-531-5900
- Marriott (A) (C) $$ 1-800-228-9290
- Master Hosts (A) $ 1-800-251-1962
- Novotel $$$ 1-800-221-4542
- Omni (A) $$$ 1-800-THE OMNI
- Outrigger Hawaii (A) $$$ 1-800-733-7777
- Radisson (C) $$–$$$ 1-800-333-3333
- Ramada International (A) (C) $$–$$$ Can 1-800-268-8998 US 1-800-228-2828
- Red Carpet (A) $ 1-800-251-1962
- Red Lion (A) $ 1-800-547-8010
- Red Roof $ 1-800-843-7663
- Relax Inns, Hotels (C) $ 1-800-66-RELAX
- Residence (A) $$ 1-800-331-3131
- Sandman $ 1-800-663-6900
- Scottish Inns (A) $ 1-800-251-1962
- Sheraton (A) $$–$$$ 1-800-325-3535
- Shoney's Inns $ 1-800-222-2222
- Sleep Inns (C) $ 1-800-221-2222
- Stouffer (some) $$$ 1-800-HOTELS-1
- Super 8 Motels (A) $ 1-800-800-8000
- Travelodge International (C) $$ 1-800-225-3050
- Welcome Inns (C) $ 1-800-387-4381
- Westin (some) $$$ 1-800-228-3000
- Westmark $$$ 1-800-544-0970

Glossary  . . . .

Advanced Purchase Excursion Fare (APEX): A reduced rate for many domestic and overseas flights, train or bus journeys, with cancellation penalties and often some limitations, for example, on length of stay.

Air Courier: An organization which transports valuable or time-sensitive material by air; an employee or agent of such an organization.

American Plan (AP): A hotel rate which includes room and three meals. See also Modified American Plan (MAP).

Bed and Breakfast: Overnight accommodation in a private home or boarding house, where breakfast is included in the room rate.

Bucket Shop: A company (often unlicensed) which sells discounted travel services, usually with few frills. May use a description like "last minute club."

Carrier: A company transporting passengers or goods.

Charter Airline: An airline operating non-scheduled services, usually to tourist destinations. It sells space to charter operators, tour companies, etc.

Charter Operator: An organization which buys transportation and accommodation space, and combines them in tours. Such tours are usually wholesaled to travel agencies for resale to the general public.

Commission: This is the amount paid by the supplier (airline, cruise company, hotel, car rental company, insurance company, etc.) to the travel agent for selling their services. It is also the handling charge made by a credit card company to the business which accepts your credit card, or a charge made for converting currencies.

Compensation Fund: This fund is established in some jurisdictions (currently British Columbia, Ontario and Quebec in Canada) to compensate travellers in whole or in part, if some part of the travel industry fails to produce services they have paid for.

Conditions: The section of a transportation or tour contract which describes in detail what is being offered as well as the parties' obligations and liabilities.

Confirmation: Notice of assurance that a service will be available. When applied to airline flights, it is the passenger's assurance that he intends to travel on a flight as booked.

Consul, consular officer: A Canadian official resident outside Canada, responsible for protecting the affairs of Canadians abroad and for dealing with local authorities on their behalf. Similar representative of other countries abroad.

Continental Plan (CP): Hotel rate for bed only, without meals.

Currency Surchage: An additional charge you will pay because of currency fluctuations when tour packages cruises, etc., are negotiated by a tour or cruise operator.

Denied Boarding Compensation: Available to passengers who are unable to board an aircraft because the airline has overbooked their flight.

Departure Tax: The cost of using an airport or ocean terminal levied against airline or ship passengers.

Direct Flight: One on which the traveller proceeds directly to a destination without changing planes. It is not necessarily non-stop.

Double Room: A room for two persons, usually with one double bed. Double room rate is the price of a room for two people.

Drop-off Charge: This is an extra fee charged by car and RV rental companies when you return the vehicle to a place other than where you accepted it.

Escort: A person who accompanies a tour to act as guide and facilitator.

Escorted Tour: A travel program, usually for a group, with an escort service and sightseeing elements.

Flexipass: This variation of a travel pass limits travel to a specified number of days within a fixed period and costs less than an unlimited travel pass (see travel pass).

Foreign Independent Tour (FIT): An international prepaid tour in which there is no accompaniment by an escort or guide.

Fuel Surcharge: The additional charge levied to compensate an airline, shipping line or tour company for increases in the price of fuel after rates were established.

Group Inclusive Tour (GIT): This is a prepaid tour, usually for a specified number of participants.

High Season: The busiest and most expensive time of the year at a tourist destination.

High Season Supplement: An additional charge for a tour, cruise or lodging during the busiest time of the year.

Last Minute Club: This type of club is similar to a bucket shop, but may charge a membership fee.

Low Season: The least busy and least expensive season at a tourist destination and a time when some services and attractions may not be available.

Modified American Plan (MAP): A hotel rate that includes bed and breakfast plus either lunch or dinner. Known in Europe also as demi-pension.

Optional Items: Extra cost items in a package. They may also be introduced in brochures by such expressions as "you may want to visit" or "take in".

Overbooking: The practice of booking space in excess of capacity, followed by airlines and other suppliers to compensate for cancellations.

Package Tour: An advertised tour comprising a number of elements which can include transportation and accommodation, meals, sightseeing, car rentals, taxes and service charges.

Port Taxes: The cost of using port facilities levied against passengers, or simply a tax similar to departure taxes charged to tourists.

Seat Selection: This allows you to select a preferred seat when buying your ticket or confirming a flight.

Service Charges: These are charges added to hotel and restaurant bills, or included in tour package prices, in lieu of individual staff gratuities.

Shoulder Season: The period between high and low seasons at a tourist destination. Prices should be moderate at this time.

Show Tour: Programs combining a number of theatre tickets, with accommodation, transportation, etc.

Single Supplement: When only one person occupies a double room or cabin there is an additional charge.

Special Fare Restriction: On lower-priced air tickets this frequently means the purchase price is not refundable if you do not use the ticket.

Stand-by: You pay less than the advertised airfare, present yourself at the airport and board only after full-fare passengers are all seated.

Standard Room: Inexpensive and often less desirable rooms in a resort or hotel, as opposed to "luxury" or "deluxe" rooms.

Tour: This is a pre-arranged, and usually prepaid, journey to one or more places and returning to the point of origin.

Tour Operator: A company or person who assembles tours and offers them for sale, either directly to the public or through travel agents.

Tourist Hotel: A modest hotel with limited facilities, often without ensuite baths and with few public rooms.

Transfer: Prepaid local transportation and baggage handling service between the airport and your hotel, and possibly to other points during a tour.

Travel Pass: A pass which permits unlimited travel on stipulated transportation systems (air, rail, bus, etc., or a combination of all) in one or more countries. Frequently they must be purchased outside the country where they are to be used (see also Flexipass).

Transfers: Prepaid services for transportation and baggage handling between airports, railway stations, cruise terminals and hotels.

Vouchers: Documents issued by tour operators to be exchanged for prepaid accommodation or other services.

Index

U

Ulysses Travel Bookshop, 46, 207
Unescorted tours, 107
University studies, 187
Uptown reservations, 59, 207
US Air, 66

V

Vaccination, 14
Vagabonding, 4
Valuables, 50
Via Rail, 21, 74, 83, 207
Visa (credit card), 31, 158
Visas, 26
Visual and Verbal Workshops, 190,
    208
Volunteer Vacations, 192-195
Vouchers, prepaid, 223
Voyageur Colonial bus system, 91, 208

W

Wagontrain Tours, 114, 208
Walking vacations, 164-166
Walt Disney World, 199
Water adventures, 163-164
Way To Go, The (travel shop), 45,
    209
Western Union, 33
Whale watching, 170
White Pass & Yukon Route, 75
Wills, 50
Wings of the World Travel, 105, 174,
    208
Wolsey Lodges, 59, 208
World Expeditions, 175, 208
Working vacations, 192-195

Notes